C000156961

This book is dedicated to my braw wee Maw.

A LITTLE PREAMBLE

People sometimes ask me if I ever got flashed or propositioned to get themselves off with a ticket. An innocuous question with a salacious undertone. A desire to hear some spicy scandal?

I got an eyeful, once, when I went to deal with a noisy music complaint.

The normal procedure is to alert the householder to the complaint and request they turn the volume down. Should they refuse or ignore the warning we can charge them with a nuisance offence and take possession of their music playing equipment - problem solved.

On this occasion, a young lady answered the door, in the background I could hear the music blaring. It wasn't the first time I had been to her home; she had regular parties that kept her neighbours awake to all hours of the morning. When she came to the door, she opened it wide and stood facing my colleague and me. She was wearing a see-through negligee that didn't even reach below the waist. There were three steps up to her front door and because I was standing on the bottom step, my eye-line was level with her bushy pudenda. As magnificent as it was, I averted my gaze and looked her in the eye. I asked her to step back into her house, out of sight, and requested that she dress herself before we spoke to her. She went inside but refused to dress herself.

Instead, she took a seat in her lounge chair, unperturbed by her near nakedness. I turned her stereo off, gave her a warning and my colleague and I made a quick exit. We were very professional. I stopped outside to note the details in my notebook and the circumstances. Maybe she wasn't trying to proposition us, she didn't make a show of her body, she just seemed comfortable being naked. I didn't grant her any favours; she received a warning like any other person.

On another occasion, night shift, alone in my office. A woman came to the door dressed in a fur coat. I didn't know her, other than I had seen her around the small town where I worked.

It turned out she was looking for the services of a police officer that wasn't part of our duties; there was nothing under that fur coat (other than a garter belt and high heels). She was a good looking woman, and I was flattered - that was until she spoke.

"Is Constable Herman not on tonight," she said, wrapping her fur coat tightly around herself when she realised she had mixed up his shift pattern.

I went scarlet.

However, the most shocking proposition I received wasn't to get out of a ticket, it was to get out of a bollocking.

I was duty sergeant and had to have a closed door session with a female cop. She was an experienced officer and good at her job. Not only was she an asset, she had a sparkling personality and made the workplace a happier place.

I had to reprimand her for something - it must have been a minor matter because I can't recall what it was. I remember her attitude to it though. She laughed it off, fluttered her eyelashes and told me she fancied me. There I was trying to be serious and professional. She couldn't care about the reprimand. Instead she suggested that I come back to her flat when we finished work.

I was aghast. How could she be so dismissive of my reprimand? What on earth possessed her to suggest such a thing to her sergeant? She must know I would not contemplate getting involved with a member of my team. That would have been totally unprofessional - a step into dangerous territory. It was a wholly improper suggestion. I need not tell you her proposal stunned me. I couldn't speak for a few seconds, appalled by her audacity.

She had a nice flat though!*

The *really* STUPID thing about being a SERGEANT is my second book detailing the funny incidents, the strange goings on, and the comic situations encountered during a thirty year and two-month career in the police. Guaranteed to make anyone with the slightest sense of humour laugh out loud. You can read these humorous accounts in any order. This book is worth reading for the one scene alone that had me, my custody assistant and every single prisoner in the custody suite laughing until our sides were sore; detailed in all its glory in the chapter entitled 'Hokey Cokey in the pokey'.

PC Penfold makes a return, but there are new characters too; Inspector Deadpan Dick who had me in stitches in a McDonald's drive-thru, Superintendent Amnesiac, and much more. There are even two bedroom scenes, the names have been changed, but my colleagues are utterly embarrassed when reminded of what went on.

*I couldn't resist this one liner - it is of course not true.**

** Her flat was actually a mess.

3

EVEN LATER ONE NIGHT

I could sense tonight would be busy. My radio chattered incessantly. Operators alerted us to an ongoing fight at The Spiral, an establishment that professed to be a nightclub. An old converted church with a spire - hence the name. The pews replaced with low seating, a DJ deck filled the pulpit, and a bar ran down the full length of one wall. The thud-thud of dance music blared as the aftershave brigade strutted around shaking their hips trying to attract the lipsticked young ladies who gyrated in the worship of their collection of handbags on the floor. A stark contrast to the previous patrons who daintily got on their knees, clasped their hands together and murmured a quiet prayer. Odd that this church converted to a disco since the old dance hall next door had also changed its use, ironically it was now a place of worship for some group who had witnessed something - not that they ever told us.

The fight started inside the foyer and spilled outside, due to the bouncers ejecting everyone involved. Once they were outside, the bouncers shut their heavy wooden doors. No longer their problem. The posturing continued and resulted in an occasional scuffle on the street. Young drunk men signalled their intention to fight by removing their shirts, puffing out their chests and seeing how close they could get to someone else's face. Punching distance. Anyone brave enough to challenge them were subjected to a flurry of fists and boots. The appeasers, indignant that their efforts to calm the situation resulted in violence, ended up trying to leave a knuckle sandwich of their own.

Such fights were an all too frequent occurrence. Every Friday night, some young men would drink too much, become argumentative and then violent. Women got involved too, their violence invariably resulting in both parties losing chunks of hair.

It was up to the police to quell these disturbances and pick up the pieces. We had measures to deal with just this type of incident. We called it the 'Weekend Policing Plan'. A document drafted by our chief inspector, which instructed that officers be at certain points in the town at certain times of the night. The plan altered on a weekly basis, changed by the analysts who examined the call distribution and crime trends. For the incumbent chief inspector, it looked like we were ready and able respond to any disorder. However, the Weekend Policing Plan did not take into account that there were never sufficient officers on duty to meet the plan's requirements. Neither did it take into account that officers had to go to calls elsewhere. Victims of a road accident, relatives of vulnerable missing persons and other victims of crime dislike waiting on police just because there might be trouble when the nightclub spilled.

As the calls to The Spiral came in, our CCTV operators directed their cameras onto the street outside the disco and described the melee. Their voices became higher pitched and more excited than normal. Control Room Operators directed all available officers to the location. Crews freed themselves from whatever they were dealing with, depending on the seriousness of the matter and their inclination to get involved in a brawl. If I could have put a bet on who would be first to arrive, my money would have been on PC Tommy 'Toolbag' McTear.

Tommy Toolbag had a tough upbringing on a farm. He had built up both muscle and resilience by working on the land. It was a small farm, though, unable to support the multiple children his mother and father bred. Tommy turned eighteen and took the first job available to him; he became a miner. He worked down the pit for much of the eighties. When the pits closed and he needed to feed his family, he had no reservations about joining the police. He had been on the opposite side of the picket lines during the miners' strike but had shown no animosity towards the police. They were just doing what police do. When Tommy no longer had a job in the mine to go to, he had no second thoughts about donning a uniform and coming over to the blue side. To him, it was just another job. Not like any other job, though, it was a job that gave him a licence to partake in his favourite hobby. Tommy liked nothing better than to get involved in a brawl. He might have taken a few knocks and bruises in his time, but he never lost a fight. He was a formidable sight when he squeezed out of his police car and stretched to his full height. Six feet six inches and wide as a Transit Van. It was always to his disappointment when his prey gave up too easily.

"That's us in attendance," radioed Tommy Toolbag, I would have won my bet if anyone had been stupid enough to have taken it.

There was a period of expectant silence from the radio as everyone waited for the result of Tommy Toolbag's attendance. It was less than a minute later that a breathless Tommy came back on the radio, "Situation under control. I have four arrested. I'll need the big van and an ambulance... On second thoughts you had better make that two ambulances."

As more crews arrived at The Spiral, everyone who didn't go to the hospital found themselves in handcuffs. A mixed bunch of angry drunk people brought back to my, already hectic, Custody Suite. As was normal in these situations, there was always great confusion as to what had actually happened. Trying to get a coherent witness statement from a dozen drunk and bleeding young adults is not an easy task. The default option is to arrest those that cause the most bloody nuisance of themselves and try and sort out who did what later on.

So there I was, in my role as custody sergeant, trying to get the growing queue of prisoners processed and into a cell before the next convoy of drunk and abusive merrymakers arrived. My patience already tested.

For classification as a nightclub the owners of such premises have to have a Public Entertainment Licence, that entertainment being free or otherwise. The Spiral charged an entrance fee, and after that, it extorted more money from its patrons by selling watered down overpriced drinks. Going out for a night on the town and ending up in a nightclub is the equivalent of playing Russian roulette with your wallet - do it often enough and it is bound to end badly.

The entertainment comprised an elderly DeeJay, Danny The Fanny, playing the same playlist week after week. Danny had got the gig many years before because he impressed the owner with his CV, which stated he had been a roadie for *Led Zeppelin*. This almost always raised an eyebrow with everyone who heard it; Danny the Fanny, at little more than five feet six inches and not a lick over nine stone, looked as if he couldn't lift more than the one record at a time, far less set up a stage. The clientele had quickly given him his adopted moniker of 'Danny the Fanny', as, no matter what record they requested, he resolutely stuck to the same playlist week after week. He nodded at all requests went back to his record decks and ignored them.

The Spiral was the only disco in town, or more importantly, the only place punters could get a drink after midnight, so they kept coming back. The drunker they got, the more likely a fight was to break out. It was a constant. Every weekend, without fail, someone got punched. Their Public Entertainment Licence should have read 'Boxing Venue' rather than 'Nightclub'. Once the bouncers poured their belligerent clientele out the door, they shut up shop, exited via a side door and resolutely remained non-witnesses to whatever had occurred.

The Custody Suite, where I was working, has a purpose-built cell complex attached to our old and decrepit headquarters building. Purpose-built by architects on instructions of senior officers who had never worked there. While it was certainly better than the cell complex in my old station, which had a narrow set of stairs to negotiate down to the actual cells. (Dangerous for us when manhandling a fighting drunk, even more so for obnoxious prisoners). However, my new Custody Suite was short on space. Just like every new government building and every hospital everywhere, the designers never factored in enough parking spaces. In our case, the Custody Suite designers hadn't factored in enough cells. Simple enough, we want to place prisoners in a single cell on their own, that way they are easier to manage. By Sunday mornings our average prisoner count was around forty, ten percent of those being female. Ideally we required thirty-six male cells and four female cells. Our purpose built custody suite only had sixteen male cells and two female cells. A lot of my time was spent moving prisoners from single occupancy to three up. (We never left two on their own in a cell - no corroboration).

For officers to get into the Custody Suite, they drove around to the rear of our Headquarters and activated the security gates with their warrant card. The big metal gates, which had big roller spikes on top, eased their way open. The van transporting the prisoners reversed in and waited for the mechanised gate to shut. The officers then removed their prisoners from the van safe in the knowledge they couldn't run away. Except that the gates didn't work. They locked in the closed position, completely inoperative. Memos flew upstairs every week requesting a repair, and occasionally an engineer would attend. Arriving on a Monday morning, he would have them working by Tuesday afternoon, only for them to be inoperative again by the Friday.

Prisoners were ushered from the police vans, through the back door past our locker rooms, on through the canteen and into the main custody reception area where I was entered the details of our customers on the computer. I had to pause when the people I was processing stopped paying attention to me and started shouting at the new prisoners. A barage of verbal abuse cascaded back and forth as the re-ignited their feud from outside The Spiral.

I finished my processing and called, "Next."

PC Tommy Toolbag McTear was first up. Nicknamed 'Toolbag' because from day one in the job he carried a black leather holdall with him, his policing tool bag. Tommy Toolbag came prepared. His heavy looking holdall contained everything he needed to complete his job, some of which would raise an eyebrow on a covert SAS operation. A flask of hot, black, double strength coffee was first out the bag. He poured himself a cup, calmly removed the handcuffs from his prisoner and returned them to his tool bag. Tommy had four spare sets of handcuffs and it was not unusual for him to find a need for all of them. Also in his bag he kept a spare baton, a non-regulation baseball bat style truncheon that he was trialling. He had been trialling it for several years in his capacity as an Officer Safety Instructor - nobody ever asked about it. He still had his regulation side handled baton tucked into the loop attached to his belt. I suspect there were other instruments of torture within his toolbag, but I didn't like to ask. When there was a brawl, we were just glad Tommy Toolbag was on hand to deal with it.

Tommy Toolbag gripped his prisoner by the arm and ushered him up to the counter in front me. We all knew Brian S. McNutt, he was a notorious local ned, not long out of jail for possessing a handgun, frightening his then girlfriend with it and then shooting his television because he didn't like what was on.

There are cameras everywhere in the custody suite, and everything gets recorded twenty-four hours a day, seven days a week. I had a process to go through, and it was time read it over. With the cameras, there are no shortcuts, but I prided myself on the fact I could process prisoners quickly and efficiently. I didn't want to delay officers any longer than was necessary.

"What's your name?" I asked Brian.

"Fuck off!"

"How are you spelling that?"

"FH...UH...K...AW...FH"

Brian S. McNutt came from a family who had adopted a tradition of giving a stupid middle name to their offspring. Thus Brian's father, Neville I. McNutt (the I. stood for Idiot) had given Brian the middle name of 'Stupid' as confirmed on his birth certificate. For the amusement of the custody staff and officers present, I tried to extricate this information from him voluntarily.

"It's okay Brian I've found your details on the computer here. Can you just confirm your middle name for me please."

"FUCK OFF," he persisted all the louder.

10

I went into my spiel. "Brian, I will be your custody officer this evening. The object of my presence here is to give you your rights and ensure that we look after you according to your needs. In order to do that, I seek your co-operation and would be much obliged if you could answer my questions as honestly as possible."

"FUCK OFF."

"Have you been drinking tonight?"

"FUCK OFF."

"For the purposes of the CCTV recording, I note that Brian's breath smells strongly of alcohol, his eyes are bloodshot and that his clothes are somewhat dishevelled. I consider that he has been drinking this evening." I typed it all into the computer before asking my next question. "Brian, have you taken any drugs this evening?"

"FUCK OFF."

"I'll take that as a no."

"Brian, you are entitled to have a solicitor informed of your arrest. If you do not have a solicitor, I can contact the duty solicitor on your behalf. Do you wish to have a solicitor contacted on your behalf?"

"FUCK OFF. I'll be defending myself!"

"This isn't judo son!"

"Naw, but I'd kick your baws tae kingdom come if I had the chance."

"Thank you for the warning. I'll make sure to limit any opportunity of you re-arranging my baws - I've grown quite attached to the way they are."

"Aw aye, Fuckin' smartarse. Hink yer funny ya bastard, well yer no, eh! Yer jist a wee wank wi a uniform. Ah widnae spit on ye if ye wur oan fire. Yer maw's a bampot and yer faither's a dobber. So hurry up ya fud, I've got hings tae dae."

11

I entered all Brian's arrest details into the computerised Custody Management System; removed his property and secured it in a sealed plastic bag in his presence. I instructed the arresting officers to take him to a cell. As Brian was led away, he turned towards me. I expected a further torrent of abuse from him. Instead, he paused a moment, smiled and said, "Any chance of a cup of tea?"

Next up was Wee Sheila McGinty. She stepped up to the bar, hardly tall enough to peer over the top of the counter. Her lipstick and makeup had long since dispersed from their original places of application and smeared lines across her face not dissimilar to the skid marks on an airport runway. While Sheila was not tall; she was somewhat round and plump-ish. All the more reason to assume that before going out for the evening she had dressed in the dark, did not have access to a mirror and had no real friends to advise her on her inappropriate dress code. A friend might have suggested she think twice about her choice of attire. Sheila was sporting a metallic gold foil boob tube and a leather miniskirt. Her life-threatening soapbox high heels, long since removed from her feet, occupied her hands. The boob tube was struggling to contain ample breasts, only just succeeding because her equally ample belly provided support for them. Her miniskirt was only just sufficient for covering her modesty due to the cheap fabric it had ridden up all the way to just short of her crotch. It looked like she had folded a black bin-liner in two and wrapped it around herself. Two chunky, blotchy legs extended down to her gold painted toenails (at least she was colour coordinated). Sheila was tearful. She was also young, just a bairn. I think I still had things in my fridge that were older than her. Certainly, I had a pair of trainers I'd purchased long before she was born. *How on earth were they letting a young girl like her into licenced premises?* I made a mental note to ensure that a detailed memo was sent to our licencing department for them to highlight it to the licencing board.

"What's your name, hen?"

"Sh... Sh... Sheila," she managed to say, in between her bubbling tears and heavy sniffs to draw the snot back up her nose.

"What age are you?"

"F... f... f... twenty one."

"What's your date of birth?

"Em..." her eyes looked up and left as she tried to work out what year she would have been born if she was twenty-one. It was a computing process too far for her tiny brain.

"You are fourteen, aren't you?"

"I am not. I am fifteen." Shiela answered indignantly.

I turned to the arresting officers and instructed them to take her to the waiting room, get her details, call her parents and have them come to the office to collect her. As they turned about Inspector Deadpan Dick entered the Custody Suite.

That night was to be the one and only one occasion I ever saw Inspector Deadpan Dick flustered. As the two cops escorted Sheila through to the waiting room, Inspector Deadpan Dick saw she was struggling to stop crying.

"What's the matter?" he asked. Sheila struggled to control herself as the tears rolled down her cheeks.

Inspector Deadpan Dick leapt into gallant action. He nipped through to the kitchen and reappeared a second or two later with a cup of water and a plastic chair. He placed the seat behind Shiela and gently guided her down onto it. Once sat down he handed her the cup of water and encouraged her to take a sip. She calmed herself down sufficiently to stop crying and take a sip. She took a deep breath back in through her nostrils to prevent more snot appearing.

"There, there," Inspector Deadpan Dick soothed her, "it can't be as bad as all that. You have a wonderful event to look forward to."

She looked up puzzled. Then as the realisation hit her and she burst into tears again, great big sobs, "Mwah mwah," she bubbled before replying, "I'm not pregnant, I'm just fat!"

I only saw the back of Inspector Deadpan Dicks' neck as he about turned and walked out. It was a strange red colour.

I got back to processing the prisoners.

Last in, was a shirtless youth who looked like he had come second best in a brawl. Blood trickled from a cut below his eye, and he was only just coming down from his vengeance-seeking state. His unkempt mop of sandy hair flopped like a seagull wing over one eye, he had cuts on his arms, and rips in his trousers. It looked like they dragged him through a bramble bush.

"Well you look as if you got a sore one," I said to him - my attempt at sympathy.

"You should see the other guy," he replied.

At that Wee Sheila McGinty perked up from her chair and shouted across the room.

"What do you mean the other guy? It was me that gave you that, and there was nothing you could do about it, ya scrawny wee prick."

My shirtless prisoner hung his head and looked down at his toes.

"What's your name?" I asked, preparing myself to get his details entered onto the computer. I had a lot to do before I could finish.

"Daffy Duck."

"Daffy Duck?"

"Aye Daffy Duck, you probably know my father."

"Donald?"

"Naw... Steve."

"Steve Duck? Canny say I've heard of him," I tried again, "Okay, perhaps you will tell me your address?"

"Buckingham Palace?"

"Well - in that case, you will be staying here at your own pleasure, your highness."

"I know you lot. You are just going to make a fool of me."

"I think you are doing that fine on your own."

"You think you are smart eh! Asking me my name and address, that's easy. I could do your job."

"You would be very welcome to it. I don't see why it should just be me that has to suffer people like you."

"Have you any idea WHO I AM?"

I turned to everyone else in the custody suite, "Does anybody know who this guy is? He seems to have forgotten, can anybody help with who he is?"

In due course he was searched, we found his wallet in his torn trousers and in that wallet a driving licence which provided me with all the details I needed. I gave him the same rights I'd given Brian then lodged him in a cell with two other drunken, belligerent youths. It would be a different story in the morning.

It was times like that I wondered why on earth I had ever bothered sitting the promotion exams in the first place. Who would be a sergeant?

Chapter 1

VELCRO STRIPES

It was the end of a busy day, sitting in the office writing up reports. Not a big office, two desks, and four computers. PC Sylvester McDougan (Uncle Sylvester) sat diagonally opposite at his computer, and I sat at mine. Heads down focussed on getting the information stored on our notebooks into the proper format on the screen. Already we were an hour past our finishing time. It was a race to input the information, change out of our uniform and get out in time to beat the rush hour traffic. Nine-to-fivers can turn our normal fifteen-minute commute into a forty-five-minute frustrating crawl. The radio was quiet, other than the occasional minor call taken by other crews.

The phone rang interrupting my concentration. A loud ring from the receiver and an even louder ring sounded from the bell outside in the corridor, a bell designed to ensure that we never missed a call no matter where we were in the office. No rest for the wicked (or the bursting). Uncle Sylvester picked up the phone put it to his ear and listened distractedly, eyes still glued to his screen. He passed me the phone.

"It's Barbeque Bill," he said.

Barbeque Bill, my old workmate, wanted me to prepare a statement for him regarding a case he was reporting. Light-heartedly, I berated him for pestering me. I told him I was in fact just about finished the statement and would email it to him in the next few minutes. We had a further bit of verbal jousting before hanging up.

"You know what you are, eh?" he said. It was a long standing joke between us.

Twenty-five years later I still get the texts, emails or Facebook messages, completely randomly and out of the blue with the one sentence: 'You know what you are, eh?'

"Now bugger off, I'm busy," I responded.

"That will be a first."

"True... a first since I stopped having to babysit you and make sure you did the job right."

"How is that retirement home you call a police office?"

"It is better than the toilet you work out of?"

"Better class of colleague here, though, now that I have got a decent partner to work with."

"Oh yes, how is your new carer getting on?"

"Will you just get that statement done ya lazy..."

"I'll get your statement done when I am good and ready,"

"Listen, ya wa..." at which point I hung up before he could insult me anymore. I smiled to myself. Barbeque Bill always makes me smile. I like him a lot.

A few minutes later I'd written the statement. I attached it to an email, addressed it to Barbeque Bill and pressed the send button. I turned my attention to the crime report I had to input. Concentrating on getting all the relevant details listed, along with all the enquiries I had carried out - if I didn't I would come back to a screed of tasks from the Crime Management Unit. Ironically the Crime Management Unit was populated by officers who knew every wangle there was to get out of doing those tasks themselves. Poacher turned gamekeeper when transferred to the unit.

I looked up when the phone rang again, Uncle Sylvester picked it up and listened for a second. He cupped the receiver with his hand before handing the phone over to me saying, "It's Barbeque Bill again, he wants to know when you are going to send that statement to him."

I grabbed the phone from him and swore into the mouthpiece, before lambasting Barbeque Bill further, "You are an idiot, are you such a complete simpleton you don't know how to read an email? Never in the service of king and country has there been such a buffoon as you. No wonder the people of Scotland despair, having you wear a uniform in pretence at being a police officer."

The voice on the other end spoke, and I flushed with embarrassment. The voice said, "Constable McEwan, that is no way to speak to your superintendent, especially when I was about to tell you that you are getting a temporary promotion."

It wasn't Barbeque Bill; it was Superintendent Rattan.

Uncle Sylvester was on the floor holding his hand over his mouth trying, and failing, to stop himself from laughing. I, on the other hand, was sitting with my big black police boot protruding from my mouth wondering how on earth I was going to extricate it.

Superintendent Rattan kindly ignored my little outburst. Despite being so unquestioningly rude to him, I got my temporary promotion. He tested me with the question, "How would you feel about having a female for a boss?"

"Well, I suppose I would feel right at home," I said.

In due course, I headed off to G Division for a six-month stint as a temporary sergeant.

It was 1998, but my move paled into insignificance to other moves that year. Rolls- Royce moved under the control of German-owned BMW, the Euro became the single currency in Europe, and there was the devastating news that Ally McCoist was moving from Rangers; along with Andy Goram, Stuart McCall, Richard Gough and Ian Durrant. What on earth were Rangers FC thinking? Mind you, the same could probably be said of my gaffers. I was maybe a bit jammy that the bosses were not aware of the nonsense and shenanigans I had taken part in up to then.

Before taking up my temporary role, the Chief Constable invited me into Police Headquarters to meet with him for a pep talk.

There would be few more important occasions in my career, so I wanted to look my best. I called into our stores to get my new sergeant's uniform. Despite the tunic and trousers being brand new off the rack, I still took them to the dry cleaners. Once they were ready, I picked them up and took them home to iron in the creases. In a further effort to impress, I also purchased a new pair of black 'Loake Bibury' shoes, which have a soft, deer leather hide, and polished patent toe cap. An elegant shoe that exudes quality and allows for a mirror finish toe. Tulliallan Police College had been pernickety about our presentation on the parade square, and I had learned that there was no substitute for elbow grease when it came to making certain of the sharpest creases and shiniest shoes. I put the effort in and, when finished, reflected in my mirror finished shoes, I saw an immaculately dressed, young soon-to-be sergeant.

On arrival at Chief Constable's Office, his secretary smiled and tried but failed to put me at ease.

"Relax, you'll be fine. If you could take a seat with the others, I'll take you through when the Chief Constable is ready."

The three others who were being given a temporary rank that day sat like tin soldiers on stiff chairs. They all looked self-assured in their pressed uniforms and polished shoes. We engaged in some idle chit chat while we waited. Before long the Chief Constable buzzed through on his intercom to his secretary, and she showed us into his palatial looking office. It was the first time I'd seen a room in a police station that didn't have a threadbare carpet. There was me under the impression that police procurement officers bought our threadbare carpets second-hand from Beirut. Either that or they spread them out on some busy motorway somewhere for a few weeks before having them thrown on the floor like a rag. It was nice walking on a soft pile for a change.

The Chief Constable indicated to us to sit in the four seats facing his desk. The moment I sat down I had to stand up again as he extricated himself from his seat and came from behind his desk to shake our hands.

"I've ordered us all some coffee and bacon rolls," he said smiling.

As if by magic, his secretary re-entered his office carrying a tray of coffee and bacon rolls. I was up off my seat again taking the coffee in one hand and the bacon roll in the other. I seemed to have missed out on the paper napkin that the Chief Constable and my three colleagues managed to obtain. On sitting back down, I had nowhere to rest my coffee or roll. The coffee cup was piping hot and already burning my knuckles. The small handle wasn't big enough to prevent my fingers from touching the body of the cup. Cautiously I tried to adjust my grip but found myself hampered by the bacon roll in my left hand. I put the coffee cup down on my right leg to adjust my grip on the cup, only to feel the burning heat radiate through my trousers and scald my thigh. Out of necessity I laid my bacon roll on my left trouser leg and used my left hand to adjust my grip on the cup. Chief Constable McDandy was speaking, but I wasn't listening. My predicament held my full attention. When I got a proper grip and lifted the cup and bacon roll off my trousers, I was horror-struck. Glaring at me, on my right leg, was a wet coffee stain ring and on my left leg a line of grease spots where the fat from the bacon had dribbled.

In a panic, I ate the bacon roll as quickly as I could, and have done with it. I was even more horrified when a greasy piece of bacon slipped from my roll, dribbled down the front of my tunic and landed on the lush carpet that bedecked the office. I looked up to see if anyone noticed. The Chief Constable was in mid-sentence, something about 'the importance of a professional attitude to take to our new roles'. The only role I could think about, however, was the roll that had stained my good tunic and trousers, half of which was now lying on the floor.

Oh my God Malky what are you going to do? What if he sees your stained uniform and decides that you are not suitable for a temporary sergeant's role?

I don't know.

Think of something.

I can't.

Why are you talking to yourself?

You started it!

Oh God, Chief Constable McDandy is speaking to you.

The Chief Constable looked directly at me, ignoring my greasy stained tunic and trousers, "Are you happy with your new station?" he asked.

I hadn't been listening. I desperately tried to rewind all that he'd said, but there was nothing. My thoughts consumed by my bacon roll and hot coffee predicament. I didn't have a clue where I was going to work for the next six months. All I had been concentrating on was a hot cup of coffee scalding my leg and a greasy piece of bacon ruining my efforts to look presentable. I mumbled something unintelligible, "Och aye, ta fur gid ah hink."

Chief Constable McDandy looked at me with the kind of disdain I normally only get at home. There was a long scornful silence before he moved on to the next in line. It was the most awkward and embarrassing start to my tenure as a temporary sergeant I could have imagined - short of turning up naked.

I felt lucky, though because there were other just as competent officers, some with more service than I had, who didn't get the opportunity to do a temporary rank. I had also been fortunate, in my career, to have worked with some of the best people. Capable, committed and kindly people whom I much admired. The brilliant PC Woolyheid behing one.

PC Woolyheid was a tall, debonair, and articulate man. If Prince Charles and John Cleese were to breed a love child and that love child joined the police after twenty-five years service its name would be PC Woolyheid. Intelligent, funny and accomplished. PC Woolyheid remained a constable for twenty-five years . Despite his charismatic presence, common-sense and leadership qualities he seemed not to fit in with management's view of what a supervisor should be. Thus he was passed over for promotion time and time again.

He seemed fairly pragmatic about it.

"How come you haven't been promoted?" I asked him.

"Well Malky, It's like this," he explained, "the bosses consider me to be something of a 'Jaggy Nettle'. When they come up with a new initiative or fancy scheme, I am the first to tell them that it is a great idea, but I also have a tendency to point out some pitfalls that go along with them. 'That's a good idea,' I say, 'but it won't work in the operational world.'"

"For example?"

"Well, it wasn't so long ago that Chief Superintendent Rattan sought feedback from me regarding his idea on how to catch our car thieves."

I was well aware of the problem. A spate of car thefts had gone undetected, and we were averaging about three stolen every week.

PC Woolyheid continued, "You may recall he suggested that on every occasion we get a report of a stolen car, we set up a road block at seven pre-identified locations surrounding the city. Thus putting a 'ring of steel', as he called it, around the area. No stolen car could, therefore, get out of the city without first passing one of our roadblocks. I told him it was a great idea but still had to break the news to him that it would not work. You see, in theory, such a 'ring of steel' would spot the stolen car as it left the city but only if, One... It was in place in time. Two... We had sufficient cops on duty to cover those areas. Three... We somehow were suddenly able to transport ourselves back in time. 'Chief Superintendent,' I said to him. 'One... These cars are being stolen during the night when our staff are dealing with other matters; some are tied up with discotheques spilling, some are in the middle of an arrest or queuing at the custody suite. Some are dealing with road accidents or are with victims at the hospital. Two... There are seven pre-identified locations, so in the unlikely event that none of the three crews on duty are busy, they still couldn't cover all seven locations. And three... We haven't had a single report of a car being stolen at the time it happened. So unless we could transport ourselves back in time when we get the call in the morning, there seems little likelihood your plan will work in the operational world'."

I could picture Chief Superintendent Rattan walking away muttering under his breath, swearing that PC Woolyheid would never be promoted, not with such a negative attitude.

PC Woolyheid seemed unconcerned. He applied for promotion when they announced the submission process, but he quietly got back to work when his application came back rejected. He didn't complain; he just accepted that he wasn't a 'yes' man and got on with his job.

PC Woolyheid competently went about his work, but he liked a bit of nonsense while doing it. That may have been another explanation for his lack of career progression. He was prone to making mischief, just to relieve the monotony. Naughty but harmless - I always thought.

For example, he submitted a report to the Procurator Fiscal, a simple case of a car not displaying a tax disc. These were such run-of-the-mill reports that we had a pro forma for them. Time, date, locus, brief circumstances, etc.

PC Woolyheid simply reported the facts, but the Procurator Fiscal was indignant about his description of the locus. The following is an extract from his report:-

'The locus of this offence is High Street, which is bordered on both sides by various shops, hostelries and a bookmaker. The vehicle in question was parked directly outside a popular fast food restaurant that was just one of many tens of thousands of a chain that are now ever-present worldwide. It is instantly recognisable by the large golden M and a picture of a clown on the frontage. At the time of the offence the fast food restaurant was offering a meal deal comprising; burger, fries and choice of drink for the princely sum of £2.99...'

The description was entirely irrelevant but quite comical in my opinion. The Procurator Fiscal, did not see the funny side and complained to the bosses (why would you?). PC Woolyheid received a reprimanded for his irrelevant humour.

On another occasion, PC Woolyheid made a trip to the canteen kitchen and found that it was in a disgraceful state. Unwashed dishes piled up in the sink, the fridge was full of out-of-date foodstuffs, and the overfilled rubbish bin had spilt its contents onto the floor. He turned away in disgust.

The next day he checked the kitchen and found it to be in a similar state. However, PC Woolyheid had come prepared. He popped out to the private car park at the rear of Police Headquarters and found a quiet space on the grass. There he ignited his disposable barbeque. Once ready, he cooked a selection of meats for himself. Unfortunately, the quiet space on the grass was directly below Chief Constable McDandy's Office and he found himself in trouble.

Once the flames of discontent had died down PC Woollyheid penned a little ode that best describes the resultant hullabaloo. He has kindly allowed me to reproduce it here.

THE ABANDONED BAR-B-QUE

Despite a certain warning
That's been passed down to me
From a certain godlike figure
Whom I've no real wish to see
I've written these few verses
To commemorate the day
When plans for a quiet bar-b-que
Most sadly went astray.

So when the woeful tale I tell
There may be those of you
Who feel the urge to commiserate
And shed a tear or two
But please feel free to do so
Let water cloud your eyes
As you hear of a simple bar-b-que
That met a sad demise.

One fine and sunny evening
As August reached its end
The thoughts of a sterling officer
Turned to the culinary trend
Full-fed up with cheese sandwiches
And stale rolls dressed in meat
He pondered some new angle
Of how to cook a treat.

So with eager passion
He set up a bar-b-que
Beside the official car park
To the rear of Police HQ
Where no one might disturb him
Or be disturbed he thought
By the smoke and smell of cooking
From the foodstuffs that he'd bought.

Six long and plumpish sausages
That smelt so fresh and new
Were placed, awaiting cooking
Beside the bar-b-que
Accompanied by hamburgers
And chopped up bits of meat
To add the right ingredients
For an outdoor cooking treat.

26

The bar-b-que was lit at last
A reddish glow was seen
Where once a set of blackened coals
With little life had been
And slowly as the minutes passed
The coals began to glow
The semblance of a cooking flame
At least appeared to show.

But all this time, unknown to him
The cook of whom I tell
There were some people round about
Affected by the smell
Of smoke that rose up to the sky
From off the bar-b-que
And felt that this here Polisman
Had no real work to do.

And so a message soon was passed
On down the line of rank
To douse the simple bar-b-que
And end a senseless prank
A senseless prank some viewed it then
Instead of how they should
A method using burning coal
To cook one's duty food

But never mind, the bar-b-que
Was soon with water killed
But not before the Police HQ
Had been with coal dust filled
For when you douse a bar-b-que
By use of water jet
The flame goes out, the fire expires
With steam and dust, you're met.

The sausages that were so fresh
The hamburgers so fine
The bits of meat so nicely cut
Had not been cooked on time
To make a meal of them was out
The grill pan at Police HQ
Could never in a million years
Compete with a bar-b-que.

Undaunted by the lack of faith
In a simple bar-b-que
The officer who was involved
Has had to think anew
And in the future, who can tell
New ventures at Police HQ
May well include a vending van
Or a car boot sale or two.

But who was he who even dared
To attempt a bar-b-que
Within the hallowed grounds behind
The regional Police HQ
I know by looking what you think
You think the cook was me
In every face, I look upon
The accusing signs I see.

Well you may be right, but all I'll say
In this bold company
The Scottish legal system states
You have to prove it's me.

Copies found their way up the tree and that type of
'taking the Michael' alienated him further from
promotion.

There were many different promotion processes over the years, all variations on a theme. When I started out, long before I was even to consider going for promotion, they had 'The Bunfight'. The Bunfight was where senior managers got together in a wee room and argued about who they should promote. There would be a ding dong barney and whoever shouted loudest, about their favourite, would get him or her promoted. I'm not sure why they called it a Bunfight, but I pictured several of our more intimidating senior officers throwing various choices of patisseries at each other.

You might think this is a fair method of promoting someone, particularly if you were in the police football team, (a disproportionate number seemed to end up with scrambled egg on the skip of their hats). However, over the years, people recognised that 'The Bunfight' was not a professional way to conduct business. It was essentially biased and not an accountable way of ensuring fairness.

So they introduced a new promotion process. The new process involved a complete revamp of the way we did things. The Bunfight found itself in the bin and the Human Resources Department (HR), who had spent months researching the subject, came up with a new system.

This new system was soon abandoned.

Our new Chief Constable was notoriously hard to please and was of the opinion that every single one of his senior officers had been promoted beyond their ability. A fact that the 'Peter Principle' would bear out. The 'Peter Principle' being a management theory that employees only stop being promoted once they reach a rank in which they are incompetent. It happens in business, and it happened in the police. Competent cops got promoted to sergeant, competent sergeants got promoted to the rank of inspector, and so on. If you were incompetent in your role, however, you did not get promoted any further. That is the 'Peter Principle'. Once you no longer perform effectively, you stop being promoted, and thus managers rise to their level of incompetence.

Chief Constable Handy McDandy ordered our Human Resources Department to come up with a new and better way of promoting people. So off they went cobbling various processes together. They looked at all other forces, read books on the subject and even asked the Royal Marines what they did. Head of Human Resources started to develop a new system, a fair system and one he felt would be the most excellent promotion system ever developed. It would be unsurpassed in its ability to identify the best candidate for the role. A lot of work went into figuring out the process. At least that is what he told our Chief Constable. There was a suspicion he had, in fact, contacted his old mate, who ran a consultancy firm operating Assessment Centres on behalf of companies and asked that they take on our promotion process.

Our Chief Constable, fed up with his (Peter Principled) senior officers, agreed that the 'Assessment Centre' system seemed fair and practical. He rubber stamped the proposal.

The 'Assessment Centre' provided an in-depth assessment of the candidates. The aim was to gauge their competencies in the role they had applied for and, after taking everything into account, rate each candidate with a final score. The system meant that the person with the highest score would be promoted to the first available position, and so on down the list. Because an outside agency administered the Assessment Centre, there could be no nepotism. The best candidate would have the highest score, and Chief Constable McDandy made a big play about how fair it would be. He guaranteed that the 'Assessment Centre' would find the best candidate, and he promised that the top ten scoring officers would receive their stripes in order of the highest score first - just as soon as positions became available. Not only that, but he also promised to promote the two highest scoring people immediately. The two vacant sergeant's posts filled on the same day the consultant agency announced the scores.

Chief Constable McDandy claimed the 'Assessment Centre' process was the best thing the police had introduced in years. No longer would they randomly promote people on a whim, they would dispense with favouritism. More importantly, there would be no more discrimination. Using the 'Assessment Centre' process meant that the best person for the role would get the promotion, no matter their gender, colour, beliefs or even how good they were at football.

Anyone, who was eligible for promotion could apply. For those who did, it meant taking a day out of their work to attend at a neutral venue where they took tests, questionnaires and more tests. The process relied heavily on practical scenarios where the candidates made decisions on mock situations as they developed. These decisions, answers to tests and questionnaires were examined and scored. The assessors had no idea who they were scoring because they had never worked with any of the officers before. The whole idea was that the best answers received the best ratings, the best outcomes from the scenarios were also rated and then at the end each candidate had their scores totted up. A final tally gave their overall score and only then was it marked beside the candidate's name. Simple, non-biased and with all intents and purposes it would identify the best person for each role.

The day came when the senior officers had their triennial planning day. A day when almost every available rank, of sergeant and above, attended the local Business Management Centre to spend a day in workshops preparing the next three years aims and objectives. They made a big fuss of these events, and on this occasion, Chief Constable McDandy decided to use it to announce the results of the 'Assessment Centre' process. At the end of a protracted and tiresome day, he stood up and gave a rousing speech. Well, it roused some from their sleep. There was quite a bit of interest in the upcoming promotion announcement. Who was it going to be? Excitement for the broadcast had everybody on the edge of their seats - either that or they knew they could soon go home.

Chief Constable Handy McDandy congratulated everyone for all their efforts and hard work. At the conclusion of his speech, he reiterated that the new promotion process was as transparent a process as it could be and that the top two candidates would be promoted right there and then. He assured us that he was unaware who had sat at the top of the list and that he too was looking forward to finding out which two officers he would hand stripes to. He then passed the microphone to the 'Assessment Centre' director to make the announcement.

The 'Assessment Centre' director stood up and explained the process they used. How the intelligence tests and scenario based exercises identified the best candidates and how the scoring system made it fair, above board and as transparent an assessment as it could be.

"So without further ado. The person ranked first and receives their promotion to sergeant using the 'Assessment Centre' process is... PC Woolyheid."

Chief Constable McDandy put his head in his hands and a little tear appeared in the corner of his eye. Shorty afterwards, the 'Assessment Centre' process got binned, and they went back to 'The Bunfight,' but not before *Sergeant* Woolyheid got his stripes out of it.

Following that perceived debacle, a working party was set up to review the promotion process. The working party comprised senior officers who convened a weekly meeting at Tulliallan Police College. Their initial findings decreed that 'The Bunfight' would continue until they, the working party, had completed another review and could recommend the way forward. The working party did eventually make recommendations. Yet another new promotion process, introduced on the back of their review. Their review took five years. Five years for goodness sake! To put that into perspective. Einstein came up with his general theory of relativity in less time. Other things that took less than five years:

1. The USA put together a space program, built the rockets and put a man on the moon.
2. The Empire State Building was erected in one-third of that time.
3. The Titanic was designed, built and sank with two years to spare.
4. The Hoover Dam was constructed in the same time.
5. The tallest structure on Earth, the Burj Dubai, was also built in five years.

In that same five-year period, our senior officers on the working party came up with something so good that all the above feats of human development paled into insignificance. I mean, it was the promotion process they used to promote me to Inspector. It didn't last as long.

Chapter 2

THE WORLD'S LONGEST PEE

In the meantime, I put on my Velcro Stripes and got to work as a gaffer.

For my temporary sergeant role, I was posted to G Division, which covered an industrial town, full of petrochemical companies. At that time, due to the potentially dangerous nature of the industry, there was a standing instruction that supervisors could not to leave the town borders, such was the prospect of a major incident occurring. If the place blew up, I had to be on hand to deal with it. It meant undergoing Major Incident Control Committee (MICC) training.

MICC training is about coordinating the running of a major incident between the police, the fire service, the council and the companies involved. Anything could happen, an explosion, leakage of poisonous gas, another explosion, toxic chemicals getting into the atmosphere or water supply. There were truly a lot of things that could go wrong - especially explosions.

I was informed that my MICC training date wasn't until four weeks after I started. I spoke to my inspector about it, "Inspector, I am not happy about not getting MICC training before I start, what if something happens in my first week?" I was due to be night shift, and there would be no senior officers around to help guide me through what I should do if something serious happened.

"I shouldn't worry about it," he said with a dismissive wave of his hand.

"Why? Is it not likely that anything will happen? Will there be someone else who comes out to deal with it? Are these things easy to deal with?"

"No. No. No. If it blows up the town is toast and you'll be frazzled along with it. Just molecules floating in a cloud of poison whether you're trained or not. So I wouldn't worry about it if I was you." My inspector smiled a smile that made me wonder if he was joking, I guessed not.

So my first official day was a temporary sergeant I worked the night shift. I did a briefing for my troops and then acquainted myself with the office. The office provided parking for all our police vehicles, but there was only sufficient room for about half of our private vehicles. Fortunately, for me, there the sergeants had a designated space. It was first to come, first served for the cops. Those arriving during the day, when we had a lot more civilian staff on, or later than the rest of their shift, had to park at a local supermarket car park and walk five hundred yards to the office. It was always to my amusement that they moaned about that five hundred yard walk, yet couldn't get away from work fast enough to spend an hour at the gym.

The ground floor of my new station contained the main reception area and housed an office behind that where our Control Room staff worked. A long corridor extended from the Control Room to the small unused cell complex. Occasionally, during big drug operations, we drafted in custody officers to open these cells up to monitor prisoners that we detained. The sergeant's office, inspector's office, and report room were all situated off the corridor. All carpets were threadbare or nonexistent. The blinds were dirty and broken. I saw chipped paintwork everywhere, and the ceilings were a patchwork of broken, punctured and dirty styrofoam. The furniture was no better; I've burned better-looking firewood. Desks and chairs that would not have been out of place in a skip. All in all, the ground floor was a bleak and depressing place to be. I rolled my eyes at the thought of spending most the next six months as a temporary sergeant there.

A set of stairs, with a middle landing, led to the top floor. Locked offices had signs outside saying 'Community Sergeant' and 'Community Office'. The community officers had learned to lock their doors. Cops are resourceful when it comes to obtaining office supplies without having to submit requisition forms - if they can avoid it. The next office had a sign saying 'MICC Suite'. It too was locked, but I could see through the glass door that several telephones were in place on the desks, two computers sat at the far side with a great big screen above them, a place where everyone in the room could see it. The largest scale maps I had ever seen covered one wall. From the maps, I saw that the industrial complex was about three times the size of the whole town itself. It all looked quite intimidating, and I would certainly feel happier patrolling the place after I'd been on my MICC training. I checked the door once more confirming it was locked and wondered where they kept the key. As the senior officer on duty, it would be a useful thing to know - in the event of a major incident.

Then boom. A thunderous explosion resonated around the office and the sky seemed to light up, sending a flood of light flashing up the corridor. A moment later an alarm bell in the MICC suite rang. I looked through the glass window into the MICC suite in horror.

What the f…?

I made my way downstairs and outside. Once in the street, I could see, at the far side of the town, a flare shooting up into the air from a metal chimney. The flare normally rose about ten feet burning day and night. Now it was shooting about two hundred feet up into the air and was dancing around like a squirrel on a barbeque. The flame started out blue and then turned orange and gold as it reached higher into the sky.

Holy cow batman!

My first night, an hour into the shift and I had my first major incident. I rushed back into the office to mobilise the troops.

To my surprise, the office clerk and everyone else on my new shift was going about their business as if nothing had happened. Several were typing on their computers, one was sorting out files, and another was making tea. "Did you not hear the explosion?" I asked all of them.

In slow motion, everyone stopped what they were doing and turned to face me. Now it was their turn to show surprise. Iain, my office clerk a solid officer of twenty years service, calmly said, "Oh, that will be the hydrocracker."

Shit, the hydrocracker! That sounds serious. Why aren't they doing anything about it? Are they waiting for me to give them instruction? I'm not trained yet. Surely they realise this? What should I do?

Iain could see I was still none the wiser. If he could read contorted looks on faces, he would have looked at mine and read; *'what the feck do I do about it?'*

He put me out of my panic stricken misery, "Happens all the time. Don't worry about it."

It was a lesson for me. In situations where things looked serious and the only sensible thing to do is to panic, sometimes it is better to watch what is going on around about me first. If the surrounding people are experienced and know what they are doing, then it might be an idea to follow their lead. They had all worked there for years. Explosions were routine, and they ignored them and got on with what they were doing. The only thing of interest for them was their new, green behind the ears, temporary sergeant panicking about it.

A month later I went on the MICC training and learned a lot. The main thing I took from it was that the petrochemical industry we had in the town was dangerous. Dangerous, as a word to describe it, is probably a bit too mild. They drummed into me that I should never get complacent about explosions. I learned that the hydrocracker is a reactor at the heart of the plant. It boils crude gas oil and cracks the heavy molecules into distillate and gasoline using a highly volatile hydrogen catalyst. Any increase in flame height or blue flame at the base is significant. In all instances where there is an explosion, major incident procedures should be considered. There is a serious risk that the whole place could go up. No matter what others are doing or saying, how experienced and how calm they are, the only sensible thing to do is worry about it.

So the next time someone tells me, "Happens all the time. Don't worry about it." I reserve the right to ignore them and go right ahead and panic.

G Division was a strange place to work, very much all or nothing. Night shifts could often be quiet. I would end up driving round in circles looking for anything to relieve the boredom. Then, about four in the morning, most young adult residents would arrive back into the town having spent the evening in the nearby city getting drunk and confrontational. The place would go from calm and peaceful to absolute bonkers. Fights, domestic incidents, road traffic accidents (caused by drunk driving) would all come in at once. All at a time when we had the least staff on and when we were most tired and at a low ebb. Time and again we made it through the night more by luck than design. I was lucky to have a shift full of bright and enthusiastic cops.

Attitude is everything for succeeding in life, and this lot were fantastic. Never once did they moan about being tired, or overworked. The only thing they left behind when they left the room was a good impression.

They moaned about other things. They moaned about the Government, senior officers, daft initiatives, procurator fiscals, lack of overtime, and (behind my back) temporary sergeants. When they were busy they didn't moan about anything. Having a mystery to solve was the one thing that united everybody. I was to discover that G Division had a long term mystery that everyone was desperate to solve.

A man caused a bloody nuisance of himself at a local bar. He'd had too much to drink and had made rather inappropriate advances to the young and pretty barmaid. The owner fired a warning in his direction, but this failed to stop him. Full of beer and bravado he continued to make suggestive remarks towards her. Several of the other regular patrons chipped in with their disapproval. Their intervention just spurred the man on, and his comments to the pretty barmaid went from being suggestive to vulgar. He received even more reprimands, but again he ignored them, and his remarks turned from being vulgar to downright filthy. Lewd enough that the owner phoned the police.

"Hello, I am the owner of The Red Lion, I'd like to report a fight."

"When did this happen?"

"In about two minutes from now.

I liked to get out of the office and go on patrol, especially on the night shifts. So I was out and about when the call came in for us to attend the fight at the Red Lion. I wasn't far away from the bar so headed round. I was the first police officer into the car park and had just stepped out of my car to lock it when I saw another marked police van round the corner into the street at such a speed it was almost on two wheels. It had its blue lights and siren activated. It screeched up to the pub, mounted the pavement and, even before it came to a sudden stop, the driver's door was open and out jumped Tommy Toolbag. Tommy was itching to get in on the fight.

"What are you doing here Tommy? This isn't even your beat."

"Oh, I was just passing boss, never like to miss a good fight."

We made our way into the bar.

To Tommy's disappointment there was no fight. At least, what fight there had been was now over. The lascivious male was prostrate on the ground with about twelve of the regular patrons using him as a seat. Some still held onto their pint glasses, supping away as the man squealed underneath them.

It was quite an amusing scene, even Tommy Toolbar, disappointed in being denied a brawl, saw the funny side and managed a great big guffaw. We allowed the clientele to remain seated on top of our suspect until we got sufficient statements to confirm that he had been a bloody nuisance. Tommy then cuffed the male, and we headed outside to put him in the van.

Just as soon as we exited the bar, something at the front nearside of my car drew my attention. It looked like a full black bin bag at first but it wasn't. It was a youth wearing a black hoodie. He was bent down letting the air out of my tyre. On hearing us behind him, the youth turned around and saw me looking at him. Peering through the hood was a pale looking face with two black pinholes for eyes. A young man only nineteen or twenty. It took me a second or two to compute what he was doing. Part of it was due to the way he reacted.

Rather than panic and run away, this hooded youth stood up slowly, gave me a sneer, turned about and walked away.

Had he really been letting my tyre down?

Tommy manhandled our prisoner into the back of our van, and I went to check my tyre. Sure enough, the tyre was half flat. I looked around for the hooded youth, but he had disappeared. I didn't think I would have much chance of catching him on my own so I radioed in and passed his description to the rest of the officers on patrol.

"Can you also see if there is a foot pump somewhere in the office so I can get mobile again," I asked.

"There should be one in the boot of your car sarge," my office clerk informed me, "We have had all the cars kitted out with one because we get a lot of this."

Back at the office, I got the story.

For about a year, someone had been subjecting the police vehicles in G Division to the regular and annoying habit of letting their tyres down. Once or twice a week, cops would find one of their tyres flat. It might have been while they were in a house dealing with a call or at the local fish and chip shop getting their supper, there was no real pattern to it. On every occasion, it was only one tyre. There was never any damage; the air simply expelled by pressing on the valve. It would have been a lot more inconvenient and expensive if he had slashed the tyres. Initially, the bosses thought it might be just a phase, a passing fancy of some idiot with a gripe against them. It kept happening, week after week, month after month, they decided to supply all the vehicles with foot pumps, which saved a lot of time. Instead of having to radio up and get another crew to come out with a foot pump or even change it for the spare tyre, they simply had to go into the boot find the foot pump and blow it up again. It was a good solution because nobody had got anywhere near catching the youth doing it.

It turned out I was the first person actually to see someone in the act of doing it. My description of the hooded youth was passed to every officer at the station. There was a genuine vigour to find the hooded youth with the pale face and black pinhole eyes.

At my next briefing, I discussed with my shift what they would do if they caught him, "What would you charge him with?"

"Vandalism," was PC Wilson's answer. It caused a general nod of agreement to pass around the briefing room.

"Well, certainly there is a deliberate intention there, but because he has let the air out, there was no actual damage caused. To constitute a vandalism, he must destroy or damage the property of another. It just doesn't quite fit," I responded.

Technically speaking, letting air out of a tyre can cause damage, particularly if the driver didn't notice and drove off. Tyres aren't designed to be driven on flat and doing so will destroy the integrity of the tyre. It had been happening for so long in G Division and with such regularity it had become second nature for all the cops to check their tyres before entering their vehicle. They checked them every time. If they found a flat tyre, they blew it up. Thus there was never any actual damage.

There was a moment of thought before PC Fyfe offered her opinion, "Well he is causing a bloody nuisance so I would charge him with a breach of the peace."

"That is certainly a competent charge; he has caused us an annoyance, and under the definition of a breach of the peace so you would be within your rights. Does anyone have any other suggestions?"

After a thoughtful pause, PC Grant came up with, "Is it an offence under the Police (Scotland) Act?"

"Yes, that would be a competent charge too. Section 41 states that it is an offence to assault, resist, obstruct, molest or hinder a constable in the execution of his duty. He has definitely hindered us. We have had to kit the vehicles out with foot pumps, and we take time to pump the tyres back up, so technically you would be correct. Any other suggestions?"

"Malicious mischief," PC Wilson suggested. I think he was miffed at being wrong about it being a vandalism. Malicious mischief is the common law charge of vandalism, but it is only applied in cases where the damage is high in value or where there is a financial cost brought about by a criminal act, the act itself has to be wilful or wanton. The main thing, though, is there has to be actual damage.

Not wishing to alienate him further I said, "Yes, I like the way you are thinking. If we had driven off and crashed the car as a result of having a soft tyre that charge would fit. Are there any other suggestions?"

That got them thinking. Was there a more competent charge?

"I suppose if we drove off and crashed because of the flat tyre, then his actions could be construed as assault, "PC Fyfe chipped in.

"Very good. That would be a possible charge too. It is like putting a stick in the spokes of a bicycle as it passes. You are not making a direct attack on the person, but if the cyclist falls off and hurts himself, then it becomes an indirect assault. Any other suggestions?

"Theft, " PC Wilson suggested, "Theft of the air in the tyre."

Now, this was a stupid suggestion. Theft of air! Where on earth was he going to put it? Even if he collected it in a plastic bag, it wasn't worth anything. Air, unless you are drowning, is valueless.

It was PC Wilson's third stupid suggestion, but at least he was thinking about it and making suggestions. I had presented them with a problem and looked for some intelligent discussion, some ideas might lack value at first sight but working on them together helps everyone feel as if they have contributed. I didn't want to discourage that participation in any way. I wanted there to be a thoughtful debate at my briefings. Even when my officers made stupid comments, I didn't want to alienate them from me. I wanted to encourage their ideas and input; it was all about developing knowledge as a group. I knew that if I made the wrong response to PC Wilson, it might stifle open discussion within the team.

"Don't be so stupid," I said - well, theft of air, REALLY!

I waited a moment as the rest of the group mocked PC Wilson with their laughter before asking again, "Any other suggestions."

They looked at each other puzzled. There must be a more appropriate charge because I kept asking.

"Attempt to defeat the ends of justice," PC Farquhar piped up, but qualified his answer with, "although I'm not sure it quite fits."

People get charged with attempt to defeat the ends of justice when they don't quite manage to pervert the course of justice, for example; by threatening a witness to not give evidence in court. It can also be infringed by obstructing an officer from doing his duty, but it is only applied to a specific case - the case=

45

the officer is investigating. His answer wasn't quite what I was looking for.

"Yes, possibly a competent charge if you were investigating a specific case and his actions prevented you from doing so. Perhaps the Police Scotland Act would cover it though. Any other suggestions?"

They looked around at each other again. I think the message was getting through that there might be an even more appropriate charge. PC Fyfe put her hand up.

"Yes, Susan, what do you think it is?" I invited her to speak.

"Is it Reckless Conduct?"

Culpable and Reckless Conduct is a common law offence in Scots Law. The offence has no specific definition but deals with acts involving a criminal degree of recklessness which causes injury to other persons or creates a risk of such injury.

"Well, if anyone of us were to drive off and not notice that the tyre had been let down and as a result, the vehicle crashed then Culpable and Reckless Conduct is an appropriate charge. Any reasonable person ought to know that letting a tyre down is a reckless thing to do and could cause an accident."

I had engineered discussion about the law. My point was that, despite the law being written in black and white, in fact, there remains a lot of conjecture on how it is interpreted. You might charge the youth with a Breach of the Peace; your sergeant might disagree and suggest you charge him with Culpable and Reckless Conduct. The Report Checker, an experienced officer who makes sure there is sufficient proof before sending a report to the Procurator Fiscal, might decide that a charge under the Police (Scotland) Act is a better fit and have the report amended. Ultimately, the Procurator Fiscal will make the final decision on what goes on the Copy Complaint, and he or she might decide that you were right in the first place and cite him on the Breach of the Peace charge. The law is not black and white; its interpretation is one big grey area.

"Okay, now let's consider another the scenario. As you are leaving the pub with your prisoner, you catch someone in the act of letting your tyre down. What are you going to do with him?"

My question; 'what are you going to do with him?' Sets up another problem for police officers - the actual practicalities of doing the job.

"I would arrest him for Breach of the Peace," chipped in PC Fyfe.

"Okay, good, but you already have a prisoner. There are only two of you, and everyone else is busy."

"Well, I'd put both of them in the back of the car."

"Very good. What if your two prisoners are in cahoots and start conniving? Or the opposite, they don't like each other and start fighting?"

"I'd take his name and address and go and see him later on once I'd spoken to you and decided what to charge him with," PC Wilson kowtowed in case I shot him down again.

PC Farquhar had clearly thought a little more about it and said, "Well it depends."

"On what?"

"It depends on who he is."

"What do you mean?"

"Well, if he was just some student having a prank, I might give him a telling off and send on his way. If he was a well-known Scroat, I might lock him up."

"Exactly. So we need more information. We need to know who he is and what his intention is. If his intention was to play a misguided prank, it is surely not as serious as him deliberately trying to interfere in our arrest and obstruct us in the execution of our duty. His intention might be that we drive off and crash, in which case it becomes even more serious. So what we do in all situations is gather evidence, assess that evidence and then act on it once we have made conclusions. The less information we have, the more basic our assumptions. That is why it is always good to delve into things, find out more and give ourselves a better chance of coming to the right conclusion."

It was the second part of the point I was trying to make. Policing is also a bit of a grey area. We have to make a lot of decisions that can have a big effect on people's lives. Thus it is important that we try to get it right. Using our discretion, based on experience and proper information will help us make sensible conclusions. I liked throwing scenarios out there and getting my troops to think about them. If they were ever to come across a situation like that in real life, it meant that they had at least thought about it beforehand. Even the process of giving it some thought would help when trying to decide on matters that they had not come across before. Happy with my briefing I got up to head back through to my office.

"Wait a minute sarge," PC Wilson stopped me, "What would you charge him with if you caught him letting your tyre down?"

"I'd charge him with an offence under Section 70 of the Road Safety Act 1986* and then send him on his way," I replied smugly, before quickly walking out the room leaving them to look it up for themselves. (It helps to research these things before you discuss them!)

*ROAD SAFETY ACT 1986 - SECTION 70

Tampering or interfering with motor vehicle without just cause or excuse

(1) A person who, without just cause or excuse, tampers or interferes with a motor vehicle owned by any other person is guilty of an offence.

While the temporary sergeant role was often demanding, all in all, I enjoyed the responsibility. Initially, I worried about making cock-ups, but I soon settled into it (the job, not making cock-ups). After a couple of weeks, I started to feel a little more comfortable about my ability to perform the role, and I even had time for a little nonsense. This time I directed it at someone who could talk for Scotland.

We had a pleasant chief inspector at the station who had an even temperament. I never saw her get angry, she was just wonderfully calm all the time. Her forte was running meetings, a fact she recognised and played on. There was not a day went by when she did not have several meetings to go to. If she found herself without a meeting to go to, she would convene one and chair it herself. She loved meetings. It didn't matter what the topic of the meeting was or who the attendees were; Chief Inspector Euphemia Miller would be at the head of the table, agenda in hand and work her way through it.

Because she was always in meetings, it was difficult to find her and make her aware of operational matters. She wasn't afraid of making decisions; it was just that we struggled to grab her attention. It is common courtesy not to interrupt meetings for trivial matters. Unless there was an earthquake, or we had an alien invasion, she was left in peace to work her way through each agenda point as thoroughly as she liked. As her meetings could take place anywhere in the area command, it was sometimes difficult to track her down.

She could be anywhere between her office, the Station Meeting Room, Headquarters, the Fire Service Meeting Room at Fire Service Headquarters, NHS Meeting Room at NHS Headquarters, Social Work Meeting Room at Social Work Headquarters or Community Council Meeting Room at the Community Council Offices.

She left one meeting and headed off to her next one. leaving a tiny time frame when she was available to run things by her. After a frustrating few weeks trying to track her down every day, I decided not to bother. I ended up deciding on her behalf. I found that, as long as I could explain my decision-making process, she would support me in whatever decision I'd made.

Some of my co-sergeants found it difficult to do the same. Not as willing to shoulder the responsibility, they would hang on well after their shift had finished, sometimes for hours, so they could catch Chief Inspector Miller coming out of her current meeting and run a problem by her. Her response was, more often than not, to ask that they put it on paper, she would deal with it in the morning as she was late for her next meeting. Waiting around to speak to her rarely achieved much. I decided not to fall into that trap. If she was in a meeting (and she generally was) I would send her a brief email stating what the problem was, what I had done about it and why. I don't think there was a single time she questioned any of my decisions. At least, she didn't convene a meeting about them.

Another thing to avoid was being called into the meetings with her. Every day she would convene a 'morning meeting' where we discussed all the previous days business - tasking meetings. We identified the priorities for the day and assigned tasks. The process, elsewhere, would take ten to fifteen minutes. The morning meetings run by Chief Inspector Euphemia

Miller could go on for hours. She identified tasks, that's true, but the process involved a great deal of discussion. Everyone had an opportunity to provide input as to what tasks were relevant, what order of priority they should go and then she discussed every infinitesimal detail regarding the best way to complete these tasks. It became a bug-bear of mine. Most of the time I had already tasked my shift with the enquiries they were discussing. I often walked out of the morning meeting to find every task we had talked about for the last hour and a half had been completed.

Sitting in a meeting didn't allow me to get on with my job. After a few weeks, I felt a bit more confident about what I was doing in my new role, and I adopted a few different tactics to avoid spending so much time in Chief Inspector Miller's meetings.

I would pop my head into her office just before the 'morning meeting' was due to start and tell her I had to go to an important call. I quickly ran over the priorities I had identified and to whom I had tasked them. She would take a note, nod and excuse me from the morning meeting. Great! Another hour saved from my day. Another strategy would be to arrange a drugs raid (carry out a search under warrant of some drug dealers house), and this always pleased her as the results reflected on her management of the station. Organising a drugs raid was a good excuse to avoid attending the meeting.

My office clerk was also first-rate. By arrangement, if I hadn't emerged from the meeting within half an hour, he would radio me up and ask to see me as a matter of necessity. I would look pleadingly at Chief Inspector Miller, and she simply nodded in agreement and off I would go.

Sometimes I got so frustrated sitting in a meeting. I couldn't help myself; I stood up, made an excuse for something I had to do; A probationer's appraisal, a custody report to check, an enquiry from the Procurator Fiscal - anything - I would just stand up and say, "Chief Inspector I need to check the thermal flange on the boiler if there is no other relevant business for me can I be excused?"

There never was any other business relevant for me. I even asked to be excused to go to the loo a couple of times and just never went back in.

On one rare occasion when Chief Inspector Euphemia Miller was neither in a meeting or going to one, she popped into the Sergeants Office and asked me who had been using the toilet next to the meeting room. Our office was an old building, and the meeting room was upstairs, it was a large room and bare of anything other than a heavy oval wooden table and chairs. Next door to the meeting room was a single toilet. The toilet had a large high ceiling and creaky old wooden floor; any noise seemed to reverberate around the room. The toilet was not for the exclusive use of anyone in particular, but only those using the meeting room, and Chief Inspector Miller, who's office was opposite, used it. I didn't know who had been using it but was curious enough to ask her, "Why do you ask?"

"Well I was using the meeting room this morning and could hear the sound of the pee hitting the water," she explained, "It was rather embarrassing as I was in a meeting with the superintendent in at the time."

I agreed that the office had poor insulation, and I sympathised with the awkwardness of the situation. Chief Inspector Miller made no more fuss and left.

A few days later I was alerted to the fact that Chief Inspector Euphemia Miller was having a meeting with the members of the Women's Police Association. There was an assortment of female ranks passing my office door as they made their way upstairs to the meeting room.

I waited until the meeting was underway, then went out to the garage and returned with a large watering can I had seen lying there a few weeks previous. It was an old green metal watering can that held ten litres of water when full. I filled it up to the brim. I carried it into the building and headed past my office and ascended the stairs, careful not to spill a drop. With my ten litres of water in my watering can, I sneaked into the toilet next to the meeting room.

The hardest part was trying not to laugh as the world's longest pee commenced. I slowly poured all ten litres of water from my watering can down the toilet, holding it as high as I could for maximum noise. My marathon pee included about twenty stop starts towards the end. (Oh, come on! That's funny, you try to do that without giggling like a lunatic.)

The next Tuesday night shift I was patrolling the town and drove into the forecourt of our Mercedes garage. I got out and had a walk round the building, checked the security but mostly just admired the cars on show. It was a clear night, and I was dreaming about winning the lottery and maybe buying one of these incredible cars. A rap on the window startled me from my daydream. Then a door to my left opened, a dark figure the size of a bear came out of the showroom entrance. My flight or fight response kicked in. The adrenaline flowed through my veins, and I panicked. I didn't know whether to run away or just tackle this monster from the off. My hand went to my baton, and I had it out and ready to thump this guy before I realised he was the security guard. He had been watching me mooning around the forecourt and decided to open up and offer me a cup of tea.

Lenny, the security guard, gave me a toothy grin. He had a boring job, so he seemed delighted to have company. I mean, all he had to do all night was wander around the place from the showroom to the garage to the offices and back to the showroom again. I think he also figured that there was less likelihood of anything happening while a marked police vehicle sat in his forecourt. Lenny's hospitality extended to a cup of tea and a tour around the showroom. Lenny was a nice guy, despite being the size of a bear he was a gentle creature. He had worked there for about twenty years, and in all that time he hadn't had a single incident to speak of. If I asked him a question, he would answer it then ramble on for another hour about the most mind-numbing drivel you can imagine. At least the tea was warm and wet, and I quite liked passing the time there than just driving my police car around in circles.

The next night was just as quiet so I stopped off to see Lenny again, and he switched on the kettle. While waiting for him to bring the tea out, I wandered around the showroom looking at all the cars. Sitting on the far side of the showroom, in pride of place, was a top of the range S-Class saloon. The black powerhouse faced the main showroom window looking all mean and menacing. I climbed into the beast, shut the door and gripped the steering wheel. If my police car wasn't parked right outside in the way, I could imagine myself sticking it into gear and smashing through the glass and roaring off up the road.

I sat there in the driver's seat fantasising that I might own one of these cars one day. Then something caught my eye. In my peripheral vision, out of the bushes on my right, a figure appeared. A youth with a hood. He craned his neck towards my vehicle, ensuring the police car in front of him was empty. Then he darted from the bushes across to the showroom window and pressed his face up against the glass, looking in. I was motionless in the black S-Class Mercedes, the low light of the showroom reflecting off the windscreen keeping me hidden from his gaze. The hooded youth was only about ten feet away from me, and I could see his pale face and black pinholes for eyes. There was no mistaking; it was the same boy I had seen letting the air out of my tyre when I came out of the Red Lion. What to do?

I couldn't open the car door and sneak out. The interior light would come on and alert him to my presence. Anyway, I would have to run back to the other side of the showroom out the door and all the way back down to where he was. By the time I did that he'd be long gone. I had no chance of catching him. My radio was in my top pocket, silent. If I radioed in for assistance, he might hear me. Even if he didn't hear me, he would be gone before anyone else could get here. It was a quandary. I sat watching him, immobile but thinking furiously in the futile hope of coming up with some way of getting out there without alerting him to my presence.

He must have decided that whoever had parked the police car was in the back of the showroom and out of sight. He edged back towards the police car and bent down to the front nearside tyre. I knew what was coming. He would let the air out of my tyre, and there was nothing I could do about it. A *Catch 22* situation. So I did the only thing I could.

I pulled on the full beam of the S-Class Mercedes and flooded him with light. He was directly in front of the beam, and it lit him up like a spotlight. At the same time, I pressed down on the horn and kept it there. The combination of being flooded with light and the noise of the horn was effective. The hooded youth jumped up in astonishment. All natural survival instincts

55

discarded, he froze. He stood where he was. His brain unable to compute how he was standing in the path of a car that was blinding him with light and confusing his senses with noise. For a split second, he must have believed he was in the path of a speeding car heading straight towards him. Right there and then he evacuated his bowels. Literally, he shit himself.

Lenny had been heading back with our tea when I had unexpectedly flashed the S-Class full beam and sounded the horn. Despite dropping two cups of tea and two biscuits he saw the youth at my car and realised what I was doing. He rushed to help. He shot out the exit door and made his way out to the forecourt.

The surprised hooded and vacated youth gathered himself enough to try to make his escape. Not quite running, because of what was now sloshing about in his trousers, he moved off. Unfortunately for him, he moved off in the wrong direction. He went to my left, across the front of the showroom and was just about to pass the entrance door when Lenny emerged and grabbed him. Lenny caught the guy who had been letting down the tyres on all the police vehicles in G division for the past year.

The police cars had been tampered with regularly. Once or twice a week cops had come out from what they were dealing with to the inconvenience of a flat tyre. Despite concerted efforts, the tamperer had remained undetected until now. With the help of Lenny, I had caught him. Now I had to decide what to do with him. The first thing I did was find out more about him. More information meant making a better decision.

"What's your name?"
"Randall."
"Mr Randall?"
"No, Randall McBrayne."

"What age are you Randall?"

"Seventeen."

I squeezed his date of birth and address out of him and radioed into the Control Room and asked for a check on the Police National Computer (PNC). I was pretty sure there would be a record of him. While I waited for the check, I asked him a few more questions.

"Who do you stay with?"

"Nobody."

"Nobody?"

"Nobody."

"You don't live with your Mum and Dad?"

"My Mum is dead. She died when I was young."

"What about your Dad?"

"My Dad left to work abroad not long after my Mum died. He came back two or three times to see me, but I haven't seen him for years."

"Who looked after you then?"

"My aunt took me in, but she got fed up and put me in a children's home."

My radio sparked into life.

"Control to Sergeant McEwan, come in, over."

"Yes, go ahead."

"There is no trace of that name or date of birth. The address is a DSS bed-and-breakfast, over."

"Roger that."

My suspicious nature took over.

"Randall, do you have any identification on you?"

Randall produced a student ID card with his picture on it. The name and date of birth checked out.

Randall was unusual, despite having been in care from an early age, unlike the majority of such wards of the state, he did not have a criminal record. He hadn't come to the notice of the police before, even for a warning. Randall was a quiet loner, with no friends to speak of. He was pretty much an anonymous entity.

57

For thirteen or fourteen months the police officers of G Division had been inconvenienced by having their tyres let down. I couldn't just let him go. Here he was squirming in front of me, worried about getting caught and uncomfortable with what was swilling around in his pants.

"Why did you do it, Randall?"

"What?"

"Why did you let the tyres down on all those police cars? You know that it caused us a lot of bother."

"Just because."

"Just because what?"

He didn't answer at first, but I waited, looking at him for an answer. Silence. People have to fill that silence and Randall did too, he broke the silence and explained why he did it.

"I bought a bike, a Raleigh Chopper, you know the one with the big back wheel."

"Uh huh?"

"I used to love bumping up and down pavements on it. I was always getting a row from the local community cop for riding it in the precinct. One day I came out of the paper shop, got on the bike and cycled off down the steps to the road but the back wheel was flat, and my wheel broke. Your community cop was there, and he laughed. My pal told me it was him that let my tyre down. I had no money to fix it, so it went in the skip."

Karma. What goes around comes around. In this case. what went around was a flat tyre. I decided to let Randall go.

First of all, not one previous incident where a police car had had its tyre let down had been recorded as a crime. The police are keen to keep detection rates as high as they can and having a few undetected tyres tampered with on the statistics every week would have

58

skewed the figures badly. Officers simply blew their tyres up and got on with what they were doing. There was no appetite to create work for themselves by writing up an undetected case. Something the bosses had conveniently ignored. They were quite happy to supply foot pumps for all the vehicles but forcing officers to record the undetected offence would reflect on the Division. After all, G Division had performance targets to meet. Secondly, I felt sorry for Randall. He hadn't had the best start in life. Through no fault of his own, he had ended up in care. I particularly felt sorry for him as he stood there squirming in his soiled underpants. I would not put him in my police car like that.

So that was it. I headed back to my station, confident knowing that we would have no more flat tyres, my warning to Randall before he waddled off would be sufficient. I was confident he wouldn't do it again. He knew I would come looking for him the second we had another episode.

So I kept quiet about catching Randall. I didn't want to have some overzealous senior officer instruct that we bring Randall in and resurrect all previous incidents. I determined that the bosses would want to see the detection figures go up but that would have been at the expense of common sense.

Of course, there was also the little matter of having to explain what I was doing sitting in that S-Class Mercedes waiting for a cup of tea

.

Chapter 3

THE ONE MAN BANDIT

After six months, my tenure as a temporary sergeant came to an end. I survived. And better for the experience. It is a responsible position and probably the hardest job in the police. There is a lot to remember, and there is always someone who wants a piece of you. Not only do you have to take responsibility for yourself but every single one of your staff. A sergeant is the conduit between the bosses and their demands and the troops with their moans and groans. Deal with a demanding public and balance what they want with what you can in fact deliver. You have finite resources but are expected to work miracles with them. The buck stops with you. It is that accountability that puts off a lot of capable officers from going for promotion. They don't want that responsibility.

The benefit of doing a temporary rank is that it allows you to experience what it is like in the promoted role. It might be that you decide it is not for you. Then again, you might not even have that decision to make; the bosses might decide that it is just not for you. It all depends on how you performed.

Before I walked out the door, Chief Inspector Euphemia Miller called me into her office for a 'meeting'.

"Thank you for coming to this meeting," she said as I sat down in a chair in front of her desk.

"No problem," I replied.

Like I had a choice. I wonder how long this will go on for?

"We shouldn't be too long, I have a few things to go over with you regarding your performance," as she looked down at a sheet of A4 paper full of bullet points in front of her.

That's not bad. Only one A4 sheet of paper in front of her, I might get out of here before lunch time.

"No problem," I answered again.

My second most favourite thing in the world is talking about myself. You might think then that I might quite enjoy sitting with a chief inspector who has my name at the top of her agenda. That was not the case. In those circumstances, all I want to do is get out of there. Being held up to critical scrutiny can be daunting. In those situations, my tendency is to go into an involuntary humble mode. I play down my abilities and forget to mention all the good things I have achieved. Is that a peculiarly British phenomenon? That isn't to say there aren't any arrogant people in the police - there are. Those who are quick to denigrate others for whatever it was they did or didn't do, even quicker to take credit for things that had nothing to do with them. People who, according to them, had dealt with every possible case you could imagine and single-handedly kept the police running. I wasn't like that. I am a worrier.

"It appears that you have carried out your sergeant responsibilities very well," Chief Inspector Euphemia Miller started off.

What does she mean by 'appears'? What is she saying? Does she know something else she is not telling me? Is it only my sergeant responsibilities that are good? Have I mucked up other responsibilities? What other responsibilities did I have? I don't know. Nobody told me. It must be my fault!

"There have been no major cock-ups," she continued.

Rats. Does that mean there have been minor cock-ups?

Well, there were, but you kept those to yourself.

61

I know. So how does she know about them?

I don't know.

Just nod and agree and see which cock-ups she knows and only admit to them if she mentions them.

Okay.

I nodded at Chief Inspector Miller, in as much to my self-dialogue as to what she was saying.

Chief Inspector Euphemia Miller picked up the A4 sheet of paper in front of her and rifled through several more sheets underneath.

Fiddlesticks. There is more.

What has she written?

How many of my cock-ups does she know?

By the amount of those sheets, maybe them all.

This will take ages. I could be here all night.

I know... I wonder what is for tea.

It's Monday; we always have Macaroni on a Monday.

I know that. I'm fed up eating Macaroni on a Monday.

Yes but you like it with that Malaysian Hot Sauce you got at Tescos.

That's right; I could have it with that…

Chief Inspector Euphemia Miller interrupted my train of thought with a cough and then went through her notes. She went through them in every minute detail. The topics she covered reflected the criteria in the sergeant's job description; leadership, motivation, report writing, management of staff, etc.

Yes, yes, get on with it.

"So, regarding report writing, you have submitted sixteen memos in total and… Blah, blah, blah."

I wonder if we can fry up some Chorizo and mix that into the Macaroni, I bet that would be nice.

Two hours later she finished up with, "So well done. I'm going to recommend that you are ready for promotion now. Unfortunately, there are no sergeants positions available at the moment, but as soon as I have a place for you, I will have you back here at my station."

What I heard was; "... blah, blah, blah, get your Velcro stripes off you are going back to being a cop."

It wasn't all bad, back as a cop. Not having the responsibility for everyone and everything made my job easier. I slotted back into my old station with my old colleagues and carried on as I left off. There were the usual pranks. Uncle Sylvester and I resumed our tit-for-tat shenanigans. He brought me right back down to the ground regarding any big ideas I had for myself, although I thought it unfair of him to ask, "How on earth did you get a temporary sergeant's role?" I mean, I was only stapling his yellow jacket to the ceiling. *What was he talking about? Of course, I deserved my temporary rank.*

I was keen to put the stripes back on permanently. As a cop, I only had to think about myself. I got sent to several calls every day, and during those calls, I would get a certain amount of satisfaction from resolving problems. I sorted out neighbour disputes, dealt with road accidents and showed empathy to sad members of the public. But it wasn't quite the same as being in charge. As a sergeant, I had to sort out cop disputes, deal with cop road accidents and show empathy to sad members of the police.

Still, I tried to remain enthusiastic. It isn't easy being a cop but having been in a supervisor's role for six months it had become a little more straightforward. So while I waited for a sergeant's position to become available, I spent my day longing for something to ease the monotony and keep me interested. Fortunately, someone came along that did exactly that. Sergeant McMachin called me into his office.

"Malky. I have a wee problem and I hoping you might solve it for me."

"What can I do for you?"

"Well, we have this lassie who is out of her probation and is struggling a little with her report writing. I'd like you to pair up with her and give her a bit of coaching. Bring her up to standard."

"Sure. Who is she?"

"It's Billie Smith."

And that was how I got paired up with the delightful and dazzling Billie Smith. Billie had six years service, was tall, blonde and had the bubbliest personality that could imagine. She could brighten any room with her smile, and I can't say I was even the slightest bit disappointed to have her as my new partner. Billie is a special person, and I found her to be a joy to work with. She was funny, knowledgeable and full of joy. Her love of life was infectious.

I quickly ascertained that there wasn't anything wrong with her report writing at all. She could write a report as well as anybody and didn't need me to be looking over her shoulder. I guessed that there may have been a little bit of friction, though, between her and our sergeant. Once I had worked with Billie for a couple of days, she opened up and confirmed as much. "I think Sergeant McMachin was under a bit of pressure a few weeks ago and we had an argument."

"What about?" I asked.

"Well, I had been back shift all week and had been going from call to call every night. Just one of those back shifts where there was no let-up. Everything I went to turned into a nightmare. Everything took forever to deal with, and everything required paperwork."

"Yes, I've been there," I sympathised.

"Trouble was I couldn't get back to the office to sit down and write it up. I kept getting sent to more calls and getting even more urgent enquiries. Then, when the back shift finished, I went weekend off. I was to be a bridesmaid at my sister's wedding in Ireland otherwise, I would have come in on my days off and completed the paperwork."

Coming into work on days off to catch up on the paperwork was a regular thing that cops just did. A mixture of dedication to duty and fear of getting into trouble for late reports. There was no recompense asked for or offered, no overtime or time off in lieu. It was just something that a good officer would do. It happened frequently.

Billie continued, "So I got back to work on Monday and no sooner had I entered the office, Sergeant McMachin cornered me and asked me for my reports. I told him I would try to get them done as soon as I could, but he went on a bit of a rant and said I had had all week to get them done. He told me I had to get them in by the end of my shift that day or he would consider them as late. I knew it would take me three days to write up all I had dealt with the week before but only if I got no more calls."

"So what did you do?"

"I told him that they could be late or they can be rubbishy. Which do you prefer?"

I pictured her smiling at him which would have put his nose out of joint even more.

Billie and I got on with our work and tried to have a bit of fun as we did it. During quiet times we would play word games, like the 'answer a question with a question game':-

"Do you want to play the 'answer the question with a question' game?"

"Why do you ask?"

"Is there a problem asking you?"

"Why should it be a problem?"

"Do you think I have a problem?"

"What makes you think I think you have a problem?"

"When did I say that?"

"Did you not say that?"

"Did I not say what?"

… and so it went on.

Another game we played was the alphabet game. The rules of the alphabet game are fairly simple. The first letter of the first word of the first person speaking must begin with the letter 'A'. The second person had to make the first letter of the first word begin with the letter 'B' and so on, right through the whole alphabet. Conversations in the *alphabet game* would go like this:-

"**A**nd what are you up to tonight?"

"**B**owling probably."

"**C**an you tell me where you bowl?"

"**D**own at the bowling club"… and so on.

Billie and I became proficient at these games. So much so we incorporated them into our dealings with the public. It was our way of making routine calls more interesting. One Sunday morning we attended to a housebreaking in a residential area. Before exiting our car I suggested we get all the information we required using the 'alphabet' game and the 'answer a question with a question' game. We agreed that we were to ask the householder all our questions alternately using the rules from both games. Then we knocked on his door.

"Are you the householder?"
    "Yes."
"Been broken into have you?"
    "Yes."
Can we come in?"
    "Please do."
"Do you know how they got in?"
    "The kitchen window was smashed."
"Every other window fine was it?"
    "Yes. I think they let themselves out the back door."
"First off. Can I have your full name and date of birth please?"
    "I'm John Galloway born 2nd June 1969."
"Great. What is your occupation?"
    "I'm a factory worker."
"Have you been broken into before?"
    "No this is the first time."
"Is there anything stolen?"
    "Yes. My wallet and some tins of food."
"Just exactly what did you have in your wallet?"
    "About twenty pounds, my bank card and some receipts."
"Know which bank you are with and the account number?"
    "Yes here are the details."
"Let's leave everything as it is until the scene of crime officer gets here, can you do that?"
    "Yes."
"May I ask if you have any suspicions as to who might be responsible?"
    "I've no idea. I think there have been a couple of break-ins in the street recently, though."
"Not heard anything about who might have done them have you?"

"No."

"Okay. What time did you notice the break in?"

"About seven this morning."

"Perhaps you heard something during the night?"

"No. I must have slept right through."

"Quite easily done. What time did you go to bed?"

"About half past eleven."

"Right. When do you think you went to sleep?"

"I don't know. I normally fall off quite quick."

"So you heard nothing at all?"

"No. Nothing."

"Tell me, is there anything else missing from anywhere else in the house?"

"No. I don't think so."

"Under what insurance company are you?"

"I'm not insured."

"Very well. We will do our best to catch them. Can you call us if you hear anything yourself?"

"Yes. I will do."

"Well, that's us. Can you think of anything else?"

"No."

"Xcellent. Can I call you next week?"

"Yes. I will be here."

"You find anything else missing can you call me too?"

"Yes. I will."

"Zippedy doo da. We'll be off then."

Billie and I left, climbed into our car. I looked at my notebook and saw a perfectly written statement from our householder. I then looked at Billie, and we both burst out laughing. Job done! The householder didn't have a clue, and we had made what was an ordinary day for us into an enjoyable game.

We used our little word games in various situations almost every day. It became such the norm that often when we worked with others, I would ask,

"And how are you?" staring at my uninitiated partner waiting for them to ask a question beginning with 'B'. Even when I tried to teach others how to do it, no-one could pull it off quite like Billie.

Do all police officers get up to such nonsense?
It turns out that what we were doing had basic advantages regarding our ability to cope with doing the job of a police officer and maintaining our mental health. I read somewhere that the job of a police officer consistently ranks in the top five of most stressful jobs. It is a career that takes its toll on the body and mind. Although, I didn't need to read that to know that. I already knew shift working is bad for your health - terrible. Night shifts affect us at a molecular level, altering our body chemistry and making us more susceptible to colds, coughs, and cancer. Combine that with the stress involved in being a police officer. One minute your glands are flooding your venous system with adrenaline and the next you are standing outside in the pouring rain guarding a scene of the crime, soaked and bored beyond belief. There are difficult demands in every situation. Dealing with upset victims of sexual abuse, those injured in an accident, the dying or the dead or even just the pressure of having to get a report written to an acceptable standard and in within a tight deadline. All these things combine to make it a job that takes its toll. There were many officers who suffered from stress, anxiety or depression and left the job long before their thirty years were up. I knew of officers diagnosed with Post Traumatic Stress Disorder, and still, they suffer years after having left.
I had occasion to meet and have an interesting conversation with a member of the Special Air Service (SAS). Dave had survived the gruelling initiation into the SAS, dumped out of the back of a van in the middle

of nowhere at three in the morning. No idea where he was and no map, he had to get back home. He had to do it within a certain time-frame, and he had to do it without being captured. With infantrymen, police and dogs all looking for him, not an easy task. For the next two days, he slept in hedgerows, ate worms and avoided contact with local farmers. Nobody could be trusted. He was on the home stretch when he met another potential recruit who had suffered as much as him. They holed up together in a shed to make their approach during darkness. It turned out the recruit was a plant who gave away their location, and he ended up captured. Despite being tortured the entire night, he escaped and completed the task, just in time.

"How did you keep going?" I asked, amazed at his endurance.

"It was a trick I learned in the regulars," he informed me, "I made it a game."

"Game?"

"Yes, I made it a game in my head. I gave myself points for every hour I could put up with it. I would sometimes break this down into minutes. It is easier to put up with something for a short period. Once I reached my target, I award myself points and move on to the next period. If I had to get somewhere, I would identify a landmark in the distance and make it a game to get there. I got points for reaching the telegraph pole and even more points for reaching the big tree. I remember my squad and I were on operations with various other sections of the army. We had to dig a hole on the moors and hide in it for two days, and it rained the entire time. Every other section gave up. My mates in the SAS unit just sat in our muddy hole and played games. It passed the time, we had fun, and it kept us sane."

It made me realise that what Billie and I were doing was the same. We got on with the job, tried to have fun doing it, and that helped. It definitely helped. Somewhere between being a kid and getting halfway through your police service, most people forget how to have fun. All adults have constraints they have to keep to, even more so in the police. A police officer has to portray himself as an upstanding member of society. He has to show patience - more than most, and he has to put up with a great deal of hassle or even downright abuse. So making a game of things helps. Having fun and seeing the lighter side of life is a prerequisite for getting to retirement age and still being able to function like a normal human being.

One of the most frustrating things a police officer comes across is having to deal with people who get away with murder (sometimes literally). I learned that it is always easier to deal with if you have a strategy to make fun out of it. Billie and I found ourselves in that exact situation.

Christmas time is a time for giving. It is a time for peace on earth and goodwill to all men. A time for celebration, happiness, and cheer. Children sense the seasonal change and the goodwill and merriment that is coming. Mostly it is about the presents they will receive and for the parents it is about the look on their children's faces as they receive their presents. It is a time of expectation. Miss Jeanie Bowes was expectant too.

Jeanie Bowes left school at the earliest opportunity she could. She left with pretty much nothing to show for her time spent there. Unable to get a job she got pregnant instead. Instead of her parents supporting her, they kicked her out of the family home. Homeless and pregnant she sought the help of the welfare state. With a lick and a spit they gave her a house, money to furnish the house, 'dole' money and, in due course, was the recipient of child benefit (her 'raise' as she liked to call it). She was the first in her class at school to have a house of her own and a steady income (provided by the welfare state). All she had done to get there was lie on her back.

This life suited Jeanie Bowes. She was so taken with her 'raise' that she adopted the legs akimbo position until she was sufficiently plump enough to confirm that another child and a secondary 'raise' was on the way. The routine repeated when she found herself up the duff for the third time. When asked why she didn't work, she openly told people that the state gave her the equivalent of slightly more than the average wage, all for doing nothing. Why would she even attempt to go to work? Nobody would give her any job that would pay anywhere near that amount.

Christmas was coming and Victor, her current boyfriend, moved in with her. He was neither the father of the children nor the one in the oven. Victor was a minor drug dealer who was not registered as a resident at her home but did stay there most of the time. Unfortunately, their relationship was somewhat volatile. Jeanie and Victor were both argumentative with a drink. One night, following a heavy session on seven percent proof cider, they fell out in spectacular fashion. Initially, they were just tetchy with each other, but that led to an argument. The argument became a brawl, and in the ensuing struggle, Victor completely lost his temper. He wrecked the house. There was not a piece of furniture in that house that didn't end up broken or damaged. Victor took a step back and realised he might get into a little of trouble for this. He grabbed Jeanie's purse, emptied it of the £150 it contained and left.

Jeanie, incensed at Victor for stealing her hard claimed cash, immediately called the police on her welfare state funded, top of the range mobile phone.

"I've been robbed," she complained, "... and I need a crime reference number."

Billie and I dealt with the complaint. We obtained Jeanie's statement and had sufficient evidence to detain and interview Victor. In Scots law, there has to be corroboration of evidence to convict someone. Since there was only Jeanie in the house, all we had was her word for it that Victor had caused the damage and stolen her money. That the furniture was smashed up somewhat corroborated Jeanie's version of events, but there was nothing to confirm where Jeanie had got £150. When asked about it, she was adamant she had 'saved it up'. Since Victor lived there most of the time, his fingerprints and DNA would be all over the place, so there was no point carrying out a scene of crime examination. We checked with the neighbours, and none of them had heard a thing. The crime might be a difficult one to prove. We would have to rely on Victor admitting to what he had done. Our only chance to secure further evidence would be to get a hold of Victor quickly and hope he had at least some money left. In any case, we would interview him and try to get him to admit stealing the money.

Billie and I went on a manhunt. Victor was our prey.

Where would we find Victor? It was ten o'clock at night, and we had to find him quick or risk losing any chance of finding the money still in his possession.

"Where is he likely to go?" I asked Billie.

"Where would you go with £150?"

"Well I might go to the pub if I had a spare £150,"

"Victor might prefer to get high somewhere. The pub might be too obvious. He will know we will look for him, so I doubt we will find him there."

"He might have gone for one pint, though."

"Where,?"

"He will go where the gear is. Who do we know who is dealing just now?"

"The obvious choice is his mate, Fergus,"

Fergus Ferguson was well known to us. Whether it be cannabis, cocaine, heroin or any other pharmaceutical concoction, Fergus was the go-to man.

"Find Fergus; we find Victor,"

Our first stop was The Seaman Inn where Fergus usually sat at a table at the back of the pub. A step away from the door leading to the toilets and the back door. An easy place to do a deal or make a run for it. Billie went in the front, and I stood at the back door waiting to see if anyone came out after she entered. Moments later she radioed me to come back around to the front.

"According to the barman, Fergus had been there. But shortly after a guy fitting Victor's description came in they both got up and left. He doesn't know Victor so we can't be certain."

"It will be him, let's call on Fergus at his house."

We made our way to Fergus' house on foot; it was just across the housing scheme. We didn't want to announce our presence by turning up in our marked police car. Again I took the back door, found a shed I could hide behind and kept observations. Even from the other side of the house, I could hear Billie knock on the front door and shout, "Open up, it's the police," There was no response. She kept knocking and shouting for Fergus to open up. I waited where I was.

A head appeared at the rear window; I wasn't sure if it was Victor, I didn't get a proper look as I ducked my head back out of sight. I waited and resisted the temptation to pop my head out for another look; I might give the game away. Instead, I listened. I wanted to hear the rear door open and footsteps on the path before I revealed myself. If it was Victor, it was the obvious thing for him to do. He would cross the small path onto the grass, pass the shed and make for the rear fence. He wouldn't go around the side of the house because Billie was still at the front door and shouting for Fergus to open the door.

But I was wrong. I didn't hear the rear door open. I heard no one on the path. The first thing I heard was the shed door opening and someone going inside. Only then did I peer around the side of the shed. The rear door was slightly ajar. Victor had made his way across the path from the back door and hidden in the shed. I noticed that there was a hasp on the door which at one time had cradled a padlock. I quietly closed the door over and stuck my handcuffs through the hasp securing the hinged metal plates together and locking Victor inside.

About the same time that I secured the shed shut, Billie stopped knocking at the front door. I assumed that Fergus had opened to door to her and was now vehemently denying that he had seen Victor. I radioed Billie and asked her to join me around the back. She joined me at the shed. I announced that I had single-handedly captured Victor, securing him in the shed. Fergus appeared at his back door looking confused. I undid my cuffs from the hasp and swung the door open - triumphant - and ready to whack the cuffs on Victor's wrists.

Only it wasn't Victor. It was Fergus' wife. I looked her up and down and scoured the shed for anyone else, but there was only her. Standing in her slippers, arms folded, and scowling. She was rather irate at me for locking her in her own shed when she was only there to collect some coal for her fire.

Further, attempts to hunt down Victor that night proved fruitless. Our chances of catching him with any money left were getting less and less.

Two days later Billie and I made our way back to see Jeanie and update her on the fact that we had been unable to find Victor so far. It was a surprise then when it was Victor who opened her door to us. He was back staying in the house. At the back of the hallway, I saw Jeanie looking rather embarrassed. Before either, he or Jeanie could object I detained Victor and whisked him off to the station.

Every cop will have at some time or other come up against someone like Victor, a recidivist offender who has been through the mill. A boy voted 'most likely to go to jail' by his classmates and did. A man who had learned to listen to the advice of his solicitor by saying nothing or 'no comment' to every question asked of him.

If you think logically about it, no innocent party says 'no comment'. If you are innocent, you explain, plead and try to persuade us of your innocence. Not Victor he sat in the back of our police van, silent the whole way. We took him to the custody suite, and the custody officer recorded his details on the computer before giving him his rights. I searched him and noted that he had no money on him, not a single penny. Other than providing his name address and date of birth, Victor said nothing.

We took him into one of the interview rooms, and we commenced our interview of him.

"Jeanie told us you stole £150 from her?" I said to him indicating with my raised tone towards the end that it was a question.

"No comment."

If the answer to my first question is 'no comment', I can expect that whoever I am interviewing has been in this situation before. I can expect Victor to stick to his 'no comment' responses throughout the entire interview. There are a lot of skilled people in the police who have a natural ability to get people talking and incriminate themselves. I liked to think I was a good interviewer because I was persistent. Whenever I came across the 'no comment' reply, I would change my approach.

"I presume you are answering 'no comment' because you are responsible for this crime. So you stole the money didn't you?"

"No comment."

"If you didn't steal the money then the appropriate answer is 'No,' thus your response would indicate that you stole it, can you tell me where the money is now?"

"No comment."

"Why do you feel it necessary to make no comment?"

"No comment."

"What did you use to smash up Jeanie's furniture?"

"No comment."

"Are you saying 'no comment' because you smashed up her furniture?"

"No comment."

"An innocent person would deny that they had done something like that."

"No comment."

"I can take it from your saying 'no comment' that you are not innocent in this matter then?"

"No comment."

"Did you spend the money on alcohol or drugs?"

"No comment."

"Are you saying 'no comment' because you spent it on drugs?"

"No comment."

"Are you saying 'no comment' because you spent it on alcohol?"

"No comment."

"I presume from the fact you replied 'no comment' to both these questions that you spent the money you stole on both drink and drugs?"

"No comment."

"Is your use of the two words 'no comment' consistent with your connotation of that phrase in that, if you have no comment to make then the implication of such a statement is that you will not say anything, yet you are making a comment. You are consistently making a comment. It is actually from the fact that you comment 'no comment' that we can infer your guilt. There is no other logical conclusion to make. Your guilt is inextricably linked with your use of those two words. Use of them again will absolutely confirm that you did damage the furniture and steal Jeanie's money. If you wish to deny it, then you should say that you didn't do it and explain to us what happened."

"No comment."

… and so it went on.

Victor would not tell me diddly squat. We knew he had stolen the money, he knew he had stolen the money, and he knew that we knew he had stolen the money. Still, he made no comment.

Victor just sat and smirked. He took great delight in replying 'no comment' no matter what. Unfortunately, with only one witness and no money recovered, we didn't have enough evidence to charge him. Victor had stolen the money, and I surmised, from the state of him, he had spent all of it on drink and drugs.

Billie and I looked at each other and shrugged in defeat. It is the likes of Victor that make policing a frustrating and stressful occupation. It is hard to let these things go. When I knew someone was guilty, but I couldn't prove it, it irritated beyond belief. I had two choices. I could let it fester away inside me and irk me for the rest of my life, or I could make a game of it. I chose the latter. After the hundredth 'no comment' reply, I called the interview to a halt. I switched the tape recorder off and put my notebook away. I then gave Billie a knowing wink.

As we tidied our paperwork away Billie, and I ignored Victor and talked casually to ourselves. The subject of our conversation got around to the quiz in the pub the night before, and I asked Billie, "What's the capital of America?"

"New York."

I nodded, "Correct."

"Where do polar bears come from?"

"China."

"Correct."

"What team are known as the hoops?"

"Rangers."

"Spot on."

Victor, clearly frustrated with our stupidity, couldn't contain himself any longer. He bit, "No it's not. It's Celtic," and then he opened right up, "and polar bears don't come from China, that's pandas. Polar bears come from the North Pole. And New York isn't the capital of America; its Washington DC."

"All right smartarse what's a 'one man band' then?" I asked him.

"A one man band is a guy who plays loads of instruments all at once. Drums, cymbals, harmonica, horns, guitar and maybe even a tuba or something."

"Don't be daft, how can you play all those at once?"

At this Victor got up off his chair and demonstrated where cymbals went between his knees, how the drum on his back would work with him stepping up and down and how his elbows going in and out would play something else. As soon as he was in full flow, Billie and I looked at each other, then turned towards him and in unison and sang, "De ra di da ra di ra dit. De ra di da ra di ra dit," giving him a rendition of the 'birdy song' as loud as we could.

We laughed Victor all the way out the office.

The next day I stopped by Jeanie's house to tell her we had interviewed Victor, but he had denied it. She showed us into her livingroom, and there was Victor sitting on the sofa drinking cider, back in her good books.

"What's going on Jeanie?"

Jeanie explained that armed with her crime reference number; she had called into the Social Security Office and put in a claim for a hardship allowance and an emergency loan. Lo, and behold 'Santa' provided her sufficient funds to refurnish her home and gave her £150 cash from the 'Hardship Fund'.

"I'm not making a complaint anymore. I got my money back from the cooncil. Me and him are back the gither."

"But he wrecked the house and stole your money?"

"Aye ah ken, but we are getting married in January."

Chapter 4

HOKEY COKEY IN THE POKEY

If I thought Victor was bad; it turned out there were worse people than him. I was about to find that out firsthand. When Sergeant McMachin called me into his office and gave me the bad news, my worries were just about to begin.

"Congratulations," he said, "you are getting your promotion."

Despite having enjoyed my temporary rank a great deal, I had been back working as a constable for four months and loved working with Billie. I had mixed emotions. I'd skip to my work - like a child heading off to the park to play with my friends. Being promoted to sergeant meant change. Did I want all the constant worry that went with being a sergeant? I gave it some thought for a moment; Sergeant McMachin was a little puzzled why I hadn't punched the air and whooped in surprise.

I was still thinking.

I weighed it all up in my mind.

Things are always changing. The police is a dynamic organisation, officers flow to different stations and departments as people retire, new recruits come in, and others move to specialist roles. Even if I declined the promotion, there was no guarantee I wouldn't get transferred someplace else.

I was mindful of the story of a cop working in Ayr who they told was being promoted to sergeant but his new station would be Oban. Oban is one hundred and thirty miles away from Ayr and at least a three-hour drive. He politely turned down the promotion, explaining that his wife had a good job in Ayr and his four children were all settled in their schools. All his friends and family lived in Ayr, and the upheaval of going to Oban was just too much. So they accepted that he didn't want the promotion and transferred him to Oban as a cop.

A good reason for me to exercise caution.

"Where am I going?" I asked Sergeant McMachin, perhaps not the reaction he expected.

"I'll leave that to Superintendent Rattan to tell you; go into headquarters and see him now."

"You know where I am going, but you won't tell me. Why?"

"That's up to Superintendent Rattan."

"Is it the custody suite?

The custody was notorious for being the worst place for a sergeant to work. Your entire working day spent locked up with all your prisoners. A lot of whom are not nice people. It can be hectic too; there can be a constant stream of prisoners brought in and all the while you have to manage the demands of the ones that have been in for over thirty minutes and are screaming for a cigarette. They need fed, watered, showered, given a change of clothes, access to a doctor and their medication requires careful administration. They need access to a solicitor, let out for an interview with CID, fingerprinted and photographed. I didn't join the police to become a prison officer and babysit prisoners.

"I'm not at liberty to say, see Superintendent Rattan, he will tell you where you are going."

"It's the custody isn't it?"

"I'm not in a position to say."

"If it is the custody, I will turn it down."

"Don't be so daft, the custody isn't so bad," he lied.

I tidied myself up before I saw Superintendent Rattan. I polished my shoes, brushed down my tunic and sorted my tie.

When I turned up at his office, Superintendent Rattan invited me straight in. I took a seat in front of his desk. There were no congratulations or handshaking. He went straight into his spiel.

"A permanent sergeant position has come up, and I have chosen you to fill it."

"Yes sir, thank you, sir."

"This is an important position that requires a solid officer to take up the reins. It is a critical piece of our business and is not to be taken lightly. There are a lot of things that can go wrong, and we need someone like you to ensure that our performance in this area is not lacking. We need you to guarantee that all our policies and procedures are properly implemented, and we have no issues."

Oh, this sounds interesting, maybe it isn't the custody suite after all.

"So," he continued, "you start in the custody suite a week on Monday."

It might not have been my first choice, as everyone who worked in the custody suite moaned about it, hated it even. It wasn't a great job, looking after all the rogues and vagabonds, dealing with their petty complaints and constant whining. I accepted my promotion, (well I had a family to feed) then settled in to learn the ropes.

The prisoners had a push button in their cell which they could press when they needed anything.

The push button set off a buzzer within my office at the other end of the cell complex. Agonisingly, the push button did not give the prisoners any sign if it was working or not, so they would continue to press it until someone came to their cell.

"What do you want?" I would ask after marching down the corridor to their cell.

"Can I get a fag?"

"You just had a fag."

"I want another one."

"I'm too busy just now," and I would march back to my office to get on with things.

Buzzzzzzzzzzzzz.

I would march back down to the same prisoner, "What is it now?"

"Can I get a fag?"

… and so it would go on.

Sunday morning was often the busiest day in the cell complex. All the arrests from Friday and Saturday nights would languish in their cells awaiting their trip to court on the Monday morning.

All of them would require feeding, watering and showering facilities. Most would also require being fingerprinted and photographed. Some would need escorting to an interview room for a consultation with their lawyer or questioning by the CID. Any drug addicts (most of them) would require a medical examination by a doctor and get pills to ease their withdrawal symptoms.

I established a routine. I arrived early to get briefed. I identified which prisoners were causing issues and who would likely become an issue. I visited each of them in turn, then asked the custody assistant to get them showered and breakfasted. I dished out the various medications they required and ensured that I

84

recorded everything on the computerised custody system.

Getting on with these tasks always depended on the prisoners not pestering us with continual buzzing. Mostly, they were just desperate for a cigarette (it was the days before we banned all smoking in the custody suite).

'Gies a fag boss,' was the most common request.

Before water, before food, before reading material, and even before medication, a fag was what they wanted.

After a while, I learned to make life a little easier for myself. I came up with a plan of action.

I walked through the cells and opened every hatch on every cell. I asked all the prisoners to come to their hatch and listen. One by one the prisoners all popped their head out through the hatches, reminding me of a scene from 'Papillon', with the exception that Dustin Hoffman and Steve McQueen were better looking (even with their toothless grins). Once the prisoners posted their heads through their hatch and were poised to listen, I laid out my plan to them. I had to be clear because they appeared to have brains similar in size and function to a bag of mushrooms.

"Gentlemen, today is Sunday, a day of peace and prayer. I cannot afford you the opportunity of attending church. However, I can afford you the luxury of a cigarette. I understand your needs. I, therefore, promise you this – if you don't buzz your buzzers, unless it is a dire emergency, and if you don't ask for a cigarette, then I will take the time out from my busy morning schedule to supply you all with a cigarette. If you can keep from pestering me by pressing your buzzer, your first cigarette will be in fifteen minutes time. After that, I will make you all a slap-up breakfast, and then I will return with a cup of tea and another fag."

"About eleven, I will once again come around and let you light up your third cigarette of the day. Lunch will be served about 1 p.m. and once devoured I will again afford you the opportunity of another cigarette. If you stick with this agreement, this treaty, this covenant, I will pass by these cells before I finish at 3 p.m. and furnish you with one more cigarette."

"But, gentlemen, be warned. If any single one of you presses your buzzer in a furious fit of pique, or I hear the words 'Gies a fag boss' even once, then you will break our agreement. Should this happen, I will have to renege on any promise and not one fag, cigarette or cancer stick will be lit anywhere within this cell complex today. I hope I have made myself clear gentlemen. This contract we make now involves you all. Cigarettes for all if you comply, but heed my warning; if you pester me even once for a fag, there will be no smokes for anybody. I hope that is clear."

There was a general murmur of approval as I worked my way back up the cell passage closing the hatches. As I reached the last cell, a wee rascal stuck his head out the hatch, looked at me with a mischievous grin and said, "Gies a fag boss."

I couldn't help but laugh.

However, not all of my customers in the cells were likeable rogues like that wee rascal.

Many of our customers were not pleasant people. Often they were drunk or high, and none too impressed with being deprived of their liberty. With nothing other than a hairy blanket to cuddle into - and make them itch - a night in a cell on a thin mattress was never anybody's idea of fun. Routinely, they subjected us to the most vitriolic and abusive language. They threatened us, assaulted us and even spat on us. It was hard to remain professional and matter-of-fact with some of them. But we tried. I was always mindful that no matter what, they were human beings and once sober they could be very different people. If we dealt with them in a fair and professional manner, then they were always easier to deal with when they came back the next time.

Early in my service, I worked in a small office in a small town with a reputation for being a violent, crime-ridden cesspit of humanity. I was once told that, per head of population, it was second only to Beirut in terms of violence. I accepted this as gospel and mentioned it as a statement of fact whenever anyone asked: "How's the job going?"

In retrospect, our local newspaper headline 'Man in court over a grossly offensive remark in an email to local MP' paled into insignificance to the Beirut Journal's regular headlines of 'Ten killed and 33 injured in machine gun massacre'.

Our wee town's violent and crime-ridden streets were down to a small core of bad apples. Most of the people in the town, like anywhere else, were law-abiding citizens.

The town was quite an insular place, in that few people came to visit (those that did would try to steal a car so they could get out again as quickly as possible). Thus most of our work meant us dealing with the small core of bad apples.

Time and time again we dealt with the same people.

Cops working in a big city might never have to arrest the same person twice. In that small town, only me and four others policed it. We couldn't help but arrest the same people repeatedly. They say 'familiarity breeds contempt'. That is especially true of rogues and vagabonds. They have a special contempt for those in uniform who 'familiarly' lock them up.

Years later the conduct of this small core of bad apples mellowed. Age does that. People get older and wiser. They dislike spending their weekends in a cell. They learn that if they change their bad behaviour, then they are less likely to come to the notice of the police and thus stay out of jail.

They get married, and their spouses get annoyed when they spend their family income on fines. Children come along and with that comes responsibility.

The cycle of criminal life means that their children grow up and get into trouble. There were the odd occasions when I would wander down the cell complex, open a cell hatch to check on a prisoner to face someone who had not aged one iota in the twenty years. I would close the hatch and look around to check time hadn't stopped, and that I wasn't in a time machine. Had I dreamt the last twenty years of my life?

No.

It often* turned out just to be the offspring of a little scroat I had dealt with years before. The identical looking spawn of a rogue continuing the cycle of criminal behaviour.

*I say 'often', I mean 'always', to my knowledge I have never been transported back in time or dreamt away twenty years of my life. Although, I did once dream I had been transported back in time.

Occasionally, I'd meet some of the small core of bad apples in other situations.

It was a strange thing, but, if I hadn't dealt with them for many years, the contempt mellowed. Sometimes we would engage in banter. I remember talking to a hardened criminal called 'Robber' Robertson. Many years previous I had interviewed him as we suspected him of stealing a car. He didn't admit to it back then. In the absence of other evidence, I had to let him go. Twenty years later, not long after I had retired, I met Robber Robertson in the middle of a shopping centre. I was sitting on a bench patiently waiting for my wife to spend all my pension. Robber Robertson spotted me and came over.

"Ah, Mr McEwan," he said full of smiles, "Are you still in the police?"

"No. I retired six months ago," I informed him.

"You are a bit young to be retired," he said.

"I feel ancient."

"Ach, away wi ye. Yer jist a bairn."

"Well, maybe all those dealings with you took it out of me."

"Ach, git yersel a job. There is always someone looking fur an old polis tae guard thur premises."

The last thing I ever wanted to do when I retired was to go back to doing night shifts, certainly not in a boring job that paid peanuts.

"No thanks. Anyway, what are you doing with yourself these days? Where are you working?"

I noticed the expensive watch on his wrist, the designer clothes and the pair of expensive brogues adorning his feet. I asked him with a genuine interest in how he had turned his life around.

"Ach, ye ken me, Mr McEwan, I've never worked a day in my life," and he laughed rather too loud and too long for my liking.

Time to put him in his place. I came right out and asked him, "See that stolen car I interviewed you for twenty years ago. You stole it didn't you?

"Aye," he said, "it was me," and at that, he turned away from me laughing; only looking back to point at me and say, "ha ha ha."

Not all of them had mellowed as much as 'Robber' Robertson mind you.

One morning, in the Custody Suite, I checked the prisoners, and on opening one hatch, I faced 'Cocaine' Wayne, one of the old core of bad apples. An old adversary. I hadn't seen for a dozen years.

They had arrested 'Cocaine' Wayne for a breach of the peace the night before and he was only just sobering up. He looked up and recognised my face.

"You used to work in my toon, eh?"

"Aye, that's right."

"What happened to that bastard McEwan?" he asked, mistaking me for someone else.

"McEwan?" I said to him with a puzzled look on my face. "You mean Detective Chief Superintendent McEwan!"

"Aw, you're fuckin' kidding. That bastard is a Detective Chief Superintendent?"

"Aye. He's a great guy, the best guy I ever worked with, I'd do anything for him. I think he might end up as Chief Constable!" and I shut the hatch on him before he realised he was talking to 'the bastard McEwan' and he was just a lowly sergeant.

My sense of justice liked the karma involved in this incident.

One Saturday morning, I signed on duty and, as normal, the first thing I did was get the background on who was in custody before going to check they were alive and well.

Angus, was in custody for stealing a pair of shoes. During the night the CCTV operators spotted him rummaging around some bags outside a charity shop. They saw him remove a pair of shoes, try them on, throw his old ones away and walk off happy with his find. The CCTV operators contacted the dispatcher who directed officers to investigate. Officers attended and based on the CCTV footage, had sufficient evidence to arrest him. The officers asked the inspector what to do.

The inspector contacted the key holder for the charity shop. It incensed the key holder that someone dared to steal their donated goods he was adamant he wanted to press charges. Thus they arrested Angus and took him into custody. The arresting officers removed the shoes he had stolen, placed them in a bag and labelled this as a production for the court. Subsequently, the charity shop key holder valued the shoes at £5.

In normal circumstances we would have charged Angus and liberated him to appear at court at a later date. Unfortunately, he had no fixed abode; he was homeless. As he was homeless and had no address to send his court citation to, we had to keep him in custody over the weekend for an appearance at court on the Monday.

I took a cup of tea and some breakfast along to his cell and Angus grinned at me like a lemon shark. It was the first time he had had a roof over his head for some weeks. And here we were throwing in breakfast to boot.

I liked Angus. He was polite and couldn't thank us enough. For the next two days, we served Angus with three square meals a day and more tea and biscuits than he could stuff into his hungry mouth.

Because of the reporting officers taking possession of the stolen shoes, Angus now had nothing to wear on his feet. The police cannot send prisoners to court with no footwear, so I took money from the petty cash to purchase a pair of shoes for him (we called it the 'imprest fund', a strange name for a fund considering the amount in it being decidedly unimpressive).

The officers tasked with this job purchased a £22 pair of loafers (the cheapest available at the nearest shoe shop).

On Monday morning Angus appeared at court, surrendered a guilty plea for which the judge admonished (reprimanded) him there and then. That was it. He walked out of the court, a free man, well fed, watered, washed and now wearing a £22 pair of loafers instead of a £5 pair from a charity shop, all courtesy of the police.

Ironically, the charity shop was a branch of 'Shelter' set up to help the homeless.

Time passed. The stock market had a bumpy ride, and you would need to have been clever or lucky to have made money. Labour was higher in the polls than the Conservatives, and the Liberal Democrats were enjoying a new found popularity. Christmas came around again, and Elvis was back riding high in the charts with *A little less conversation'*.

I was on the roster to work an early shift Christmas day, which fell on a Sunday. Christmas day in the custody suite with every cell filled with all the ne'er-do-wells from all over our area. Marvellous!

All sergeants had a custody assistant to help them, now known as a Police Custody Support Officer (PCSO). Most of them could put in a good shift but I was fortunate enough to work with the best.

Whistling Wally was great. He always arrived in sharp and never needed to be told to do anything. Before I even thought about it he was getting it done. I would finish processing a customer and decide it was time the other prisoners received their prescribed drugs. Whistling Wally would already have their medications out, the paperwork marked up and ready for me to check before we dispensed them.

If I decided it was time to feed the prisoners, Whistling Wally already had their meals cooked and on trays ready for them to eat. If I decided we had time to fingerprint and photograph prisoners, Whistling Wally would already be halfway through doing it.

He was great.

There was never a moment when he didn't anticipate what I required. He was a hard worker, he had a great sense of humour and he was easy going. The only downside to working with Whistling Wally was that he was always happy.

Irritatingly happy.

Don't you hate it when someone is always happy?

Come rain, hail, sun or snow he came into his work whistling away to himself. All day every day he whistled the same tune. The same few bars, over and over again. It was infuriating.

Whether it was my inherited inability to distinguish the difference between tones (I come from a long line of musically inept and tone-deaf forefathers) or Whistling Wally was just a poor whistler I don't know. But I could not put my finger on what tune it was that Whistling Wally always whistled. It was just a few bars of the same tune, whistled repeatedly. I am not even sure he knew he was doing it. It was his habit to purse his lips and whistle the same tune no matter what he was doing. After a day in the custody suite with him, I often went home with the tune stuck in my head. Like a Trojan horse, it would wait until I was lying in bed trying to get over asleep then it would pop back into my thoughts, repeating over and over again in my head.

It was torture.

On Christmas morning the cells were full. All sixteen of them were in use. Much of them trebled up, three prisoners, three mattresses, three blankets. I would release some when sober but most were staying in custody to appear in court on Monday. Whistling Wally entered the Custody Suite full of seasonal cheer, whistling that tune - the same few bars duplicated by his pursed lips. He paused for a second to greet me, "Good morning. Haaappy Christmas," before resuming his contented whistling.

"Good morning Wally," I replied, "and a Merry Christmas to you too."

There is an unwritten rule that police officers abide by on Christmas Day.

The rule is that they only do what is necessary. There will be no operations to arrest people on a warrant. No planned drugs raids. Nobody stands with a speed gun trying to catch speeders and no minor enquiries carried out. Not unless there is a serious crime to investigate.

The police don't pester members of the public on Christmas Day. It is not the police being lazy or even altruistic. It is just that the police need to rely on the public for their information and co-operation. Pestering people on Christmas Day just alienates them. People want peace and quiet. It is a day family want to celebrate without having a man in a uniform knock on their door asking if they had seen anyone in the area the week before when their neighbour's greenhouse was vandalised. Not unless there is a call will they do anything other than have an extended breakfast and catch up on some paperwork.

This unwritten rule meant that we didn't have a trail of police officers coming into the custody suite with prisoners. We only had to cater to the needs of the people we already had in the cells. Instead of rushing around with medication, food, and cups of tea in between processing more prisoners we could spend a little more time ensuring they got showered, fed and watered. I headed down to the cell passage with Wally.

There is a metal barred gate at the start of the corridor and we locked this behind us to ensure we didn't have any unfortunate escapes. I opened all the hatches and went into my Christmas day spiel.

"Gentlemen, today is Christmas, a day of celebration, a day for swapping presents, a day for enjoying with your family. Unfortunately, you are locked up in here with us, so today Wally and I will be your family. We can celebrate this joyous day together. Wally and I will bring you all a sumptuous breakfast prepared by our own fair hands, a cup of tea, fresh blankets and a cigarette to puff upon. Before we do that, I'd like to give you the opportunity to have a shower and a shave. I'll start at cell one and work my way around. Everybody happy?"

There was a general murmur of agreement from the cells.

We got the prisoners out two at a time and supplied each with soap, a razor, and a towel. Afforded them the use of either of the two showers and allowed the use of the small sink and mirror.

Things were moving along nicely.

Until I got to cell number four. I looked through the hatch and standing naked on his mattress was a ginger man. A man with unkempt ginger hair and pubes to match. A remarkably hairy ginger man. He was standing staring at the open hatch, his eyes frenetic. Darting from my left eye to my right eye in quick succession. He reminded me of an angry orangutan.

The naked ginger man was a serving prison officer, hence he had a cell all to himself. They had arrested him the night before following a domestic incident at his house. He'd assaulted his wife and under those circumstances, no matter what your occupation, our guidelines were that he had to remain in custody to appear at court on the next lawful court day.

"Are you okay?" I asked, cautious of his reply.

"What the fuck is he whistling?"

"What?"

"He is doing my fuckin head in."

I looked up at Whistling Wally. He was whistling that small bit of a tune he always did. Over and over again. I had become so accustomed to it that it was just background noise. Something you don't notice. At least not until it stops. Then it becomes something you can't quite remember. You don't have an awareness of it when it is going on but when it stops there is a strange feeling you are missing something. Like that uncomfortable feeling when you climb into your car for a long journey and can't remember if you locked the house door or not. No matter how hard you try to replay the event of leaving your house in your mind you can't ever be certain you didn't lock the door.

"Do you know I have no idea," I turned to Whistling Wally and asked him, "Wally, what on earth are you whistling?"

"The Hokey Cokey."

"The Hokey Cokey?" I said.

"The Hokey Cokey!" my ginger orangutan repeated with disbelief in his voice.

"The Hokey Cokey!" Gerald, a prisoner who had just stepped out of the shower and was towelling himself down, said with amazement. "That sounds nothing like the Hokey Cokey; this is the Hokey Cokey."

96

And at that Gerald whistled a much more recognisable version of the Hokey Cokey. The prisoner in the second shower got into the spirit of Gerald's whistling and sang it, "Oh, hokey cokey cokey, oh hokey cokey cokey..."

The three prisoners in the cell nearest the showers then joined in.

"You put your right hand in, your right hand out..." and at that, a hand shot out of the cell hatch and then back in again. "... your right hand in and you shake it all about." The hand shot out of the hatch again and shook all about. I burst out laughing as did Wally. Spurred on by our obvious merriment all the other prisoners within their cells sung along.

"You put your left foot in, your left foot out..." they made efforts to stick a foot out of the hatches. "... your left foot in and you shake it all about, you do the hokey cokey and you turn around. That's what it's all about. Oh hokey cokey cokey, oh hokey cokey cokey..."

I couldn't stop laughing. Almost every cell took part in the impromptu sing-song.

"You put your head in, you put your head out. You put your head in then you shake it all about..."

The sight of half a dozen heads sticking out of their cell hatches and shaking about was the funniest thing I had ever seen. There were tears of laughter flowing down my face, dribbling onto my shirt and spattering onto my legs. I don't think there are many prisoners locked up on Christmas Day or any other day, for that matter, who end up laughing so much. The entire cell complex filled with great big guffaws. Everybody found it hilarious. A simple, spontaneous outburst of a song had cheered everyone up and given us all sore sides.

When it quieted down and the laughter reduced to chuckles and sniggers I looked through the hatch at my naked ginger orangutan and said, "It appears that he is whistling the Hokey Cokey in the pokey."

Chapter 5

INSPECTOR DEADPAN DICK

In charge of my group was Inspector 'Deadpan' Dick. Deadpan Dick is a highly intelligent man and too smart for the police. I don't mean that all cops aren't smart. There are loads of clever people in the police. Some police officers have university degrees, some can play instruments, some can solve *The Scotsman* crossword in their coffee break, and some can even write a book. Deadpan Dick was different in that if he had wanted to be a rocket scientist or a brain surgeon, he could have been. If *Stephen Hawking* hadn't already penned *'A Brief History of Time'* then Deadpan Dick could have written it.

It seemed to me that Deadpan Dick joined the police because he wasn't sure which direction his immense intellect should take. He saw the police as a stopgap, something exciting he could do until he decided what course to take in life. A man of Deadpan Dick's undoubted intelligence would surely enjoy the police life for a few years then move on to spend his time on some noble goal. With focus, he could have achieved anything he wanted to. Unfortunately, it didn't work out like that.

Deadpan Dick passed through his probation with flying colours, and soon they identified him as a high flyer. They transferred him to various roles in different departments and excelled in them all - challenging projects worthy of his undoubted intellect. He was enjoying himself, so he delayed achieving a noble goal in an occupation other than the police. This was cemented with his pearly promotion to sergeant. With the plaudits he was receiving for his work, it was accepted that he was destined for greater things. A senior officer in the making - a potential Chief Constable perhaps.

After impressing in every role, Deadpan Dick found himself transferred to a project that involved computerisation of police systems. The police had moved with the times; they needed to keep up with technology. We needed computerised recording systems to record all crimes, offences, events, missing persons, road accidents and even custody records. At that time there were no specific computer programmes available that could do all those things. They tasked Deadpan Dick with designing and implementing a software programme that would do the job. Not an easy task, but a task for which he was ideally suited. On that project, he discovered that not only was he a genius with computer technology but he enjoyed it so much it became his passion.

They provided Deadpan Dick with four powerful computers and three civilian IT guys to help develop the new system. For two years they beavered away on the project. In the world of computers, two years isn't a long time. There were companies with hundreds of engineers working for many more years on similar sophisticated projects. So what Deadpan Dick produced in such a short time frame, with his limited resources, was nothing less than brilliant. It was the most elegant of computer systems and way ahead of anything else out there. The search facility could fire up tens of thousands of results almost instantly, only rivalled by what *Google* could do twenty years later. The Chief Constable recognised his brilliance, and Sergeant Deadpan Dick in charge of a project became Inspector Deadpan Dick in charge of Information Technology (IT). The Chief Constable was keen to see him oversee the continued development of the software for the next few years and he promised that there would be further promotions in the offing in recognition of his brilliant work. Inspector Deadpan Dick was, without a doubt, destined for higher things.

Times change, projects are never permanent, posts become redundant, and people move on. The Chief Constable, who supported this bright high flyer, came to the end of his service and retired. A new, younger chief came in. He didn't have the same opinion of Deadpan Dick that his previous incumbent did. As is often the case, the fresh chief took his bristling new brush and swept the departments clean. They handed Deadpan Dick's project over to the civilian IT guys, and Inspector Deadpan Dick was unceremoniously dumped back to the front line. He became the Inspector in charge of my group.

Deadpan Dick no longer had an exciting project on which to work. He was back in a job he had last done ten years before. The exciting challenge of developing new software gone. By this time he had over twenty years service and sight of his pension. Too much to lose if he were to leave the police. With nothing worthy to focus his superior intelligence on, he turned his passion to smoking cigarettes and making mischief.

I first met Inspector Deadpan Dick standing at the back door to headquarters. Casually leaning against the stanchion and blowing smoke into the air. It was his first day on shift, and he waited for us all at the back door. Despite his relaxed body language he was immaculately turned out. His precision pressed uniform, shiny shoes and a full head of well-groomed silver hair gave him a presence. His sharp looks reflected his razor sharp mind. His eyes sparkled with intelligence, or was it mischief? I couldn't be sure.

"Good morning Inspector," I said to him.

He took a draw on his cigarette, blew more smoke into the air and lazily looked up at the cloudy blue sky as if to inspect whether it was a good morning or not. He replied, "Aye, McEwan," in a lazy drawl that neither agreed nor disagreed with me but also seemed to say, 'I know everything there is to know about you McEwan, I can read your thoughts.'

Despite his ability to unnerve, it wasn't long before I took to enjoy working with him. Nothing was ever a problem. He had a remarkable ability to take a brief look at a situation, identify the problem and come up with a plan of action to get the job done. He never got flustered or angry. Deadpan Dick effortlessly solved any issue we brought to him.

"Inspector, I've got a problem I'd like to run by you."

"Put the kettle on," he'd say.

He probably had it solved before the kettle boiled but he liked to entertain himself by sitting me down and playing out the scenario. And in as much time as it would take to drink a cup of coffee he'd help me solve the problem for myself.

If it were a legal issue, he would ask, "What does the law say?"

It would force me to think about what we could do legally and by doing so guide me in the right direction so I figured out the answer on my own. It was his way of making me think for myself. It was a good way to learn.

"If that is what the law says, then that is what you should do," he would finish with, as I walked out the door.

If it were to do with staffing issues, he would come away with, "What do the regulations say?"

I would have to work out what our course of action based on the regulations. Sometimes he had to prod me in the right direction, but his interpretation of the laws and regulations made it easier to come to a sound conclusion.

"If that is what the regulations say, then that is what you should do," he would say.

I would walk out confident I would do the right thing.

My respect for him grew in other aspects too. He supported the troops, and he stood up to senior management on many issues. He would be full of condescension whenever he felt that the demands from the senior management were unreasonable. That kind of unconcealed disdain for senior officers disenfranchised him from further promotion.

Inspector Deadpan Dick made mischief but did it in such a deadpan fashion it sometimes took a while for us mere mortals to realise he was just having fun with us. He was also exemplary in his time-keeping. Every day he reported for duty a perfect five minutes late, in this he was faultless. He would then spend his day standing at the back door smoking cigarettes, taking any opportunity to make mischief and play with the minds of those coming and going. All the time he remained deadpan. Those that did not know him would sometimes walk out of his office and two hours later start laughing when they got the joke.

He could do this all day long because he had an ability to deal with all his work in the space of twenty minutes. It wasn't uncommon for me to nip to the toilet then come back and find his desk cleared

It meant that he had a lot of time on his hands. When I covered the street role, Inspector Deadpan Dick would cajole me into going out on patrol with him.

One day, about lunchtime, he was driving me around looking for things to amuse himself with and not finding much. He asked if I was hungry; I confirmed I was, and we agreed to eat. He drove the marked police car into the *McDonald's* drive through and joined the queue. We reached the service counter, a young girl with a pony tail and clean overalls popped her head up to the server, she clocked the uniforms and marked car and smiled her best smile, "Yes, can I help you?"

Deadpan Dick in the deadest deadpan voice and deadest deadpan face turned to her and nodded, "Yes," he replied, "Can you direct me to *Burger King*?"

So that was how Deadpan Dick passed his working days, smoking cigarettes and making mischief. If anything serious happened he would remain calm, get control of the situation and delegate. He was like a big three litre Jaguar cruising along the motorway, with enough power under the bonnet to get himself out of trouble whenever needed.

One afternoon Deadpan Dick and I were sitting in his office chatting. Talking about this and that. Interested in what made him tick I asked, "I'm curious, how come you haven't been promoted further?"

Deadpan Dick reached down, opened his desk drawer and pulled out a file. A bright blue folder used by the Professional Standards Department for collating complaints they were investigating. They gave these out to inspectors to carry out the enquiries and report back. He passed it over, "This might be one of the reasons."

I pulled out the paperwork and read the contents. It was a disciplinary matter.

Two years previously Deadpan Dick investigated a complaint against a cop. The cop had charged someone with a minor road traffic offence but took three months to report the offender to the Procurator Fiscal.

Police set timescales for submissions. The stipulated time given for road traffic offences is four weeks. For various reasons, four weeks is often an unattainable time frame.

According to the paperwork, Inspector Deadpan Dick was due to attend a hearing for failing to properly investigate the disciplinary case.

"Why didn't you investigate it?" I asked.

"I did. The Chief Inspector handed me the investigation and twenty minutes later I provided him with a report."

"Twenty minutes? What did your report say?"

"It detailed why the officer's report was late."

"Why was it late?"

"He was busy."

"That doesn't seem like much of an investigation?

"No, the Chief Inspector didn't think so either, but I did all that was necessary. I spoke to the cop, and he explained that he had been on annual leave. When he returned, they seconded him to a murder enquiry team and had other more important cases to report. But that wasn't the real problem."

"What do you mean?"

"It was a road traffic case, and the timescales weren't met."

The law states that the prosecution process (issuing of a copy complaint) for offences under The Road Traffic Act must start within six months of being committed. If this process doesn't get instigated in that time, the cases are abandoned.

"But it was reported in time, wasn't it?" I queried.

"Exactly, despite the Procurator Fiscal having three months to progress it, they decided that wasn't enough time, so they abandoned the case. They blamed the police for submitting the report late."

"I understand that he didn't submit the report within the stipulated four weeks but the Procurator Fiscal still had time to send out a copy complaint and deal with it, didn't they?"

"You are right. We only stipulate four weeks so that we pretty much guarantee the reports reach the Procurator Fiscal in plenty of time."

"So why is there such a fuss?"

"Well, the Procurator Fiscal have to submit accounts for all of their decisions. These are the checks and balances to ensure that they are dealing with criminal matters efficiently. Questions get asked if they abandon too many cases. They have to collate all their decisions, and when they blame the police for abandoning a case, we get a notification of what cases and why."

"I take it that is when our Professional Standards Department look at it?"

"Well, they don't even look at it, they automatically send it out for investigation. The presumption is the cop is at fault because the Procurator Fiscal says so."

"So how come you are getting into trouble for not investigating it?"

"Ah, now this is where it gets interesting. There was nothing to stop the Procurator Fiscal sending out a summons the day they received the report, but that didn't happen. In fact going by the date they signed it off as abandoned, it looked like they hadn't even read the report until two months after the last date for prosecution. I don't see how I could get a cop into bother for being too busy to write a report for three months, but the Procurator Fiscal is not at fault for not even reading it for five months."

"That seems reasonable."

"Chief Inspector Higler didn't think so. He concluded that the cop should have reported it sooner, so it threw my investigation into question. They served the cop discipline papers for submitting the report late, and I have to attend a hearing for failing to investigate the case properly."

There were the odd occasions when cops submitted late reports. When that happened, the bosses sent out reminders to progress matters timeously. If someone repeatedly failed to submit reports on time, their supervisor would be instructed to 'get it sorted'. If that didn't work, then they would be referred to the Training Department for remedial instruction. If the officer still submitted late reports then, and only then, the Professional Standards Department would get involved, and initiate discipline procedures against the cop. I had never heard of a cop being disciplined for a one off incident or of an Inspector getting disciplined for failing to investigate a discipline case properly.

"How can they discipline a cop for a single late report?"

"That was one of my arguments. They wanted to, but I informed them I had already reprimanded the officer and that was the end of the matter for him. They can't get two bites at the cherry in discipline cases."

"So because they couldn't discipline the cop, they disciplined you? I don't see how they can discipline you for not investigating it properly?"

"Well, there might have been a little more than failing to investigate the case?"

"What else?"

"Insubordination."

"Insubordination?"

"Yes, well, when Chief Inspector Higler told me I would be disciplined for failure to investigate the case properly, he asked if I had anything to say. I told Chief Inspector Higler that I stood by my investigation. While the case was late I had spoken to the cop about that and, in fact, the case had been abandoned due to the Procurator Fiscal Service failing to read the thing for five months after they received it. I also suggested that Chief Inspector Higler discipline himself while he is at it."

"What for?"

"Well, he took four months to investigate and submit his report. He gathered no more information than I did in twenty minutes. The only difference in our reports was that he came to a different conclusion."

"You are getting disciplined for insubordination for that?"

"Well, not that exactly. That came later."

"What happened?"

"Eighteen months and twenty minutes after they tasked me with carrying out an enquiry into a cop for submitting a report two months late, they served me with discipline papers. I picked them up and wandered down to see Chief Inspector Higler and we had words."

"Words?"

"I pointed out that he had taken longer to submit his report than the cop took to submit his road traffic offence. Perhaps he should be the one getting disciplined. Then the Professional Standards Department should pull their finger out their backsides because they had taken over a year to read it and serve papers on me."

"What did he say to that?"

"He said he had been busy!"

I laughed at the ridiculous irony. "That doesn't sound like insubordination?"

"Well, I might have put him straight on a few things. Then he accused me of having no respect for him."

"What did you say to that?"

"Chief Inspector, I am leaving now to go to the toilet, and I can assure you I have more admiration and respect for the turd that I am about to expel from my body than I do for you."

I later heard that during his discipline hearing Inspector Deadpan Dick had remained calm and self-assured. When it was his turn to speak, he re-iterated the ironic nature of the investigation against him and caused, not only, Chief Inspector Higler but the entire Professional Standards Department to squirm in their seats.

At the end of the discipline enquiry, he was fined £100. Inspector Deadpan Dick smiled at this decision, took out his wallet and asked if they took cash. His wallet contained exactly five £20 notes.

The next day Inspector Deadpan Dick arrived in for work an exemplary five minutes late.

"Let's go on patrol," he instructed me - as if nothing was the matter.

As usual, he was wearing his perfectly fitting and immaculately turned out uniform. His coiffured silver hair gave him a look of distinction. He always carried himself with an upright deportment. He even moved with a slow, measured gait that expressed his high standards and confident manner. That was how he was when we walked into the local *Kentucky Fried Chicken* for lunch.

Inspector Deadpan Dick glided to the serving counter closely followed by me. The young spotty server behind the counter didn't serve many police officers. It was unusual for police in uniform to walk in and buy lunch. It was even more unusual for an inspector to walk in. A seriously deadpan looking inspector. He had the braid on his cap, and his face showed no emotion. He was expressionless when he asked, "Can I have a fried egg sandwich please?"

"Er um er," said the young server, somewhat confused. "We, er um, we don't do fried egg sandwiches."

"Can I have toast and scrambled egg then please?"

"Er um. Scrambled egg isn't on the menu, sir."

"I'll just have a boiled egg then, thank you."

The young server looked even more confused. He even looked behind to check the menu on the wall in case he was missing something. He turned back to Deadpan Dick and said, "Err um, we don't have any eggs here at all."

Deadpan Dick's appearance didn't change. He looked at the young server straight-faced, paused and asked.

"Then where do your chickens come from?"

Inspector Deadpan Dick remained so expressionless that the young server still didn't know if he was being serious or not.

"We get them delivered," he said then quickly asked, "Can I help you with anything else?"

"Yes. Do you do take away?"

"Um, Yes of course."

"Okay, what's twelve minus six?"

It was hard not to laugh when he came away with things like that.

It was a few months before I was once again covering street duties. During one night shift, in the lead up to Bonfire Night, we received a call informing us that someone had blown up a telephone box. Initial attending officers confirmed that the telephone box had been blown up and Inspector Deadpan Dick decided that this was an interesting enough call for us to attend.

The telephone box was the old style red box, with the small windows and big heavy door. It sat twenty yards down a small path leading to a play park. We parked on the narrow road along with several other police cars, blocking the one-way street, and off we went to examine the scene of the crime.

The perpetrators had placed an outsized firework in the phone box, lit it and then shut the door. The subsequent explosion in such a confined space caused a massive expansion of gas within the phone box. The sudden build-up of pressure had been sufficient to blow the telephone box apart. The roof had shot off and landed fifteen feet away. With the lack of a roof to hold the box together, the door and two side panels had fallen to the ground. All that remained standing was the back wall of the phone box. The telephone handset dangled on its cord, dislodged from its cradle, although still attached to the back wall.

Shortly afterwards, a *British Telecom (BT)* van bounced down the road and parked up behind our cars. It was your typical BT transit van; full livery advertised BT on the front sides and rear, a picture of the earth depicted the global nature of BT's business.

The driver stepped from the cab. His overalls emblazoned with the BT logo and colours. He deliberately removed his toolbox from the rear of the van. The tool box was also in BT colours and bore the BT logo. Only then did he wander across towards us. It was patently obvious that the BT engineer was there to deal with the exploded telephone box.

Inspector Deadpan Dick met him on the path and in the driest deadpan way asked him.

"Yes. Can I help you?"

The BT engineer checked his tool box and overalls to confirm for himself that he was wearing his identifying uniform.

"Um, I'm from BT."

"BT!" Deadpan Dick reiterated unnecessarily, "Good," he said, "I've got a complaint to make," his face remained steadfast.

The engineer looked aghast, like a ten-year-old schoolboy about to get the belt for something he didn't do. You could see him racking his brain, trying to think what he had done wrong. Was it for taking so long to get there? But he had gotten there as quickly as he could. Was it for parking his van in the street and blocking traffic? But the police cars were also blocking the traffic.

"Um, What is it?" the engineer asked rather worried he had upset this senior police officer.

Deadpan Dick looked at him, then turned and pointed at the phone box lying in pieces. Still, with that deadpan voice, he stated.

"This phone isn't working!"

As I say - hard not to laugh.

Chapter 6

OPPORTUNITY-ISED

When Deadpan Dick wasn't amusing me, it was the public who made me smile. When the duty sergeant, covering the street, went on holiday I would step into his role, and a senior cop would cover in the custody suite. It was on those occasions when I policed the street that allowed me to go out and meet the public - especially those who have a tenuous grasp on reality.

There are some who believe the world revolves around themselves and the police service is there solely to cater to their every need. I often raised an eyebrow in disbelief. One such a moment, I was in the Control Room when the operator answered a treble nine call. The caller was phoning from the same area I was covering, so the operator put the speakerphone so I could hear the call firsthand. This was what I heard:

Operator: "Hello police, how can I help you?"
Caller: "There are some youths outside my house pouring Sunny Delight* through my letter-box."
Operator: "Excuse me?"
Caller: "There are two youths pouring Sunny Delight through my letter box."
Operator: "Are you sure? How do you know?"
Caller: "It is the same two youths I battered earlier."
Operator: "What did you batter them for?"
Caller: "They called my dad old."
Operator: "Your Dad! How old is he?"
Caller: "He has just turned eighty."
Operator: "So... er... He is old then?"
Caller: "Yes."
Operator: "So... er, did you need to assault these youths then?"

113

Caller: "Yes they deserved it. I mean they are pouring Sunny Delight through my letter-box."
Operator: "When did they do this?"
Caller: "They are doing it right now."
Operator: "But how do you know it is them and how can they possibly be pouring it through your letter-box?"
Caller: "I am outside watching them."
Operator: "'You are outside? But this is your house phone you have called on how can you be outside?"
Caller: "I climbed out the front window so I could see them. I have an extra stretchy cord."
Operator: "I take it they have stopped now? Are they still in the area?"
Caller: "No. They are still there pouring Sunny Delight through my letter-box. They have a big crate of the stuff, and they are opening each bottle and pouring it down a traffic cone into my letter-box."
Operator: "Why haven't you stopped them?"
Caller: "I don't want to put the phone down."
Operator: "I will get someone round. (sigh)"
        And at that, he hung up.
Operator: (*taking next call*) "Hello Police, how can I help you?"
Caller: "Hello. It's the paper shop on James Street. Someone has just stolen our delivery of Sunny Delight."

Then there are others who keep themselves to themselves, but we ended up having to deal with them for different reasons, as was the case when Tommy Toolbag and I attended at the home of Gershwin Sleekit. We were early shift, it was a nice spring Saturday morning. The sun shone, people were behaving themselves, and I could concentrate on checking reports and other admin. There was the occasional minor call to attend but generally it was a catch-up day. A day when the cops found time to follow up their enquiries and write their reports. They tapped away on their computers, making phone calls to complainers or out chapping doors. Not the usual frenetic pace they normally operated. They were getting on with their business, yet when they fancied a coffee, they got up and made one. When they were hungry, they made their way through to the canteen and sat down, munched on their sandwiches and chatted amongst themselves. It was a good day. Like normal people doing their work. No running to get to a police car, blue lights or woo woo of the sirens.

My radio burst into life. The Control Room Operator made me aware of a complaint, "Sergeant McEwan, we have just received a call complaining about a television being too loud, who do you want to attend?"

"Where about is it?"

"Ten Orchard Street, the complainer is a neighbour."

It seemed like an innocuous call, but there were two strange things about it. First, it was 10 a.m. Nobody complains about televisions blaring at ten in the morning. Late at night yes, in the middle of the night when people are trying to sleep, but not ten in the morning. Second, it was Orchard Street. Nobody in Orchard Street complained about anything unless it was murder. Orchard Street comprised two rows of council owned flats extending about 100 yards up either side of the street. Each block comprised three levels with two flats on each floor making six. It wasn't the most pleasant of places to stay because of the proximity to everyone else, but the tenants had all learned to keep themselves to themselves. When there were problems, they sorted it out without ever involving the police. There were some problematic people there who would make life hell for anyone that complained about them, and there were life's unfortunates, those who bore the brunt of living in such an area. Not bad people but sad people and they had learned not to tell the police anything because if they did, they'd be clypes (tell-tales), and their lives would be unbearable. So no matter who you were in Orchard Street you abide by the unwritten code; Tell the police feck all.

Tommy Toolbag sensed there might be a fight, and no sooner had the call come over the radio he popped his head around my door and said, "Do you want me to go to that Sarge?"

I knew that the rest of the staff were eating their lunch, not wanting to disturb them and happy to get away from my desk for an hour I informed the control room I would attend with Tommy.

"Roger, that's great, and just for your information we have had another two calls in from two other people complaining about the noise from television."

Another two calls? That is strange. What on earth is going on? It is just a television blaring. We should get it sorted pretty quickly; maybe then I can go for my lunch.

Gershwin was an ugly guy in his mid-forties, six feet six inches in height and weighing in at about twenty-four stone. He was a loner and an odd character. Occasionally we had to attend at his home for minor matters. These calls were normally resolved by contacting his health worker who would take over.

Gershwin was the oddest sort of person you could ever meet. He wasn't one for conversation; I once found him sitting on the step outside his flat, in the pouring rain and wearing just his underpants. I asked him what he was doing, and all he could do was stare into my eyes with a glazed uncomprehending look. I checked his flat and found his door closed but insecure; he hadn't locked himself out. With help from my colleague, we helped him to his feet and get him back into his flat. We left him on his sofa with a dirty towel we found in his bathroom. All the time he never said a word. About ten minutes later I drove past his flat, and there he was again, still in his underpants, sitting on the outside step in the pouring rain.

Tommy and I headed off to Orchard Street, it was only a ten-minute drive, but during that time the Control Room Operator informed me they had received a further four calls complaining about the same thing. It was getting stranger and stranger.

Gershwin's flat was right in the middle of Orchard Street. Grubby and neglected. Tommy and I arrived and parked on the side of the road nearest to his flat as we could get. Before we could even open our doors, we could hear the noise of Gershwin's television blaring, through his slightly open front window, the noise reverberating into the street.

Out of the car, it was louder. It wasn't just the volume that was disturbing; it was what we heard. Gershwin Sleekit was, by the sound of things, watching a porn film (I won't go into detail, but I can assure you it was obvious). There were several rather concerned faces at the windows of the surrounding flats watching our arrival with expectation. Three old women, in their sixties and seventies, stood on the pavement opposite next to a sodden and abandoned sofa. They looked at us, folded arms and glowering, expectant. Determined that we put a stop to it.

Tommy and I made our way into the block of flats and rapped on Gershwin's door. The noise of the TV continued unabated. We waited on the porn stars to have a break in their exertions, at the first pause in the noise we banged on his door again. Nothing. The porn stars went back to their business. Tommy and I were ignored. I tried the handle; the door was unlocked.

117

I pushed it but there was something at the back of it preventing it from opening. We had a gap of no more than an inch. Barricaded in, Gershwin Sleekit was free to watch whatever he chose.

We went back out front and tried looking in the window. It was high up, and Tommy had to help me stand on a bucket so I could reach. I stretched enough to put my hand through the partially open window and move the curtain back just a fraction. I caught a glimpse of the back of the couch and the top of the television. I couldn't see anything else. The window wouldn't open any further the security catch was on. There was nothing more I could do.

I presumed that Gershwin was on the couch, engrossed in his salacious choice of breakfast television. I shouted to him to open his door. However, there was no movement or sign he heard me.

Tommy and I went back to the flat door. I decided that Gershwin's actions were tantamount to causing a bloody nuisance and, with his failing to desist, this gave us powers of entry. I reasoned that he might not be well and could require medical intervention. Perhaps all the excitement had caused him to have a heart attack, and he was lying there dead. Either way, we needed to get in.

We pushed and pushed at the door, but it didn't budge. We tried shoulder charging it individually and even in unison, our efforts rewarded with a slightly larger gap, but that was all. Now we could see what was blocking the door, but we still couldn't get in. A large rolled up carpet pushed up against the door and stretched down the hallway. No matter what we did, the door wouldn't budge. We had managed to make a gap of about three inches, but that was all. The porn film still blared away forcing us to do something, but what?

118

Tommy Toolbag's jaw set rigid as he foamed at the mouth. He didn't like to admit defeat at anything.

"Wait here Sarge, I have an idea," he informed me and disappeared out the close. I stood at the door hidden away from the eyes of the neighbours, powerless to do anything. A minute later Tommy arrived back. He held a massive axe in his hands.

What the bloody hell was he carrying a massive axe on duty with him for? Did he keep that in the police car? I need to have words with him - perhaps now is not the time, though.

I moved out the way, and before I knew it, Tommy Toolbag had shredded the door to pieces. The axe ripped its way through the heavy door, sending splinters of wood in all directions. The door crumbled about the lock and the axe worked its way down from top to bottom, and we pulled and pushed bits off until there was room to allow us entry to the flat. Council Housing would not be best pleased.

We scrambled through the shattered door. Habit made me want to check each room. I had been on the job long enough to know that unwanted surprises are not good. I signalled to Tommy to check the first bedroom on the right while I clambered over the rolled up carpet and peeked into the room on the left. The curtains were pulled closed, and I had to let my eyes adjust to see that the room was bare, except for a rusted pedal cycle lying in pieces in the middle of the floor. Tommy let me know his room was clear, and we moved further down the hallway. I pushed open the door to the bathroom; and I recoiled - my eyes and nose offended by the toilet. The seat was up, it hadn't been flushed and was half full of dirty toilet paper. I made an involuntary gag which seemed to amuse Tommy Toolbag standing next to me. He smiled at my discomfort.

119

We made it into the livingroom. The porn stars were still at it. Grunting and groaning nearing climax by the sound of it. We discovered Gershwin Sleekit wasn't dead; he hadn't had a heart attack, he was just smashed. He lay prostrate in an alcoholic stupor on an old brown fabric settee mottled with indeterminate stains. His trousers were at his ankles (not a pretty sight). We switched the video off and silenced the television. I tried to rouse Gershwin, but he just groaned and rolled on his side, knocking over the empty litre bottle of cheap vodka by his hand.

On the floor, surrounding the television, were enough naughty videos to fill three black plastic bin bags (gloves used). I arrested Gershwin and tried to sit him up, "Wha tha fu ur ye doin?" He protested.

We tried to haul his trousers up so he was half decent but they kept falling down. Gershwin was oblivious to this so as we manoeuvred him out of the flat he kept tripping up. The more unstable he became, the more we had to manhandle him to keep him upright. The more we manhandled him, the louder he protested, "YA FUH BISTARDS, FUH LEAVE ME, WHA THE FUH UR YE DAEN TAE ME."

Tommy Toolbag lost his patience.

"Look, can ye no jist come quietly, this is fur yer ain good."

"If he could come quietly, we wouldnae be arresting him," I pointed out.

We managed to bundle Gershwin to the back of our van. I managed to get the rear doors open, but Gershwin had started to sober up a little and protest a little more vehemently.

"WHA THE FUH. AM NO FUHHIN GOIN IN THUR. GEH FUHHIN AFF ME."

Gershwin turned to looked at us, his bleary eyes clouded with fury. He stood up of his own accord and then raised his fists. He was a big man - 6' 7", wide shoulders and paws like shovels. I could see this going badly. Just as he stretched himself out to his full height, his trousers once again fell prey to the effects of gravity and dropped to his ankles. Gershwin's natural reaction was to bend down to pick them up. As quick as a striking snake Tommy pushed him back, and he tumbled over right into the back of the van ending curled upside down with his trousers covering his face and his hairy arse bared towards us. We slammed the doors shut.

Once we got Gershwin safely locked in the van, we returned to his flat and took his entire stash of porn as evidence.

We lugged him back to the office, and once the custody officer got all his details, we decanted him into a cell to sober up. The last time I ever saw Gershwin Sleekit was when I closed that cell door over on him.

When I think about it now, it was a strange thing I never saw Gershwin Sleekit ever again. I discussed the circumstances of his arrest with the CID, who took an interest in the three black bags full of pornography and lodged it in their production cupboard. We reported Gershwin Sleekit to the Procurator Fiscal for being a bloody nuisance. I think the Procurator Fiscal must have ordered a psychiatric assessment, a regular request before an appearance in court. I went off duty and never saw him again. He just disappeared, never went back to his flat, and I never found out where he ended up. Come to think of it; I saw none of those three bin bags full of videos ever again either.

There were other cases like that. A guy who we caught masturbating in the bushes of a local park, was held in custody and appeared in court the next day and I never saw him again. He never returned home. There was a middle-aged music teacher charged for masturbating at his front window. He appeared at court the next day and disappeared after that. I know not what happened to him. A butcher we caught masturbating in the changing rooms at Marks and Spencer was taken to court and then never heard of again. It would appear that the quickest way to disappear off the face of the earth is to masturbate in public. Murderers, vandals, thieves and fraudsters, in due course, all came back to the community where they committed their crimes. However, if you were to play with yourself in public, you would never be seen again.

After working in the custody suite for six months, getting out to work the street a few days to cover colleagues when they were sick or on holiday, wasn't enough. I knew that a lot of custody officers had been there for years. You could see it in the pallor of their skin and the way their heads went down. After years spent dealing with the dregs of society, their cynicism for their fellow man was almost tangible. All faith in humanity lost to the dark recesses of the custody suite. I didn't want to end up like that.

In charge of all transfers at the station was Chief Inspector McPherson. He was a nice fellow, a tall, intelligent ex-traffic officer who showed a great deal of concern for his staff and as a result was able to run the station without having to wield a stick. I decided it was time to drop a few subtle hints to him.

"Chief Inspector McPherson, I've been working in custody longer than any sergeant living or dead. It is about time I got a change," I lied, I hadn't been there longer than anyone else, but I didn't want to be too unassuming. He might not get my gist otherwise.

It worked.

A year and four months later I got my transfer.

Every day for a year and four months, I walked into his office and suggested, asked, pleaded, and cajoled him for a move. When he wasn't there on the weekends, I left a post-it note. Then on the 485th day, this happened:-

"Ah. Sergeant McEwan, I think it is about time you got a move," Chief Inspector McPherson informed me as if it was his idea.

"That's great sir. I really appreciate it. Where am I going?"

"I have a great opportunity for you," he said smiling as if he was Santa Claus.

Alarm bells rang in my head, is that what intuition feels like? A crawling feeling started in my stomach and crept its way through every bone in my body. He used the dreaded word - 'Opportunity' was police speak for 'shafting'.

"Space has come up for a sergeant in the Community Safety, Media and Operation Planning Unit," the department name unsheathed from his tongue, formed a rapier-like sword, swung up in the air, did a flip and came back down in a big arc and stabbed me straight through the shoulder blades.

FLIBBERTY JIBBER! What the hell did I know about Community Safety? Nothing. Media? Nothing. Operational planning? Nothing. C.O.S.M.O.P. - Jeez!

I stood there dumbstruck. I didn't want to go there. I fought desperately for an excuse to turn it down.

"The Chief Constable has agreed on the move. You will deal directly with him as it is his baby. Well done."

FECK! I have been well and truly, right royally, opportunity-ised. I didn't want to be answering to the Chief Constable. He was notoriously difficult to please.

This is bad. This is really bad. I need to turn this down. I can't go there; I would be a complete fish out of the water. I want to be a sergeant on the street. I want to be a real policeman. That's it, tell him you are not going. Just turn it down. Even if you have to go back to the custody for another year, it would be better than working there. There is no way I am going to the C.O.S.M.O.P. unit.

"Thank you, sir. When do I start?" - Well, I find it hard to say 'no'.

Chapter 7

C.O.S.M.O.P.OLITAN.

I spent my first day in my new role getting a handover. I was taking over from Sergeant Guy McRoper, a squat, outdoorsy, rugby player type who was the exact opposite of the person I imagined would be suitable for the job he was doing. Guy was hands-on as a sergeant; he liked to get dirty. He used to work at a nearby station to me that operated on the same radio channel. Whenever he was on duty, he kept up a constant commentary as to what was going on, and always he was there attending calls, taking charge, running things, getting people involved, issuing instructions and generally being at the centre of everything. It was a surprise to everyone when he transferred to C.O.S.M.O.P. He wasn't the type for Community Safety, Media, and Operational planning. Some say it was a prudent move by the bosses to prevent a murder. I wasn't sure that his officers would have gone that far.

Guy had been at C.O.S.M.O.P. for a year and was now being transferred to a little station in the back of beyond - the rumour mill circulated (unkindly) that he was being bumped out of the way. Guy itched to get out and about, he wasn't comfortable sitting in an office all day and requested a move to a smaller working station to get back to being the biggest fish, albeit in a smaller pond.

Monday morning I walked into Headquarters nice and early and made my way to the canteen where I had arranged to meet Guy.

"Hi, how's it going? What's the agenda for today?" I asked, keen to find out what I would be doing.

"First things first," he replied, "breakfast."

We ordered bacon rolls, which were filled to the brim with greasy, artery clogging, fat dripping bacon, wrapped in soft rolls slobbered with chunks of full-fat butter. Tastiest bacon rolls I ever ate. We washed them down with stewed black coffee.

I finished my delicious bacon roll, drained my coffee, wiped my hands on my trousers and readied myself for a busy day learning my new job.

"So, what's the agenda for today?" I asked again.

"Well, I have to take you to see the Chief Constable at ten, so we would be as well to sit here and have another coffee until then."

It was a quarter past eight in the morning. I was getting the impression that there wasn't a lot of urgency to do anything in the C.O.S.M.O.P. Surely there were things we could get on with? I was keen to know what my job entailed, what my responsibilities were and even where my office was.

"Do you not have things to do?"

It was a Monday morning. Monday mornings are busy, hectic even. Bosses return from a weekend off and want to know every single thing that has gone on while they were away. Hindsight meetings take place, faults found, blame apportioned, and tasks identified. Everyone who has more than three chevrons on their shoulder wants to justify their existence. Monday mornings are manic - unless it is a statutory holiday, if it is a statutory holiday everything runs smoothly enough for an extra day, cops and sergeants get on with their jobs, and the work gets done. Tuesday mornings after a statutory holiday are torture. The bosses return to the chair at the head of the hindsight meeting and have three days worth of work to find fault with instead of two.

"I did everything I needed to do," Guy informed me.

"What time did you get in?"

Worry lines appeared on my forehead. How early did I have to be in on a Monday morning? What were the reporting structures for the C.O.S.M.O.P. sergeant? I knew Guy had to organise weekend operations and that the Chief Constable took a personal interest in how they had gone. C.O.S.M.O.P. was the Chief Constable's idea. His baby. A personal project of his. It had come to him in a dream and he'd implemented the next day. Everyone thought C.O.S.M.O.P. was a brilliant idea - at least to his face.

"Ten minutes to eight," Guy said smiling.

"You did everything you needed to do in the ten minutes before we met?" I asked, somewhat surprised.

"Oh yes. It is just a case of collating the returns from the weekend operations and sending them on via email to everyone on the mailing list."

"How many returns? Who from? What's the format? How do you collate them? Where do they go?"

"Oh don't worry, it's easy. I'll show you later."

"So what else do you do on a Monday morning?"

"Well, that's it really. We have to organise the press release, but we do that with the Corporate Media Office, but we can't see them until this afternoon. They are busy on Monday mornings, but I'll introduce you to them when we go to see them at three."

"Three! In the afternoon?"

"Yes."

"What do we do until then?" I asked, amazed that we were expected to sit around until then doing nothing.

"Well, I normally go for a run at lunchtime. If you want to go home and get your running shoes and gym gear, you can come with me."

"You go running instead of having lunch?"

"Oh no! I go running, come back get showered and changed, then I have lunch."

"Doesn't your inspector have something to say about that?"

"My inspector? No, he is happy keeping a low profile too. He doesn't want pestered with anything that will upset the apple cart."

"How long do you spend with the media office organising a press release?"

"Well, Andy McCoist is the Marketing and Communications Manager, and he is good, he sorts it out in ten minutes, but sometimes he is quicker than that. Once that's done we can go home."

I often wondered why we needed a Marketing and Communications Manager. We were a police service. It is not as if we were selling mobile phones.

"So let me get this right. On a Monday morning, you collate the weekend returns and send them on by email, then suit yourself until 3 p.m. Then you go to the media office and arrange a press release, which takes about ten minutes. And that's it?"

"Yup," Guy said smiling.

I swallowed the last dregs of my coffee and decided that the only thing to do was have another one.

Chief Constable 'Handy' McDandy kept us waiting twenty-five minutes before he got his secretary to show us in. Just enough of a wait to show he was a busy man with more important matters to attend to than welcoming a sergeant into his new role in C.O.S.M.O.P. and not too long a wait to signify that he was inefficient or overwhelmed.

Handy McDandy directed Guy and to sit in chairs positioned in front of his desk.

"Thank you for the returns this morning Sergeant McRoper. Good results once again. A lot of positive feedback from the community. How are the press releases coming along?"

"Working on them right now, sir. Should be ready by late afternoon."

"Good. Good," Chief Constable 'Handy' McDandy smiled and nodded at Guy then turned to me.

"Well Malky, I thought I would personally welcome you to COSMOP. This is a very important role. I can't stress how much of a challenge this will be. There will be a lot of hard work for you, but I have high expectations. It is a high profile position, and I demand that it works. I think you will already have seen this morning, working with Guy, that it will be busy. I would like to assure you I am placing a lot of faith in your ability to promote the 'Safer Communities' message to all our stakeholders and over the next year I am looking for you to organise some of the largest proactive operations this force has ever seen. You will also be in charge of getting the message out there. I want you to take a hands-on approach with the website and liaise closely with the media office. Are you up for it?"

"Sir, I'll do my best."

"Good. Now I don't want you to feel you are on your own and that it will all be down to you. If you have any problems, you can pop in and see me anytime. You can take it from me you are my direct representative in this, you are acting on my behalf. If you come across any stubborn senior officers who put obstacles in your way, then feel free to put them straight, or they will have me to deal with. I intend to give you every possible resource we can to make sure the 'Safer Communities' message is at the forefront of everything we do. Any questions?"

"Do I have a budget, sir?"

"Yes, of course, Guy will keep you right with where you are with that, anything else?"

"Who will be involved in the major operations and how do I get them relieved from other duties?"

"Everyone... everyone will be involved. Guy will keep you right with that. So if there is nothing else."

"You mentioned the website, sir. I haven't any experience with that side of things, will I be trained?"

"Yes, of course, Guy will keep you right with that. Now, if that is all."

"Em, just one more thing, sir, regarding these large proactive operations, is there a format you have in mind?"

"Yes, yes, indeed, Guy will..."

"... Keep me right with that. Yes, thank you, sir."

"Remember, I can't stress how important this whole project is. That is why I am happy for you to use every resource available. I want C.O.S.M.O.P. to introduce new values and incorporated throughout the force. That is why your office is on the top floor. People should know the standing you have in this role."

With a wave of his hand, Chief Constable McHandy excused us. Guy and I got up and left.

"So we have an office on the top floor?" I asked Guy, surprised that he hadn't mentioned this before.

"Well, I'm just about to take you there now."

My new office wasn't so much an office as a cupboard under the stairs. There was a standard snib lock on the door, and clearly, it had been a cleaners cupboard at one point in time. The desk was tucked under the staircase, and the computer screen was jammed as far back us the risers would allow. The rest of the desk taken up with the keyboard, so there was nowhere to rest your wrists as you typed. I looked at pulling the desk out a little, but in doing so, it made access in and out of the door all the more of a squeeze. It was claustrophobic and dusty. Not a nice place to be if you suffered from allergies. I understood why Guy didn't like to spend too much time in there.

The dust inveigled their way into my nasal passages, and I sneezed. Guy squeezed by me, stretched down behind the desk and produced a plastic wrapper which still contained four standard white toilet rolls, further evidence that the original purpose of the cupboard was something other than an office. High profile position - indeed!

I took the proffered toilet paper and blew my nose.

"So Guy, I have a budget. How much is it and how do I use it?

"You don't have a budget. It has all been spent."

"Spent?"

"Yeah. The Chief Constable wanted flyers made up, so we got them made up."

"Flyers?"

"Yeah. We had fifty thousand flyers produced at his request. They basically say 'Safer Communities - working for you', that's the message he wanted to convey."

"So where are they?"

"In those two boxes behind you."

I looked behind me and saw two large boxes tucked into the corner of the cupboard. I opened the top one and saw bundles of the flyers Guy was talking about.

"Why didn't you hand them out?"

"Oh, we tried that. We got Community Cops to accompany the Drugs Unit when they did a raid and asked them to pop them into neighbours letter-boxes. They delivered about half a dozen, then threw the rest in the trash. We got Weekend Policing Plan officers to hand them out to late night revellers, but the revellers just threw them away. Half of them got charged for littering, so it became counterproductive."

"So we have no budget and no staff prepared to do anything?"

"Pretty much."

"The emperor is wearing his new clothes?"

"What?"

"Never mind. What about the website? I didn't realise that I had to manage that.

"Yeah. Well, the Chief Constable wants us to add good news stories to it and keep it up to date. Also, any enquiries that come in relating to COSMOP through the web enquiry form, will be your responsibility."

"How do I keep it up to date?"

"You have to get I.T. to give you editor authorisation so you can use the functions on it."

"Is it easy to manage?"

"I don't know. I have been trying to get I.T. to give me editor authorisation for twelve months, and I still don't have it. I've no idea how to work it."

"So who is editing it now?"

"Haven't you seen it? The website hasn't changed for three years."

"What about when someone sends in something through the web enquiry forms?"

"Oh well, I occasionally get an email passed from I.T., I decide who is best to deal with it and pass it on to them."

I sat dumbfounded. Here I was ten minutes after having had a pep talk with the Chief Constable and being told I had an important job to do, yet the reality was somewhat different. I had a cupboard under the stairs for an office, no budget, fifty thousand flyers I couldn't give away, no technical support and, evidently, there was no appetite from anyone else other than the Chief Constable for his C.O.S.M.O.P. idea.

I went home, got my running gear, and Guy took me for a jog. I wasn't what you would call a runner, but it looked like I would be.

The Media Office, by that time, was situated on the ground floor opposite the gym. The furthest point away from the Chief Constables Office. Before Handy McDandy became Chief Constable, our police force had never had, or indeed felt the need for, a Corporate Media Office. Handy McDandy decided it was an essential part of any big organisation. An office was vacated on the top floor, a disgruntled Chief Superintendent moved out of the Complaints and Discipline Office with his staff and banished to some out of the way station across the force. The name on the door changed to Corporate Media, Communications and Marketing Office. Andy McCoist, a journalist who used to work for *The Daily Record,* became the new Communications, Media, and Marketing Manager. He hired two more assistants, and the three of them set up shop in their new office just along the corridor from Chief Constable Handy McDandy.

Initially, it all went swimmingly. The Chief Constable liked to pop into the Media Office and took great delight in all the good news stories they were getting spun about the force. Andy McCoist came up with some great ideas to promote the force and extol the virtuous performance of Chief Constable Handy McDandy. The press were delighted to have their work done for them and cordially obliged with half page spreads, written by Andy McCoist and supplied with photographs. Journalists happily cut and pasted a half page news story and inserted it into their papers if it meant they could take the rest of the afternoon off.

Andy McCoist promoted the news Chief Constable Handy McDandy had taken on eighty-one more cops to the force since the beginning of his tenure. He ordered all eighty-one of them into headquarters for a photo shoot. Wearing full uniform, yellow jackets, hats and polished boots, they were organised to stand to attention in the car park, arranged in such a way that from above they looked like the figure '81'. The senior police photographer made his way to the roof and took an overhead photograph. The public relations machine rolled out a positive message to go with it and inserted a photograph of the self-serving Handy McDandy smiling like Sir Walter Raleigh after winning the Battle of Waterloo.*

History tells us that The Duke of Wellington won the Battle of Waterloo against Napoleon. But like Sir Walter Raleigh, Chief Constable Handy McDandy wasn't shy of taking credit where credit wasn't due. The real reason the force had been able to recruit more officers was that the Scottish Government had provided the finances for it. It was like coming to work with a box of sweeties and taking credit for sharing them with your workmates - even although it was your maw's idea and she gave you the money for them.

Then reality set in. Andy McCoist was in a new environment. Working with the *Daily Record* was a relaxed affair. He could walk into his editor's office any time of the day or night and ask questions, propose stories or even just chew the fat. That was the editor's job. Once the journalists had finished, and the paper went to press, everyone toddled off to the pub. The editor was first to dip his hand in his pocket and set up the round.

The chain of command operates differently in the police. There is a hierarchy. If a cop wants to run something by the Chief Constable he has to put it on paper and send it to his sergeant, his sergeant has to read and agree with the content and send it to his inspector, the inspector does likewise and sends it to his chief inspector. The chief inspector will read it too, append comments and pass it to his superintendent; the superintendent will also read it and pass it to his boss, the chief superintendent who will do the same and pass it to the assistant chief constable who passes it to the deputy chief constable. Only once the deputy chief constable has scrutinised it and sent it back twice for amendment will he consider passing it to the Chief Constable. At any stage of that process any boss can, and often would, send the report back to the cop for amendment or simply file it in shredder No. 1. The Chief Constable is a busy man and need not know every single thing that goes on. He doesn't have to decide on every single minutia of business. The likelihood of a cop's memo being passed to the Chief Constable is rather remote. Not like the workings of a newspaper. Thus Chief Constable Handy McDandy was quickly pissed off when Andy McCoist came running to him every two minutes to ask what he wanted done with every bit of business that came Andy's way.

The Media Office moved down a floor, under the pretext they needed their top floor office as a meeting room. The physical act of walking up one flight of stairs to speak to the Chief Constable was a small hurdle that reduced Andy McCoist's visits to Chief Constable Handy McDandy's office. Although, it wasn't sufficient to deter him altogether. In due course, he thought up another excuse and the Media Office permeated its way to the opposite side of the building away from

135

Chief Constable Handy McDandy. The physical distance and growing experience allowed Andy McCoist to get on with his job and Handy McDandy to get on with his.

Andy McCoist met us with a great big grin when Guy and I walked into the Media Office and we got a cheery wave from his two assistants. All three had big desks to cater for the two large computer screens sitting on top. They had the best of technology. Very different from the abacus with missing beads that the cops had. Newspapers sat in bundles on the remaining furniture and Guy and I had to move boxes of flyers off chairs to find somewhere to sit. A large television, set to the *Sky News* channel, adorned the far wall. The sound was on mute but headlines scrolled across the bottom of the screen. Some walls had framed newspaper articles depicting the good news stories that the Media Office had spun to the press. It wouldn't be too long before there would be no more room left on the walls.

"This is Malky, the new COSMOP sergeant," said Guy introducing me.

I shook hands with Andy and got another wave from his two assistants.

"Welcome to the team, what do you think of your new job so far?" Andy asked smiling conspiratorially at Guy.

"I'm not sure yet. I might be a little less anxious when I find out exactly what it is I'm doing," I replied.

"Well, it's easy. All you have to remember is that everything we do is good news."

"Good news?"

"Yes, that's our job here. We have to make sure we roll out good news stories."

"What do you mean?"

"Well, for example," Andy explained, "last week we had a lot of vandalism in the city centre, there were about a dozen windows smashed and we even had two police cars damaged. The officers were dealing with several disturbances at the nightclubs and came out to find their windows smashed."

"That isn't good news," I pointed out.

"Of course it was," said Andy positively adamant, "Here is the press release we got printed in the local paper."

I read the article:

VIOLENT CRIME REDUCED TO ZERO

Intelligence lead policing has shown the way to increased uniformed police presence in the city centre and has cut violent crime in the area. Chief Inspector McPherson, who covers the area, said, 'Proactive patrols have been a success in the city centre, last weekend there wasn't a single incidence of violent crime...

I looked up at the smiling Andy McCoist and raised an eyebrow.

"Well, it's true," he spread his hands out palm upwards showing that he was innocently reporting the truth.

"I thought there was a young lad stabbed last weekend?"

"Ah! Yes, there was, but that wasn't in the city centre. The article is still accurate."

"So what are you going to report on this week?"

"Well I've had a look at the returns Guy sent me and there isn't a lot to report on is there?"

"No. It was a pretty quiet weekend by all accounts," Guy answered. "It is disappointing that out of twenty officers deployed across the area command over Friday and Saturday nights, the only bit of proactive policing was a guy locked up for being drunk and a couple of underage youths that had their alcohol confiscated."

I was aware that the weekend had in fact been unusually busy. Officers had gone from call to call dealing with domestic disturbances, thefts, road accidents, sudden deaths and various other matters that required immediate responses. Under those circumstances, any proactive policing has to take a back seat.

"How are you going to come up with something positive about that?" I asked Andy.

"I've already done it," he said, and passed me another article:

UNDERAGE DRINKING CRACKDOWN
Proactive policing patrols have netted a haul of alcohol including lager, cider, and fortified wine. Several youths were issued warnings in front of their parents. Sergeant McEwan, who is now overseeing anti-social behaviour in the area said: "We are working to reduce instances of alcohol related anti-social behaviour and keep our communities safe. All confiscated booze has been poured down the drain."

Underneath the article was a picture of numerous half-empty bottles of alcohol. 'Déjà vu' - I had seen that picture somewhere before. It was the same picture we rolled out every time we reported on underage drinking.

"I never said that?" I queried with Andy.

"Don't worry about it. We make up all the quotes for these news articles that's our job."

"But what if it is something important, and I get asked about it later?"

"Never happens. I started off asking senior officers for quotes, and every single one of them asked me what they should say. So it saves time. We make

138

them up to keep the corporate message the same, and it saves me pestering people for quotes."

Guy and I were in and out of the Corporate Media Office in under half an hour.

"Well that took longer than normal," said Guy as soon as we were far enough away from the office they couldn't hear him. "Now we can bugger off home."

I was taken aback. It wasn't what I expected my job to be. I still wasn't sure if I would enjoy it or not, this wasn't police work.

The following day saw Guy and I follow the same breakfast routine. We met in the canteen at dead on 8 a.m.

"Hi, how's it going? What's the agenda for today?" I asked.

"First things first," he replied, "Breakfast."

We ordered bacon rolls for the second day in a row, and I gobbled down my greasy, artery clogging bacon roll with a hunger that was probably down to the previous day's jog. I followed this up with two cups of stewed black coffee.

"So, what is the agenda for today?" I asked again.

"Well, I suppose I better take you to see your boss, Inspector McScotty. I thought Inspector MacGundridge was my boss?" Inspector MacGundridge was the inspector in charge of the Community Safety Team and worked from the same office as them on the middle floor. I expected my job would require a lot of liaison with him.

"No. No. Inspector MacGundridge has nothing to do with you. He is in charge of the Community Safety side of COSMOP. He has nothing to do with media or operations."

I looked at Guy, and from my confused expression, he guessed I needed an explanation.

"Your role is all about organising operations and promoting good news stories for the force. Inspector McScotty is your boss."

"Inspector McScotty? But he is in charge of the Public Order Team and the Diving Team." I couldn't quite figure how that worked.

Inspector Innes McScotty had been a career detective. He had joined the CID with five years service and stayed there for twenty years. Promoted to detective sergeant after serving his time, he stayed in that position for another ten years. The bosses liked that he was professional and trusted him to do his job without ever worrying about him cutting corners. If there was sufficient evidence to prove a case he'd find it. Nobody was more methodical. What they didn't like about Innes McScotty was his candid approach. He told it like it was. Certain senior officers didn't like that - they preferred their bottoms licked to his outspoken assessments of their incompetence. So they left him to get on with it. He didn't need babysat to do his job, and they avoided getting in his way for fear of his bluntness causing them affront. Then the incumbent of his present post retired, so he bosses looked around for a replacement. They picked Innes McScotty. Promoted him to the inspector in charge of the Public Order Team and Diving Team. It was a strange appointment because he had no background or training in public order or diving. I presumed that they were freeing up his detective sergeant role for an officer with a more obliging tongue.

I didn't know Innes all that well, but on the occasions I had met him I found him interesting to listen to. He had an intensity of purpose about him.

Conscientious and capable, I thought. I didn't mind that he was my gaffer, I just couldn't see the logic behind it. For a start he worked at a different station, he had no involvement in C.O.S.M.O.P. and would be totally detached from of my day to day work.

"Yes, I know, something to do with the total amount of yearly appraisals they have to do." Guy explained.

"But Inspector MacGundridge has about a dozen people in his unit; Inspector McScotty must have responsibility for hundreds of officers?"

"Yes, but most of the Public Order Team officers are only there for training exercises or when they get called out. Inspector McScotty has few permanent staff he has to do appraisals for - thus they gave him line management responsibility for this role."

"Do you have much to do with him?"

"Well, funny enough, that's our agenda for this afternoon. We have a meeting with Inspector McScotty every Tuesday."

"So what have we got on the agenda this morning?" I suspected jogging might be involved.

"We need to liaise with the group sergeants, then we can go for a jog."

"I take it we will promote the COSMOP side of things with them?"

"Naw, we just need to cadge a car off one of them for this afternoon so we can meet with Inspector McScotty."

"We don't have car allocated to us?"

"Naw, that's one problem you will have. Trying to get transport anywhere is a nightmare."

To my surprise, it took all morning to borrow a car off the group sergeant. We asked, bribed, cajoled, wheedled and coaxed - all to no avail. Guy got down on his knees, clasped his hands together and begged - when that didn't work, we tried bullying. Guy sneaked up behind him, grabbed the duty sergeant in a bear hug, pinning his arms to his sides. While Guy grappled with him, I rifled his trouser pockets and whipped out a set of car keys for his marked Vauxhall Astra and ran off down the corridor, closely followed by Guy and an irate duty sergeant. We jumped into the car and headed off out of headquarters to the Public Order Team office.

Inspector McScotty's office was in a remote police station. He had a small room at the rear of the station near the back door. Chosen because it was close to the large storage unit across the car park where the Public Order Team and the Diving Team kept their gear. Giving him an office there was pointless. Because Inspector McScotty had no background in either Public order or the Diving Team he had no need, or desire, to be next to the storage unit. He had only been in it once to nod at all the shelves stacked with shields, protective kit, helmets and scuba gear.

His desk was piled high with papers on either side and documents protruded out of the in-tray. He looked up from the haphazard array of documents lying on his desk and smiled, glad of the respite.

"Good afternoon lads," Inspector McScotty, welcomed us into his room, "coffee?"

He was instantly likeable.

"Coffee would be great," I replied.

Guy backed me up, "Indeed."

For the next hour, Inspector McScotty listed everything he had on his plate. He had taken over a role he had no experience in and was now in charge of many people, who required a lot of training. Not only that, any or all of them could get called out for a live incident at the drop of a hat. Despite his lack of knowledge of the department, Inspector McScotty had started to get a handle on it all. He had an analytical brain, and he was thorough. He looked at every aspect of the department and questioned everything. The department operated on the 'we have always done it that way' principle. That didn't sit well with Inspector McScotty. He looked for a reasoned and logical argument for doing anything. If something wasn't right, he set out to put it right. Opposition to him was intense. He related an example.

"We got a bill in for seven nights dinner, bed-and-breakfast for the Diving Team training. They were staying at some hotel in the North West coast of Scotland. Two sergeants and ten cops went up with the Diving Bus."

When he mentioned the sum involved Guy looked at me, astonished and gave a low whistle, it was a lot of money.

"Thing was," McScotty continued, "when I asked why they did their training up there, they told me it was because they always go there. That made little sense. They spent a day travelling up, five days training and a day coming back. The petrol alone was costing a fortune, but the whole diving team also claimed two days overtime for travelling. Surely there was somewhere closer they could have carried out their training. So I suggested they do their training at the dam - half a mile from the office. No need to travel the length and breadth of the country. Apparently that wasn't suitable because it wasn't deep enough. I suggested a nearby deep loch. That wasn't suitable because it didn't have flowing water. I suggested another loch only a mile further away, but that wasn't wide enough. Every suggestion I made, they would come back with some other argument for going up the North West coast. I got all sorts of excuses; there was no access or no parking. I was even told they couldn't go to one place because they would disturb some protected bird population. I suggested over a dozen locations to carry out their training all within a ten-mile radius of us, but they kept coming up with excuses why it wasn't suitable. Basically, the training week was an all expenses paid holiday for them, and they didn't want to lose it. I put my foot down. What if they had to do a real job at one of these places? I reasoned that the only place they were training to do a search and recovery was the sea loch on the North West coast - and they had never yet been called out for a real search on it."

"I take it they now do their training nearer home?"

"Well, no. They still get their week away. Friends in high places."

"Friends in high places?"

"Yeah, a couple of them are on the football team."

"That must irk you a bit?"

Inspector McScotty waved his hands to show that he wasn't bothered, "I have other things to worry about."

"You seem to have a lot on your plate," I said as I looked at all his paperwork piled up on his desk and in his in-tray.

"I have a lot, yes. There is this one thing I'm trying to get sorted that has the potential to be a serious embarrassment to the force. That is what I am working on now."

"What is it?"

"Every once in a while we have a military convoy that travels through our area. We get little notice, a couple of days at most and we have to implement an operation to ensure that it passes through without incident. Nobody takes it seriously. Yet, there is an acute threat to us and the public if it doesn't. There are also people out there plotting to obstruct the route, and there is even potential for a terrorist event."

"There are protocols in place for these things, though?" I posed it as a question because I'd been involved in one operation before.

"There are some old protocols in place, but they don't take heed of the potential seriousness. You've been involved before - what was your impression?"

"Come to think of it; it was all a bit blasé."

"Exactly."

"So what did you do?"

"I highlighted the potential problems to the Chief Constable."

"Has he done anything about it?"

"Oh yes. The Chief Constable ordered an immediate review of our whole processes. He wanted a comprehensive report detailing everything we did, everything we didn't do and everything we should be doing."

"So who got that?"

"Who do you think?"

"Have you completed it?"

"It has taken me three months solid, and I have eighteen pages of recommendations to take to him. I go for my brushectomy tomorrow."

"Brushectomy?"

"Yeah. When I present this to the Chief Constable tomorrow, he will remove the medium-sized brush from my backside and replace it with an extra large one. The only person he can give responsibility for implementing the recommendations will be me."

I saw his point.

"Is there anything I can do to help?"

"Well, there are these," he handed me four names and phone numbers.

"Who are they?"

"Just some local organisations, the community council and Rotary Club looking for a police officer to give them a talk, you can do that can't you?"

Standing up in front of a group of people and giving a talk was not something I relished, I hadn't done any talks like that before. I'm sure I read somewhere that people are more afraid of public speaking than getting shot in the head. I didn't have a phobia about it, but I suspected that it might not be my favourite thing. I'd stride into a pub and break up a fight without thinking, but I hadn't had any training giving talks - either in making them up or presenting them. I think it is something that most people baulk at the thought of. There are few natural speakers who are born with that ability but I'm not a comedian or a politician. Inspector McScotty could see my nervousness.

"Oh come on! All you have to do is stand there, scratch your balls and look out the window," he assured me.

"Okay, I'll do it," I answered.

Well, I find it hard to say 'no'.

Our Wednesday and Thursday weren't much busier. Guy ran me through what he did (very little), and we went for a run at lunchtime - then we showered, changed and sat down to have lunch. We weren't the only ones to have an extended lunch. I had my eyes opened. Until then, I had been on front-line duties or in the custody suite, where I could be called upon at a moment's notice. Lunch, if I got a bite, I spent at a desk typing reports. Even then I could be called away to attend the next incident. There were many a time that a bowl of soup was left all on its own to ping in the microwave as I rushed out the door to attend an emergency.

In headquarters, there were plenty of nine-to-five jobs that didn't require the officer to be available on the other end of a radio. I met these nine-to-fivers as they changed in the gym. Some went running, some used the gym equipment, and some played badminton. The other half who weren't on front-line duties, sauntered downtown to go shopping.

On Thursday afternoon Guy informed me he was taking the Friday off, it was his last day on the job, and he felt his handover was complete.

"Okay, so what do I do on Fridays?"

"Fridays are your busy days. You have to produce the operational order for the weekend policing plan, organise the staff, carry out the briefings, prepare the return templates, ensure the front-line sergeants know what they are doing and are on board with it all. Then you have to organise transport, arrange special constables, send the orders to senior officers, risk assess staffing for the custody suite and keep the control room in the loop. There might be occasions when you get interested councillors coming out on the operation as well. Make sure that there is a full itinerary for them, hire vehicles to show them about, arrange a driver and, hardest of all, persuade an inspector to lead them around the operation." Guy rattled it all off as if it was second nature.

I looked at him with a cynical squint in my eye, "Cheers," I replied.

Guy was correct. Fridays were busy. Over the next few weeks, I organised things a little differently. Instead of waiting until Friday I pulled things together on Monday. As I settled into the role, I still went for my jog at lunchtime but my days filled up.

My first task I set myself was to get access to the website, so I could make changes and bring it up to date. From what Guy told me this would not be an easy job. I walked into the I.T. office and asked for the necessary editor authorisation. I prepared myself for a fight. According to Guy, he had been waiting a year to get those functions authorised and was still waiting. He said he had filled in the I.T. request form and emailed it to them every week for a year and still, they hadn't given him the functions. He turned up at their office with the I.T. request form printed off, and they told him they couldn't accept it and that he had to email it to them.

I would not put up with that kind of incapacitation. I took a haversack with me containing a flask of coffee, sandwiches and a pocket radio. I was going to get a password, and I wasn't going to leave until they gave it to me. Which they would once they realised I was in for the long haul. If they didn't give me editor authorisation right there and then, well they would have to put up with me dancing around their workshop to the sounds of *Radio 2.* I even had a picnic with me. Determined, I would wait there until I got it - as long as it took.

I walked into the I.T. workshop, plonked my haversack on a chair and asked to speak to the head honcho. Billy McGrieve looked over the top of his spectacles and wandered up to see me.

"Hi Billy, I need a password for editor authorisation for the website," I folded my arms and stared at him.

"Ok, no problem," said Billy, as if it was the easiest thing in the world, and two minutes later I was hauling my haversack off the chair and heading back to my office under the stairs with a new user name and password.

I sat at my desk and stayed there until I figured out how to update the website. I soon got up and running. For the first time in three years, it got introduced to new content. I changed things around, added good news stories and once it took shape, I let people know about it. It worked. Within a week I.T. informed me that unique visitors to our site had increased from three in the past month to... twelve. Fantastic! Although I suspected that my mum, my dad, my sister, my aunt and uncle in Canada and my two brothers accounted for half them. The rest were probably senior police officers or I.T. themselves. It wasn't my main worry. I had talks to present.

The four names and numbers Inspector McScotty had handed me were requests for police talks. Four innocuous names and numbers, heads of community groups, round table secretaries and the like. All of them were keen to have a police officer attend their meeting under the guise that they were interested in what we had to say. Of course, all the invites were for the Chief Constable; he can't do them all of them (or any, as it appeared). So the requests slid down the chain of command and ended up with me.

The first name on the list was Mary McSheen, secretary for a local community group. The group had a small number of elderly members, all local residents, who would meet once a month in the community hall (a converted public toilet). I called Mrs McSheen and introduced myself.

"Hello, I'm Sergeant Malky McEwan, I was asked to call you and see if I can help," I informed her, with my nice and polite posh voice.

"Oh, fantastic," Mary McSheen, said in an excited voice, "could you come and give us a talk on drugs?"

"I don't do drugs, but I could do it on a few glasses of wine. What do you want me to talk about?" I replied.

"I don't know about wine, but you will get a cup of tea and a biscuit. We all get a cup of tea and a biscuit, a wee blether and then hear what our guest speaker has to say. It's all very civilised. Could you come a week on Thursday?"

I agreed.

So a week on Thursday I turned up prepared to give a talk about drugs. I spent my week digesting all the information I could. I spoke to just about everyone in the drugs unit; I quizzed the experts, researched the subject myself, I even went to the library and pored through books on the topic and then put together an interesting and informative talk about drugs, their effects, the law and our enforcement of that law.

I was welcomed to the meeting and shown to a chair at the far end of the small hall. The chair faced the crowded room, full of elderly blue rinse women and bald men. I made polite conversation with Mary McSheen while the audience filled themselves up with tea and biscuits. After a while, Mrs McSheen stood up and addressed the group, welcomed everybody, did a little housekeeping and then introduced me.

"This is Sergeant McEwan who will give us a little insight into what is going on in the police."

A couple of people clapped, but it didn't last.

"Good evening, ladies and gentlemen. I've been asked to talk to you about an important topic, one that is very much in the news these days and of which I know most of you will consider a great problem in today's society. I will go into a little of the history behind the laws that we have, how the drug problem affects everyone and what we are doing about it. At the end, I hope to have time to answer any questions you may have."

I was interrupted by a tall and scrawny looking gentleman at the back of the hall, "What are you doing about the speeding in the Main Street?" he asked in a thunderous voice. There was an echo of approval to his question from the rest of the room.

"I want to ask what you can do about my neighbour leaving all her rubbish in her front garden?" a slight woman in a heavy coat, sitting at the front of the room asked.

Before I could think of any form of response, I was bombarded with questions from all around the room.

"I want to know what you are doing about the kids hanging around the shops at night?"

"Why don't we see any officers walking the beat in Grange Avenue?"

"I want to report that my shed broken into two months ago."

"Where is PC Harry... er um whats-his-name working now, has he retired?"

"How do I report a drunk driver who nearly ran over me last month?"

I knew people like to read about what the police do. Even more than reading, they like to hear about what the police do. What I learned from giving that talk was that even more than reading and hearing what the police do, people like to moan about what the police don't do. They love it all the more when they can moan to a police sergeant in person.

The meeting went from bad to worse. My half hour talk about drugs forgotten as I went on the defensive and tried to justify my existence. I felt ambushed. Blindsided by the geriatric Gestapo interrogation squad.

"We paid for that uniform on your back, you know," were the last words I heard as I walked out after an hour of making excuses. I entered that hall aged forty-one and left feeling like eighty-one and a half. Older and a little wiser. That's what the police does to you. It makes you older and wiser. I say 'wiser'; I mean 'cynical'.

During my next meeting with Inspector McScotty, I was overflowing with excitement as I recited to him how well the meeting had gone.

"It was such a pleasant evening; everyone was so nice. They served me tea and biscuits, and I had a great time with them all. It is not like real police work at all. You might like to try doing the next one. It might give you a break from all the other stuff you have on your plate. You would be fantastic at it. I can help you out with your other work if you like.

He didn't fall for it.

"Do you think I was buttoned up the back in a diaper suit when I came in this morning?" He replied almost laughing.

"If you enjoyed it so much you carry on and do them all." Then he did burst out laughing. Sometimes Inspector McScotty wasn't so likeable.

The next two talks I gave went slightly better than the first one. I learned to project my voice, deflect questions with, 'I'll come back to that' and keep on the topic. I still got several pelters from the audience, but I now understood some of the techniques required to keep them engaged in what I was saying rather than what they wanted hear. A lot of it was to do with preparation. Proper preparation prevents piss poor performance is better advice than 'just stand there, scratch your balls and look out the window'. By the time I gave a talk to the Rotary Club, I was ready to hook the audience and distract them from asking awkward questions.

The Rotary Club comprises business leaders, people of influence and concerned citizens who work to help solve some of their communities greatest challenges. They have great projects across the world that helps to promote peace, fight disease, provide clean water, support education and help people in growing their local economies. They asked me to come along and tell them about the new C.O.S.M.O.P. idea that our Chief Constable had implemented. They were interested in finding out how it would improve the lives of their local community.

Walter Dinkins, a retired minister, introduced me to the group.

"This is Sergeant McEwan, who has kindly come along to explain what our local police force is doing with their new initiative; Community Safety, Media and Operation Planning Unit and how it will reduce crime in our area."

I stood up to a smattering of applause.

"There's been a murder..." I said, pausing for effect, "Last week I was called to a disturbance on Hamilton Street. A man was found lying in the middle of the road badly beaten to death."

I know if you are beaten to death you don't have to justify it with the adverb 'badly', I mean if you are dead it is the worst beating it could be. However, I was there to engage the audience and hold their attention for as long as I could to prevent them asking me any questions. I continued without pause.

"As duty sergeant, I was one of the first officers to attend. I parked at the bottom of the road and instructed the cop I was with to barricade it off and let no-one through without my express permission. I wanted no one interfering with any evidence. Every interaction leaves a trace. As I walked up Hamilton Street, I was careful to watch where I stepped and followed a route up one pavement. About a quarter of the way up I saw a brown furry left slipper lying upturned on the roadway. A little further up was a bloodied and bashed baseball bat. Then, right in the middle of the street, was a man about forty years of age lying all twisted, his face mashed and unrecognisable. He was dead for sure. Not a breath of life. Battered to a pulp. Murdered with a ferocity rarely seen. I set things in motion. Closure of the road, CID attendance, extra officers to the scene and all the things necessary to preserve evidence and kick off a major enquiry."

"In due course, I looked for witnesses. There was no-one hanging around. We needed to knock some doors. Basic policing. We don't get anywhere without talking to people. Information comes from what we see, what we hear but mostly from what people tell us. The nearest flats to my dead body was a block of six. As soon as the first detective constable arrived (a promising young detective called Tucker) I accompanied him into the block of flats. Time to knock those doors. Someone might have heard something, hopefully even seen something. We knocked the two doors on the ground floor, police knocks. Hard, loud and many. There was no reply. We did the same again on the second floor. Two doors both given hard, loud, repetitive knocks. There was no reply. We went up to the top floor. A tired and drunk woman came to the door of the first flat. She took a moment to gather herself. I asked if she had heard anything unusual this evening. 'No,' she replied, 'only them arguing downstairs' and she pointed to the flat below her. At that moment, I heard a door opening from the middle flat. I moved to the top of the stairs and saw a middle aged male poking his head out of his door. 'What's going on?' he asked me. This was much more interesting."

"Detective Tucker and I made our way to his door and asked to come in and see him. He obliged. We followed him through to his small kitchen, and he sat on a stool beside his bunker. There was only room for us to stand. 'What's going on?' he asked again. I looked him up and down. My eyes settled on his feet. His left foot was bare and on his right foot was a brown furry slipper. I knew right then that I was looking at a murderer."

I paused again - purely for effect - the room was silent. I looked at each of the Rotary Club members in front of me, making eye contact. Unsmiling, trying to convey the seriousness of it all. I let the gravity of what I had told them sink in. Each one of the Rotary Club members held my eye for a second. They also looked solemn. As I scanned the audience I saw wrinkled faces, ruddy complexions, bald pates, a beard and then a face I recognised. Not a serious or solemn face, an angry face. Sitting at a table at the back of the room, it was my Chief Constable.

Chief Constable Handy McDandy was a bloody Rotarian.

Feck. Here I am supposed to be giving a talk on how my Chief Constable had introduced a new unit that would reduce crime and save the world. But no. I'm frightening them all with a story about a murder. What are you going to do? You can't continue with your presentation now. I know - he won't be best pleased if you tell them they are all doomed to be murdered. I need to change it! Okay, okay.

"So the reason for me telling you this story is not to put the wind up you. Let me reassure you that murder is the most uncommon of crimes. Murders are few and far between. We, the police, are skilled at detecting murders. We pull out all the stops. A well oiled investigating machine rolls into place, and we set about putting all our resources into ensuring that the murderer is apprehended, incarcerated and convicted in court. I have been in this job for twenty years, and I can't think of a single undetected murder during that time. The number of murders in Scotland has been on the decline. In the last ten years the murder rate reduced by thirty-six percent and we are not talking about large numbers to begin with. There have been about the same amount of murders in Scotland in the last ten years as committed on an average day in the United States of America. Males perpetrate most of the murders we get, most of those the victims are males. Most victims know their murderer as in the situation I related. Two drinking buddies had fallen out, had a fight, things got out of hand, and one ended up dead. Despite the horrible nature of the events I have just related to you, don't be afraid. The likelihood of you being the victim of murder in Scotland is very remote. The likelihood of you getting away with murder in Scotland is even remoter. We do a great job with serious crimes like these."

I paused for breath and thinking time, all the while trying to avoid looking in the direction of the Chief Constable.

"What our Chief Constable has introduced with the Community Safety, Media and Operation Planning Unit is a way of us getting as good at everything else we do just like the way we deal with murder…"

156

Oh wow, Malky! That was great, what a comeback. Now you can go on and tell them all the good stuff we do and then wrap it up. Hopefully, Handy McDandy will be pleased with that.

I finished up my talk and received a hearty round of applause. My original intention was to sit down and then get out of there as soon as I could. However, buoyed by the positive response, I made the mistake of asking if anyone had any questions. Stupid I know. Leave on a high if you can. Never try to milk it.

"So what exactly are your responsibilities?" a squat looking grey-haired man in the front row asked.

Hmm. How do I answer this? The truth is, I email everyone on a Monday, meet with my boss on a Tuesday and organise work for everyone else to do on a Friday.

"Do you know," I replied, "If I had a job description it would probably say 'Everything else' I couldn't define it all. I have responsibilities for organising some of the biggest operations our force has seen to keeping the police website updated. I just get on and do what needs done."

If Carlsberg made COSMOP sergeants, eh?

Then I saw it. The dreaded hand in the air. From the table right at the back of the room. Chief Constable Handy McDandy had a question for me. I looked in his direction, and that was enough for him to take it as an invitation to speak.

"You mentioned the police website, how has that bit of work being going?" he asked. The poisoned chalice question. How do you explain that we were averaging a dozen visitors per week? That's pretty rubbish, isn't it?

Who the hell is interested in our stupid bloody website, anyway?"

"Oh hello sir," I said, pretending I had just seen him, "As you well know we have had a four hundred percent increase in unique visitors to the website since COSMOP have taken over responsibility for it. The content is being updated daily, and as a result, there has been a marked reduction in enquiries through the online form. People are getting the information they require much more quickly. I think it is working very well."

I wasn't going to tell him that the four hundred percent increase was from three to twelve or that the online enquiry form was now much harder to find. He sat back looking pleased with himself.

I spent over a year in the C.O.S.M.O.P. role. Inspector McScotty completed his reports and got things working efficiently in his department then got himself transferred. My new inspector, Alex McFleming, had been a member of the football team and was going places.

Within about three seconds of taking up the role, Inspector McFleming took credit for all the good work that Inspector McScotty had been working on. He was shameless about it. I didn't mind him all that much as a person - he was a nice guy. However, he came with a reputation for taking credit for things that had nothing to do with him. Everyone knew he was like that. Nobody believed he came up with anything original or did anything that involved hard work. For some reason, it still grated on me. I always believed in giving credit where credit was due. It galled me when bosses would claim successful outcomes to be down to their brilliance as a leader and the same people were the first to have slopey shoulders when things went wrong. My new inspector would be the first to run to the superintendent to inform him that 'we' had recovered a load of drugs in an intelligence-led operation. It didn't matter he didn't even know of the operation and was tucked up in bed when it happened. On the opposite side of that if something were to go wrong his first response would be 'I sent them all a memo telling them not to do that' - no matter that the memo he sent was a generic thing he sent out three years previous.

Sometimes it is difficult to identify those bosses who take credit for the work of others. Looking out for the clues can be tricky. Physical signs are slopey shoulders, Teflon coated uniform and a darker area around the tip of the nose. Another sign is that you know the sight of the back of their head better than their face - if you give them any good news they immediately about turn and run off to tell their boss and anyone else who will listen. Newton's third law states: For every action, there is an equal and opposite reaction. That applies to those who take credit where credit isn't due. When you bring them bad news, it is never their fault, they never take responsibility and are quick to disassociate themselves from whoever is the bearer. It is just another occasion when you will see more of the back of their head than their face.

So how do you deal with a colleague or a boss who takes credit for your work?

You can sit down with them and discuss the situation. Let your colleague or boss know you feel aggrieved that your contribution wasn't fully recognised. Reiterate your support for them and your commitment to the team but stress that in future, you expect your effort to be acknowledged in the future.

Or...You can do what I did.

Tuesday afternoon arrived, I closed down my computer and headed downstairs to borrow a car. It was my day to visit Inspector McFleming. We keep the keys for operational police vehicles within a secure lockfast cabinet in the duty sergeant's office. The duty sergeant holds the key for the cabinet and divides the keys to officers. Next to the cabinet, a whiteboard lists the vehicles, and a marker pen dangles from a piece of string so that officers can mark up on the board with which vehicle they have. A sergeant can see at a glance who has which vehicle.

I introduced the whiteboard when I worked there. After searching frantically for a vehicle to go to an emergency call and later discovering that three of the vehicles we had were in the garage and a cop, who had been on night shift, had gone home with a set of keys in his pocket (not an unusual occurrence).

A temporary inspector introduced the lockfast cabinet and the crazy system of the sergeant holding the key to the cabinet who issued each vehicle individually as the cops required it. It was crazy because sergeants have better things to do than issue keys all day and if he is not around (out on a call, having lunch, or indisposed reading a paper on the loo), then no-one has access to any vehicles. I mean, if you can't trust a copper!

Anyway, as soon as the temporary inspector finished his stint in the role and added his 'inspired lockfast cabinet initiative' to his CV, the sergeants simply left the cabinet open so people could get access. I wandered into the sergeant's office and saw that the cabinet was bare. There wasn't a single ignition key hanging from any hook. The whiteboard told me that every vehicle was out, including the nicest car, our Honda CRV, which was being used by the duty sergeant.

"Can I borrow your car for an hour, Sergeant Vince?"

"No, I am just about to go out to view a sudden death at the mortuary."

The mortuary is a short walk away. Ten minutes at most. I used to walk there all the time.

"Could I drop you off there? Your cops could give you a lift back."

"No, I might need it."

"I'll only be an hour. I will be back by the time you get finished at the mortuary."

"No!"

"Pretty please?"

"No!"

"Pretty please with sugar and spice and a pint of beer?"

"No!"

"Okay, thanks."

I walked out of his office. Just as I got to the door, I turned back to him as if I had forgotten something.

"Oh, and by the way, the chief inspector wanted to see you."

"What about?"

"Some overtime claim or something, I don't know."

You may or may not have heard of *'Evidence-Based Policing (EBP)'* it is an approach to policy-making and tactical decision-making for police. I am a great believer in EBP. It is the use of the best available research on the outcomes of different approaches to police work. It

161

makes sense, doesn't it? It follows a basic principle: Do what works and stop doing what doesn't - simple. I am also a practitioner of *'Evidence-Based Pranking.'* So my previous evaluations of experimental pranking stood me in good stead here.

I knew that if I wanted to get Sergeant Vince out of his office, I had to create a ruse he wouldn't twig. My dodge to get him out of his office relied on two proven elements in my last statements to him. First, I told him the chief inspector wanted to see him. If I had used a lower rank, it might not have worked. If I had said a cop, or a sergeant wanted to see him, then he wouldn't care. They could come and see him if they wanted to see him. If I had said the inspector wanted to see him, then he might have gone along with it, but it was fifty-fifty. He would reason he could always explain away to the inspector that he was busy. If I used a higher rank than a chief inspector, then his suspicions would be aroused. *Why would a superintendent want to see me?*

Second, I gave him a good reason to see the chief inspector. If I had said I didn't know why he wanted to see him, he would guess it was a hoax. If I didn't come up with a plausible reason, it was fifty-fifty if he fell for it. My in-house tried and tested focus on what works best told me that using 'overtime' as bait would work. Sergeant Vince would take in the information that the 'chief inspector' wanted to see him and that it was about 'overtime.' He would think two things; had he wrongly submitted an overtime claim or was there overtime going a begging? Either thought would have him legging it to the chief inspector's office sooner rather than later. He would worry he would get in trouble for submitting a wrong overtime claim or he would be too greedy to let someone else in on the overtime that was going a begging.

162

I headed off down the corridor and stepped into the report room where I sat waiting. Thirty seconds later Sergeant Vince briskly made his way past the report room on his way to the chief inspector's office. I waited a further ten seconds before slipping back into the sergeant's office and rifling Sergeant Vince's tunic pockets. I found the keys to the Honda CRV and headed off to the custody suite to see my mate, Whistling Wally. After leaving Wally my instructions, I hot-footed it out the office and drove to see Inspector Alex McFleming for our weekly meeting.

Inspector Alex McFleming was sitting with his feet up his desk, phone to his ear. He motioned me to sit down and indicated with a single tap on his shoulder that he was speaking to a superintendent. I gathered that the 'chief' superintendent must have been busy.

I waited while my inspector related all the recent successes that C.O.S.M.O.P. had achieved and noted that he used a lot of "I did...," "We did...," and "I lead the way with..."

Eventually, Inspector McFleming hung up the phone. He took out his hanky and wiped the brown stains from his nose. I updated him on what I had been doing and discussed what operations were in the pipeline. Then my radio chattered into life; it was Wally.

"Sergeant McEwan, come in over."

"Yes, go ahead."

"Just to let you know, intelligence has just confirmed what we discussed."

"Roger, does it confirm that there are plants there?"

"It looks like quite a farm, yes."

"And do we know if it is young MacDonald or his Dad?"

"Looks like it is just the Dad involved."

"Roger, thanks."

Inspector McFleming moved his feet off the desk, and he leaned towards me looking for more information.

"A cannabis farm?"

"We won't know until we search it, will we?" I said smiling.

"How big?"

"We won't know until we get there, will we?"

"What kind of money are we talking?"

"We won't know until we assess it, will we?"

He sat back in his chair; I could see he was itching to tell someone what he had just learned.

"I need to go into headquarters," he said as he stood up.

The meeting was over.

I headed back to my office and met by Whistling Wally at the back door.

"What was all that about, getting me to radio that message?" he asked.

"Oh, nothing much," I said, "but I would just love to be a fly on the wall when Inspector Alex McFleming tells the Chief Superintendent that Old MacDonald has a farm."

My time in C.O.S.M.O.P. served me well. I learned a lot of new skills; family life had improved as had my health. Not working shifts, especially night shifts, was a boon for both. On top of that, I had ran my first half-marathon, an achievement for anyone my age and weight. However, I felt it was time for me to move on. I put in a request for a transfer. By coincidence, on the same day, another sergeant landed himself in hot water and required a move off front line duties. So it wasn't long before my new inspector chapped my door and ducked into my cupboard.

164

"I've got you a move," he said, yet again taking credit for something entirely outwith his sphere of influence. In taking the credit he was impossible to embarrass.

"Somewhere more respectable than a cleaners cupboard I hope?"

"No, somewhere a little more manic."

"F division?"

"Yes. F division."

"Great, I'll cancel the papers."

Chapter 8

SEE SEE TV

My transfer to F Division happened in April. Spring had warmed things up, and we headed on into a gloriously hot summer. Throughout the country, the Queen's Golden Jubilee Celebrations cuddled the cockles of all the royalist's hearts. Will Young and Gareth Gates, two successful talent show contestants, were popping in and out of the charts but it was the old stalwarts of Elvis Presley and Enrique Iglesias that held the top spot for the most part. Elvis, revived from the dead, with a remix of *'A little less conversation'.*

F Division was commonly believed to be the worst division in the force - hence graded 'F'. The station was an impressive enough building when first built in the sixties but was now woefully inadequate for use as a modern day police office. Second and third planned phases of construction did not happen. It was a grandiose granite building right in the middle of town. Unfortunately, the main arterial route ran right past the front of the building. The roadway outside, thus splashed with double yellow lines on either side, and bold warning signs promised punitive fines for even thinking about stalling your car there.

There was a car park at the rear of the building that just about catered for the police vehicles, but not personal vehicles. It had a designated spot for the Chief Inspector's car, a spot that became a free-for-all when he wasn't on duty. There was insufficient parking for everyone else, and it meant that most officers and civilian staff had to park elsewhere and walk to the building. The office itself was in direct contrast to the cramped car park.

Inside the building, the rooms were spacious and decorative. Classic high Georgian ornamental ceilings were the order of the day, albeit the condition of the building was poor. It looked as if it had been built in 1690 instead of 1960. A wide sweeping staircase with polished wooden bannister and brass posts was at the centre of the building. It split the building into two spaces. Upstairs were the senior officers and their typists, assistants and administration staff. Downstairs were us plebs, the sergeants, the cops, the cells and the janitor's hidey-hole.

Members of the public entering the reception at the front of the building were met with a glass screen. They could press a button on the counter sounding a buzzer in the control room alerting their presence to those in the office.

The control room is the place where it all happened. The hub of all our police business. Of all the places I have worked that one office was undoubtedly the best place to manage anything. A big heavy door on a spring ensured that it always swung back to the closed position. A small hatch, situated to the side of the door, made clear the intention that the front office was designed to keep people out. Office clerks dealt with queries from the public through the glass screen, and queries from police staff were supposed to dealt with through the hatch. Except it didn't work like that. While the members of the public remained at bay, cops and sergeants congregated in the front office, and for good reason.

The town centre had a Closed Circuit Television (CCTV). A system that fed back live footage to our screens in the front office. Monitored by CCTV operators situated right in front of our office clerk. That was the best set up you could imagine; communication was instant. As a supervisor, it was like having a bird's eye view of incidents, and it meant that directing officers to the right area and arresting the right person was easy and efficient. When trouble brewed, the CCTV operators were on it. They were able to give a running commentary to the troops via radio. The office clerk provided guidance as and when required, alerted the troops when a serious incident was brewing or merely put things into perspective for the CCTV operators. They might get upset at some drunken youth piddling at the side of the chip shop but if all the crews were tied up dealing with something more important, the office clerk would tell them to leave it. It was a great way of managing ongoing problems. As a sergeant I spent a lot of time in the front office assessing what was going on, seeing what was required and passing out instruction. Often it was better than being on the ground because it was easier to decide what was necessary because I had the big picture. Occasionally, however, it helped me decide to put a jacket on and get out there to do my bit.

When CCTV picked up on an incident, I would take up a position in front of the screens and direct the officers on the ground. The CCTV operators working the cameras were efficient and on the ball. The office clerk was on the radio behind me, and he could see the screens, assess the situation and instruct officers as necessary. Fights got resolved before they started, we could follow robbers on camera and direct officers to their current location. Often we caught them red-handed, still in possession of the stolen goods. The CCTV system was one of the best tools we had to prevent and detect crime. That's not to say we didn't have fun with it either.

One night shift, in the early hours of the morning, the CCTV operators saw a drunk male totter through the town centre. The discos had long closed, and everyone else was tucked up in their beds sleeping off the copious amounts of shots they had consumed. Even the taxis were heading home.

The drunk male staggered into a shop doorway, tripped and fell onto a large black plastic bag, which cushioned his fall. Despite his fortuitous landing, the black plastic bag burst open revealing copious amounts of shredded paper. The drunk, in a playful mood, began kicking the bag along the street strewing its contents all over the pavement. He stopped at a post box and stuffed the shredded paper into the slot. Due to his intoxicated state, this proved to be a difficult task, but he persevered long enough for a crew to saunter round and catch him.

Under my direction, the crew pointed out the trail of shredded paper which led all the way back to the shop door. They informed our drunk it would be his responsibility to clear it all up.

The crew then stood and watched as the drunk made his best efforts to avoid a charge of littering. He gathered up a handful of shredded paper, staggered to a bucket fifty yards away and deposited the contents. He must have had about two dozen trips before the street looked a bit more orderly. His protestations of being tired and altogether more clear-headed satisfied me that the punishment meted out was sufficient restoration, and we allowed him to go.

The most trouble occurred at the weekend. Young lads tanked up on Tennent's lager, tequila and testosterone would come into contact with young men full of beer and bristling with bravado. It didn't take much to antagonise either group. Fights broke out but were over with fairly quickly. The aftermath that we had to deal with wasn't as quick to sort out. We could spend weeks gathering evidence, following up medical details, interviewing witnesses and trying to trace the protagonists. The CCTV was brilliant for identifying problems before they started. If we got troops into those areas quickly we could prevent someone from getting a sore face and avoid getting ourselves tied up with lengthy enquiries.

One night I was watching the CCTV cameras and saw a belligerent young male approach a young couple and start an argument for no clear reason. The young couple walked off, and the youth followed shouting abuse at the couple, trying his best to provoke a reaction from them. He pushed the guy a few times, but the guy continued to walk away with this girlfriend, trying to avoid confrontation. The youth followed them for six streets, goading the guy to fight with him. The couple kept walking away.

Then the couple stopped at a cash machine, and the guy inserted his bank card. (He had decided to get a taxi to escape the attentions of the youth instead of walking home, and he needed money to pay for it.) As the guy typed in his pin number, the belligerent youth spat several times on the cash machine covering the screen and keypad with spittle. The guy had had enough, despite all his efforts to avoid a confrontation his anger boiled over and he punched the youth on the chin knocking him to the ground. It was just one punch, a soft, slow punch that was more of a push. The kind of tap that showed the guy had had enough but was still reluctant to enter into a full blown fight. It didn't seem like a strong enough punch to knock the youth to the ground, but he fell anyway. A theatrical fall almost. It was like watching Raheem Sterling in slow motion. The youth remained on the ground, produced a mobile phone and dialled nine nine nine. Within a minute the control room radioed for a crew to attend and deal with the assault.

170

I already had a crew heading in his direction, and they arrived moments later. It appeared to them, from the injury to the youth's face, that he had been assaulted. Had we not seen the whole situation unfolding before us on CCTV the likelihood would have been to detain the poor boyfriend and bring him in for questioning. The evidence from the belligerent youth and a medical examination would have been on his side. There would have been a good chance that the guy would have appeared in court charged with assaulting the obnoxious youth.

As it was, I instructed the officers to wait there with everyone until I attended at their location. It was just a short walk from my office. I made a trip to the cleaner's cupboard before making my way up the street to them.

On arrival, I ensured that the officers obtained everyone's details. I then pointed out to the belligerent youth the cameras dotted around the town and in particular the one trained on him right at that moment in time. I further informed him he was clearly seen baiting the young couple, pushing the guy and spitting on the cash machine. If he wished to pursue a complaint of assault, I would be happy to take a note. However, I made it clear that if he did make a complaint, he would also be charged with assault, vandalism, breach of the peace and possibly wasting police time.

The belligerent youth looked a little less quarrelsome once he realised that from start to finish his actions had been caught on camera. I then suggested an alternative that avoided anyone going to court.

After considering his options, the youth apologised to the young couple. I then handed him a bucket of soapy warm water and cloth I had collected from the cleaner's cupboard. He could go once he had cleaned the cash machine to my satisfaction.

Regrettably, some people never learn. As he walked away, I asked the CCTV operators to keep an eye on him. As soon as he turned the corner out of my sight, the CCTV operators watched him as he ran across the road and kicked the side of a black BMW parked on the opposite side. He ran off further down the street where he saw another cash machine and spat on that several times before running off once again. I nipped round to see the damage. The front driver's door was now concave. I knew the car belonged to a bouncer from the local club, so we spoke to him. It crossed my mind to give this big bruiser the youth's address, summary justice, but I couldn't be sure the bouncer wouldn't go too far. He was furious.

The youth arrived home ten minutes later to find two of my officers waiting to arrest him. The youth was charged and allowed to go in the morning after he had sobered up. I told him who the BMW belonged to and clarified that if he ever saw him in the town… the rest went unsaid.

I never saw that youth again, but it wasn't the last time I was thankful for having CCTV. This next incident was recorded on our CCTV cameras and later proved to be an interesting watch when things were calmer.

It was a Saturday night about midnight. I was on foot patrol in the town centre with a young cop. Our control room radioed that they had received a call from a male who stated there would be trouble at one of our pubs called 'Bacchus' (named after the God of wine and merrymaking). I radioed back that I would attend as we were just around the corner.

Our CCTV operators also picked up on the message and swung their cameras to cover the pub in question. They picked up a male in his twenties standing outside the door kicking at it. He had a mobile phone up to his ear and realised that this was the male who had phoned in with the warning. It turned out the bouncers had thrown him out of the premises. Too much drink had made him so obnoxious that they decided they no longer wanted his money.

The CCTV operators watched the male as he made his way to a nearby car. He opened the boot and took out a baseball bat. He remained on his mobile phone the whole time talking to our service centre operator. The service centre operator, now and then, relayed the message that the male kept repeating that 'there would be trouble at the pub if they didn't let him back in.'

I didn't quite understand his logic. Under what circumstances did he think the bouncers would allow him re-entry to the premises? Arming himself with a baseball bat and then asking the police to get him back in before there was trouble seemed a tad optimistic.

The CCTV operators kept their cameras trained on the male as he made his way back towards the front door of the pub, still holding on to his baseball bat and talking on his phone.

When I watched the footage later, the next bit seemed surreal. The male was shouting down into his phone (the service centre operator could confirm his threatening behaviour) and that CCTV showed that he was in possession of a rather large and intimidating baseball bat. Yet, a teenager standing next to his girlfriend in the shelter of a shop canopy emerged, approached the male and apparently asked him if he had a light (why on earth would you approach an angry male with a baseball bat and ask for a light?).

Our angry male told the service centre operator to 'wait a minute,' tucked the baseball bat under his arm then rummaged about in his pocket. He produced a lighter and lit the teenager's cigarette. The teenager walked back to his girlfriend, puffing away and our male got back on his phone and continued to make all sorts of threats about what he would do to the bouncers who had thrown him out of the pub.

I headed on to his location. I rounded the corner with my colleague and saw this angry young male, still there, holding his baseball bat. My colleague and I withdrew our side handled batons and spread out. As we approached the male, I shouted to him to drop the baseball bat. That was the last the service centre operator heard from our male as he dropped his phone and took up a threatening stance. Holding his baseball bat in both hands as if I was going to bowl a fastball at him.

My colleague and I edged towards him, and I barked at him, "Drop the baseball bat!"

"Calm down!"

"Drop that bat now!"

He backed off onto the pavement and stood outside a butcher's shop still brandishing the baseball bat. His anger transferred from the bouncers towards us. He ignored my commands. We kept sidling our way towards him and surrounding him as best you can with only two people.

As I moved forward my eyes fixed on the male and his baseball bat, wary of what he might do. My senses heightened, my adrenaline flowing. I was totally concentrating on this male and the danger he posed to us. That explained why I accidentally stood on his phone.

The instant I stood on it, I realised that it was his phone. I dared not look down at it. I didn't know if I had

174

caused any damage to it or not but I didn't want to look. I didn't want to draw his attention to the fact I might have damaged it. He had a baseball bat brandished in his hands and if he realised that I had destroyed his phone, whether or not unintentional, it might push him over the brink.

I edged further forward and tried to put myself between the male and the phone so he wouldn't notice I had crunched it under my big police boots.

Then the male stated, "Right, if it's a fight you want!"

He started to remove his jacket in readiness for a ding dong battle with the police. He put the baseball bat between his knees to free his hands so he could extricate his arms from his jacket. As his jacket slid off, it got to the point where both his arms were down, and both hands were still inserted into the sleeves. I made a snap decision. I wouldn't get a better opportunity. I dropped my baton ran towards the male and rugby tackled him. My shoulder connected with his torso and I slammed him into the butcher shop window. My colleague also dropped his baton and joined in. The force of my rugby tackle was enough to make him drop his baseball bat and lose his footing all in the one go. He fell to the ground, and as I had a grip on him, I had no other choice but to fall with him. All three of us ended up wrestling on the ground. The male put up quite a struggle, but I held on to him for dear life. I didn't want him getting free and give him the chance to grab his baseball bat again.

As I lay on the ground grappling with the male, I got my bodyweight onto his body and hold him under me. My colleague got a grip on his left arm, and effectively we had control. Now he wasn't going anywhere. All we needed to do was to hold him like this until the cavalry arrived.

I was lying on top of him facing the road, and I could see his phone sitting about three feet out from the kerb. Thankfully, it looked as if it was undamaged. The male remained squashed on the ground, but he too was facing out onto the road. He saw his phone, and despite the weight of two police officers on top of him, his right arm started to stretch out towards his phone.

Then the cavalry turned up in the form of a marked police van with two officers therein. They arrived with blue lights flashing and sirens blaring. The van screeched to a stop on the roadway next to us. In the process, the van drove right over our prisoner's phone, demolishing it. It burst into a hundred different pieces as the two-tonne van screeched to a halt right on top of it. The male, on seeing his phone smashed to smithereens, commenced another strenuous effort to escape our grip. He went banzai. We had to get the help of another four officers before we secured him with handcuffs and get him into the back of the van.

Viewing the CCTV footage later, I could see the van arrive and spray his phone into pieces. In the same freeze frame is my face with a look of complete and utter consternation.

There is a real danger in having to wrestle a baseball bat from a madman like that. It is one of many dangers that police officers up and down the country face on a daily basis. The job is full of potential dangers. Every day we hear of such stories where police officers are hurt or even killed. It is estimated that 23,000 police officers are assaulted in the UK every year. It is probably a lot more. Despite health and safety regulations dictating that such injuries on duty are properly recorded, I suspect that a high percentage go unreported. Bravado will prevent officers recording an injury, some will be too embarrassed and others too lazy - there are forms to fill in and to be honest police officers have too much paperwork to do as it is.

Protecting the public is a big part of the job. The police are the first and last port of call when a drunk man is reported to be wielding a baseball bat outside a nightclub. I turned up with a young cop to deal with the baseball wielding madman. I don't think either of us thought through the danger to ourselves. We had to get on with it. All part of the job. We didn't stop to think if it went wrong, we could end up injured or dead. A baseball bat is a lethal object when used as a weapon. We didn't stop to think what would happen to our family if we ended up with our heads bashed in. We arrived, saw the madman with the baseball bat and recognised it was our duty to prevent him from assaulting members of the public. We couldn't walk away from him. We couldn't allow members of the public to come into contact with him. We couldn't leave him to sober up, get tired and go home.

I didn't imagine all the things that could go wrong. I pictured no other scenario than a successful outcome. I knew I had to get that baseball bat off of him before he did someone some damage. I didn't stop to think of what damage he could do to me. Still, I was mindful of my colleague. I wanted nothing to happen to him. So I was careful. I did nothing rash, but I had to do something. Fortunately, it worked out. We confronted a drunk baseball wielding madman and walked away. Uninjured. The man in handcuffs.

You get a buzz when you survive things like that. As much out of relief as pride in doing a good job. The sight of closing the cell door on someone who has threatened you harm releases the built up tension. We relax, let go and laugh. Our job complete, and for that moment, we can thank our lucky stars we escaped the situation without our friends or family having to visit us in a hospital or worse.

Then the radio buzzes into life again, and we head off to the next call.

Perhaps the judge would see our baseball wielding madman as a genuine threat to society and mete out a severe sentence commensurate with his actions - actions that had the potential to have a lot more serious outcome.

Our drunk baseball bat wielding madman experienced police hospitality in the form of bed-and-breakfast. We provided him with free transport to visit a nice man with a white wig. He apologised to the nice man in the white wig, who was sufficiently bewildered by the pleasant nature of the man before him that he found it difficult to comprehend that he could ever have been so aggressive.

"I'll admonish you on this occasion," the man in the white wig decreed.

Nowadays, CCTV operators work from a site miles away from any police offices. The police no longer have immediate and direct access to the screens. Police officers cannot gain access to the CCTV offices unless it is Monday to Friday between 10 a.m. and 4 p.m. Even then; they aren't allowed access to the screens. Should an officer require help from the CCTV operators, he has to radio his request to the control room. The control room operator has to phone the CCTV office and request the operator listen in to the appropriate radio channel. Precious seconds or even minutes lost before they get their instructions.

It was a money saving exercise. Having fewer CCTV operators meant less cost, but it also meant fewer eyes are looking at more screens. As a result, they were often busy with another incident elsewhere, unable to help everybody. Fewer CCTV operators also meant they often lacked local knowledge. They didn't know the streets or the people.

It could be weeks before we found the time to send an officer to the CCTV offices to trawl through hours of recordings and find the evidence we needed.

Cost cutting needs to be cost effective. Why save money on a CCTV operator (who is paid very little) who can spot things as they happen and prevent incidents escalating, then instead have an expensive police officer sitting in front of a video screen analysing footage for hours on end?

Chapter 9

SUPERINTENDENT AMNESIAC

The job of a sergeant is the most difficult of jobs in the police. A sergeant has to manage staff, know their every call, sort their reports, ensure cops' welfare, audit productions, develop skills, instruct, mother, cajole, beg, borrow, steal and listen.

A sergeant has to attend the serious calls, deal with complainers, tidy the office, wash the cars, manage the cleaners, keep on top of resource issues, go to court, plan events, be present at incidents, deal with belligerent prisoners, identify threats, create daily logs, progress priorities and never falter.

She is also a conduit between the cops and the bosses. She has to take instruction, take the blame when it goes wrong, give credit to others when it went right, balance call demand with ever increasing fanciful initiatives, know the answer to everything, give up staff, drive performance and take a whipping. The list goes on.

There are obstacles put in a sergeant's way to prevent him from doing all these tasks. No matter how busy she is. No matter what is going on. There is always someone, a boss or an officer from another department, who was looking to expand the time they have to complete their work.

This person will pop into the sergeant's office looking for a chat. They couldn't care less that the sergeant is run off her feet. They will stay and chat for as long as they can, the object of the exercise for them is to waste time. It is all about letting the clock tick closer to their finishing time. Then, 'whoosh' they are out the door faster than the *Road Runner* on speed. I wasn't a sergeant for long before I developed a strategy for dealing with such time wasters.

It took a little while to perfect, but I came up with an approach that worked every time. An amazing strategy. It offended no one; it cost nothing, it made the time waster get up and go away. I found that I could use this strategy right at the start of a conversation. I could use it the second a time waster walked in the door, and it would work. Alternatively, I could just decide mid-conversation they were wasting my time. I would use the technique on them; they would just stop talking and walk away. I could get back to my work with no further delay.

This brilliant little strategy worked every time. It would work for anyone. From a cleaner who wants to complain about another cleaner, a boss who wants to dump his work on you or a colleague who just wants to chew the fat. It was the most effective tool I had.

No longer did I have to put up with time wasting. It is a technique I used whenever I liked as often as I liked and on anyone I didn't like. It was a simple way of maximising my valuable time, without causing offence or creating friction. At any time I wanted I could use the technique, and miraculously people would get up and leave me on my own. I think most people thought better of me after I had used it, not that they realised I was using a manipulation technique.

Now, I know you will wonder what this powerful technique is. What is it? How does it work? I'll tell why I am reluctant to tell you.

I walked into my inspector's office one day and got chatting with him. We discussed the demands of the job, and he identified that there were several 'time wasters' in our building who were worth avoiding. He had wasted hours that morning with a certain chief inspector who was working on a project.

"God knows how long the project will take him because all he seems to do is saunter around the building seeing who he can cadge a coffee off and rabbit on about his holidays."

My inspector looked frustrated. That is when I told him I had the solution. I told him I had a technique and that my strategy worked every time. Simple and effective.

"What is it?" he asked me.

So I told him.

"What I do, mid-conversation is glance at my watch or look at the clock on the wall and say, 'Oh my! Is that the time?' That get's their attention. Then I follow up with, 'Listen, you will have to excuse me, I need to phone my Mum.' It is as simple as that."

My Inspector looked at me with what could only be admiration bordering on adulation. I had given him the full, unadulterated manipulation technique, and he sat back and nodded, pleased with himself that he now had such a beautiful and elegant solution to this problem.

"Of course, I don't leave it at that. I then pick up my phone and look at whoever is wasting my time anticipating they will leave. Every time I use it they get up and leave me in peace. So that I am not telling a lie, I then phone my Mum and say, 'Mum, I am just phoning to tell you I love you.' And you know every Mum appreciates being told that."

I sat back pleased with myself for having come up with such an ingenious solution.

My inspector nodded and smiled.

He looked at me again, looked at his watch then looked back at me. Then he said, "Oh my! Is that the time?"

He went straight in and used my technique on me. "You will have to excuse me," he said, "I need to phone my Mum."

I had no choice but to get up and walk out.

That is why I now keep it to myself.

Later, as an Inspector, I made up a little sign, only two inches long that said 'Headquarters' and I stuck this above my office door. When I was particularly busy or needed to get something done, I would close my door and my secretary could honestly say to those looking for me, "Sorry he's in Headquarters."

Dealing with members of the public was often easier than dealing with colleagues and bosses. However, sometimes we were frustrated with those who worked in other public services.

Doctors are magicians and nurses are absolute angels. At any hospital, the accident and emergency (A&E) you will find the most dedicated and caring of people. They work under the most gruelling conditions, let's face it - if they get it wrong then people die. Daily they see the most awful of injuries and have to care for the old, the infirm, the seriously ill, the drunk and the belligerent. A difficult job at the best of times. They also have to deal with police officers.

In the early hours one morning, we received a call from a female who reported that her brother is missing. She was at the hospital with him as he had 'taken a funny turn'. He was hallucinating, convinced he saw 'zombies' and that they were chasing him. At the hospital, she was asked to sit and wait until a doctor could see him. During the wait, her brother found a plastic cup, urinated in it and then drank it. Then he stood up and left the hospital. His sister could not get hospital staff to assist (he wasn't their concern once he left the building) so she called the police.

A few minutes later we received a report of a break-in at a shop in the town centre. I arrived with my partner at the time, Constable Ronnie Runcorn, and we quickly traced the brother outside the shop. He had smashed the window with a half brick and was trying to climb in. He told us he had broken in to get a gun to shoot the 'zombies' (Good luck to him finding a gun in an optician's, mind you).

The Mental Health Act allows police officers to remove a person to a place of safety if that person is in a public place and he suspects he has a mental disorder. A place of safety should be a hospital where the person could receive due care, psychiatric assessment, and help. Protocols are in place to fast track those people the police bring to hospitals. There have been, and continue to be, some high-level meetings between hospital administrators, senior doctors, and senior police officers. They agree on these protocols because it makes sense to free up the officers as soon as possible and get them back on patrol. Following each of these high-level meetings, our senior officers would send out a memo detailing what procedures had been agreed. These were always positive and stated that we would receive appropriate assistance and preferential treatment when we attended at A&E with a prisoner or problem person who required medical attention.

Unfortunately, the hospital administrators and senior doctors were not so efficient at relaying their agreements to A&E staff. I never 'ever' found a nurse or doctor who knew the protocols - at least not one that admitted to knowing them.

PC Runcorn and I returned the brother to the hospital. We sat with him until he could be seen and certified or given medical help, a foregone conclusion you might think. He was drinking his pee for goodness' sake. One nurse suggested we leave him there and they would see him in due course. Experience told me we could not. Despite the fact that we were the only crew on at our station and calls were mounting up, if we left him and he was to go wandering again, there would be nobody there to stop him disappearing. In those circumstances, a full-scale missing person enquiry would begin, and instead of tying up just us two cops we would tie up every available officer from all the surrounding stations.

It was forty-five minutes before a triage nurse examined him. Another two hours went by before an A&E doctor gave him a cursory examination. The doctor referred him to the psychiatrist. A further three hours went by before the psychiatrist examined him. The psychiatrist took all of three minutes to carry out his examination, after which he concluded that as he had been drinking, he was not psychotic. He deemed him 'fit to be detained' by police. We had to take him back to the police station and give the custody sergeant the bad news. PC Runcorn ended up sitting outside his cell watching him all night.

I had sat with this prisoner for most of the night. I knew he had been drinking his pee, I knew he had smashed an optician's window and climbed in looking for a gun to shoot zombies. I knew he was incoherent, suffering from hallucinations, delusions and disturbed thoughts. I could not get a sensible conversation from him. He would flit from one subject to the next, and he was completely unaware of his bizarre behaviour. That was not the ramblings of a drunk man - I had seen so many of those. He was a man who needed help, psychiatric help. Yet, the only answer that the psychiatrist seemed to take an interest in was when he answered, 'yes' to 'have you had a drink tonight?'

There was a time when the police used to deal with bad people, increasingly their time is taken up dealing with mad and sad people. The cells are full of alcoholics, heroin addicts and others with unresolved mental health issues because there is nowhere else for them to go.

It wasn't an isolated incident. It happened just about every night. Walk into any A&E anywhere in the country at night, and you will be almost guaranteed to see two, three, four or more officers sitting waiting with their sad case. Hours and hours of police time wasted, babysitting the sad and the mad. No wonder the bad find it easy to get away with things.

It riled me enough to put it on paper. I drafted a rather long memo to my bosses. I detailed examples of the time wasted waiting in A&E. I detailed that the hospital staff were not adhering to the protocols. I cited that the A&E staff didn't know about the protocols in place to fast track police officers back to their beats. I could evidence that not one of them knew anything about them. I could sympathise with the A&E staff, I wholeheartedly agreed, those needing immediate treatment should take priority - that was a given. I saw no reciprocal sympathy. Often there seemed to be a distinct lack of interest in getting police officers back out where they belonged.

My lengthy and well-researched report went up through the chain of command. I waited for a response. A week passed, then a month - nothing. I wasn't one to rock the boat, so I bided my time and bumped into Superintendent Amnesiac, to whom my memo had been addressed. We were walking by each other in a corridor at headquarters, and I took the opportunity to bring up my memo after we had exchanged pleasantries, "What did you make of my memo sir?"

"Er... which one?"

"The one regarding the hospital protocols not being adhered to sir."

"Em, I don't recall that... can you send me that again please?"

So I sent it to him again. This time I bypassed all my supervisors and sent it direct to his email. I was to learn from this that not everyone in a position of rank is as efficient as you think they might be.

I don't know where my original memo went missing. The process is simple. I write a memo and address it to the person highest in the organisation with the authority to act on it. Thus if a cop is concerned about a broken chair, he would address his memo to his sergeant, who has the authority to submit a furniture request from the purchasing department. If he were looking for a transfer, he would address his memo to his chief inspector who has overall responsibility for staffing. All memos are passed to the immediate supervisor although addressed to the chief inspector he would still hand it to his sergeant first. The sergeant should make comments on the memo, either giving supporting evidence for the transfer or otherwise suggest that it does not go ahead and his reasons behind it. He, in turn, would hand it to his inspector who would consider the contents of the memo, the comments made by the sergeant and add his thoughts. After that, it should arrive on the chief inspector's desk with all the arguments in front of him, sufficient for him to make a decision.

With my hospital memo, I had addressed it to Superintendent Amnesiac because he had overall responsibility for policy and was, in fact, the senior officer liaison between the Police and the Health Service. He was the one who had attended all the meetings with the hospital administrators and senior doctors. Superintendent Amnesiac attended the meetings where they had drawn up the protocols. He had a vested interest in my memo (or so I thought).

The process, in getting my memo to him had broken down somewhere. Perhaps my sergeant had binned it, or maybe my inspector had disagreed with my suggestions and decided not to pass it on. The chief inspector might have been so busy that my memo could have lay unread on his desk for so long he decided that it was unimportant enough to not bother with. I just don't know. The likely scenario would be that Superintendent Amnesiac received the memo, skimmed over the content and comments and either not realised he had to do something about it or just put it to the back of his mind and forgot about it.

So I emailed it to him again.

Another month later I bumped into Superintendent Amnesiac in the corridor at headquarters again. We exchanged pleasantries, and I again asked him about my memo.

"Er, I don't recall that… which one?"

"The one regarding the hospital protocols not being adhered to sir."

"Em… can you send me that again please."

It was a lesson I took on board. As a supervisor, I always made a point of progressing paperwork quickly and efficiently as I could. I took pride in it. I also lowered my expectations regarding some senior officers. So I sent my memo to Superintendent Amnesiac for the third time. This time I clicked on 'options' and ticked the boxes requesting a 'delivery receipt' and a 'read receipt', then waited. Seconds later a 'delivery notice' informed me it was sitting in his Inbox. Two days later a 'read notice' informed me that Superintendent Amnesiac had opened my email to him.

A couple of weeks passed before I bumped into Superintendent Amnesiac again.

"Hello sir, was there anything of value in my memo?"

"Which memo was that?"

"The one relating to the hospital protocols, sir."

"I don't think I got that. I have been having issues with my email."

"I have a delivery receipt telling me it arrived on the 7th and a read receipt telling me you opened my email on the 9th... sir."

"If I didn't get it, I didn't get it," and he walked away looking rather indignant.

I mumbled away to myself for a little while and put it to the back of my mind. Then, the same day, I had six officers on my shift tied up at A&E, leaving no-one to attend any calls. It was hours before they were freed up.

The next morning I printed off my memo, marched up to Superintendent Amnesiac's office, barged in and laid the memo on his desk right in front of him.

"Sir, that is my memo relating to the hospital protocols not being adhered to. It really is too important to ignore." I about turned and left.

I expected to hear nothing more about it - but at least I had tried. It was with some surprise then when Superintendent Amnesiac phoned me back the next day.

"I've read your memo," he said, "and I think you have some valid points."

"Yes, I think I do. We waste hours of our time at the hospital because they are not adhering to the agreed protocols."

"Well, I think we need to do some research on the matter. Can you do a report for me detailing how

189

much time we wasted, what the issues are and make recommendations on how to solve it."

I tried to hide my groan, this was a mammoth task, and I was busy enough with my own job. I had little experience in carrying out such a project; there were people in the organisation trained for such things. We had, in fact, a unit called the Policy and Strategy Unit whose job it was to do that type of research and compile those type of reports before presenting them to senior officers at policy meetings. I could not be expected to do that report while carrying on with my sergeant's job. I didn't have the time. It was impossible. There was no way I would cow down and accept that I had to do it.

"When do you need it by?" I answered. (I'm such a pussy cat).

"Oh, take as long as you need. There will be a lot of information to gather, and your recommendations will be important so make sure you get it right. If it takes six months, it takes six months."

His timescale surprised me. Six months! I got up from my chair and headed through to my inspector's office.

"When does Superintendent Amnesiac retire?" I enquired.

"I think he only has about five months to go."

I pushed the boat out. I worked hard on my report, I engaged the help of every custody officer in the force and had them get cops to complete questionnaires every time they took a prisoner to the hospital. I emailed every sergeant and asked for evidence. I contacted other forces to see if they were experiencing the same problems. Within two weeks, I had gathered pages and pages of information. I ploughed my way through all the information and got to work on my report. I came in early to work on it; I stayed late to work on it. I came in on my days off and worked on it. If I wasn't working on it, I was thinking about working on it.

Six weeks after being tasked with doing the report, I called into Superintendent Amnesiac's office and handed over a well researched and detailed report identifying the problems.

What I had discovered was crazy. There were days where almost half the entire police strength on duty had spent time waiting in an A&E Department. There wasn't a single day that officers weren't there. The average time spent on any enquiry at A&E was three and a half hours. That meant two officers waiting, so seven hours of police time taken up with sitting around in a hospital. That was just on average. In one instance a crew of two officers got the job of taking a prisoner to A&E because he had a headache. The officers spent twelve hours waiting for a doctor to see him. The doctor prescribed two Paracetamol.

On other occasions, we had prisoners in custody who feigned injury. We took them to the hospital, 'just in case'. Sometimes they kept them in overnight for observation. We had to give up two officers to sit with them the entire time; this could be a third or even half the police strength on duty. Prisoners were taking liberties, almost literally. Rather than spending a night in a cell, they claimed they had a fuzzy head or pain in the chest. Often the result was a much more comfortable and warmer bed in the hospital for the night.

My recommendations were not radical. I made several sensible proposals that would ease some of the problems. Simple suggestions that were obvious and easily implemented. Nurse practitioners, for example. Why waste twelve hours waiting in a hospital because of a sore head when a nurse could issue two Paracetamol within minutes. Other recommendations I made would require liaison with senior administrators and doctors within the health service, to appeal that they publicise the existing protocols to the people that mattered most - those working within the A&E department. Adopting my recommendations across the board would save thousands of police hours. I was proud of that report. I had invested a lot of time and effort into that report. Shocked into writing it by the inefficiency of the existing system, flabbergasted at the waste of police time and distraught with the lack of consideration for police officers. My determination stretched to making sure that my recommendations were worthwhile, simple to implement and had commonsense solutions that would make the difference. Yes, I was proud of that report because I knew that if acted upon, it would make a massive difference.

I wonder whatever happened to it?

Even today, I still wonder if Superintendent Amnesiac even read it before he retired.

Sometimes nothing much happens if it doesn't affect the person who has the power to change the system, things move as slowly as the tectonic plates.

I learned the fifty/fifty/fifty rule applies to superintendents. The fifty/fifty/fifty rule states that only 50% of all superintendents will read 50% of the paperwork that crosses their desk and of that only 50% will decide on it. For those of you who are mathematically challenged that means you will have a 12.5% chance of getting a reply. That drops away to zero if the superintendent in question is due to retire in less than six months.

Anyway if you find yourself stuck waiting in an A&E and happen to see police officers with a prisoner in tow, then take the opportunity to have a chat with them. They will have all the time in the world to listen to your gay wit and sparkling repartee, they will be so glad you helped them pass the time.

Chapter 10

THE POLIS ATHLETES

Over the course of my career, I had the honour of working with Gentleman George and the great pleasure of being in his company during our involvement in police sports. Gentleman George is an all round good guy and a great sportsman. He excelled in snooker, golf, pool and fishing - you know, the sports that required supreme athletic prowess and a sturdy liver. Because of his proficiency and skill in these endeavours, he qualified to represent the force at the Scottish and British Championships. Thus two or three times per year he would travel across the country for an overnighter or two.

The Police Sports UK (Scottish Region) fund part of the expenses incurred but insisted on the cheapest method of transport and accommodation. Thus anyone taking part had to share a room with a fellow competitor.

Gentleman George is one of the most charming people you could ever meet. Intelligent, amusing and entertaining, a great person to have with you on any outing. He is a natural storyteller, quick-witted, and the most companionable person in any social environment. It is always a delight to be in his company - until you had to share a room with him.

Gentleman George, suffers from obstructive sleep apnoea (OSA) a symptom of which is loud snoring punctuated with silence as he ceased breathing. The length of the pause in his breathing is exactly the length of time that the unfortunate roommate takes to assimilate the information in his brain that George is no longer sucking in life-giving oxygen and goes through the following thinking process; *'he'll be all right, wait he still isn't breathing, holy cow! What if he is dead? Och, leave him… shit, he is still not breathing, maybe I better check'*, then just as he gets up to check Gentleman George has a loud intake of breath, like a sinkhole opening up and swallowing two cars and a bus. He would then continue, oblivious, and get right back to the job of snorting and snoring.

If sharing a room with him, you would be subjected to a night of torturous gasping and worry he was choking. Darth Vader would be a better roommate. The older he got, the worse his sleep apnoea became. His snoring became so unbearable that nobody ever shared a room with Gentleman George more than once (other than PC Penfold who would drink himself comatose first).

As an example; Gentleman George went on a golf trip with a group of his friends. They were an odd number, so they agreed Gentleman George could have a room to himself. They had all had the 'Gentleman George room share experience' and were unwilling to go through that again. They'd chop their own willie off rather than share a room with him.

The outing started well. They enjoyed a round of golf during the day and one or two pints at the nineteenth hole. After a bite to eat, they made their way to the bar of their hotel and settled themselves around a heavy wooden table with plenty of beers mats to cater for their pints and drams. During the evening's drinking session another colleague joined their company. Sam, had been passing through and bumped into them by accident. They bought him a drink, after which, Sam made his excuses, telling them it was time for him to head home. There was much protestation, and they persuaded Sam to stay for a further pint. Before long Sam was in no fit state to drive and they agreed that he should remain in their genial company and spend the night in the hotel. After all, there was a spare bed in Gentleman George's room.

Gentleman George explained to Sam that the reason he was on his own was that he was an appalling snorer but if he was willing to put up with that he was welcome to share the room. Sam dismissed this warning with some bravado.

"Och I can sleep through a thunderstorm," he informed Gentleman George, "I used to live right under an airport and never once woke up with the noise. Once I put my head on the pillow, I am out like a light. Your snoring won't bother me."

Thus agreed they had as much hospitality as their bladders could cope with, then retired to bed.

Due to the number and frequency of libations consumed during the evening, Gentleman George woke at 2 a.m. in urgent need of relieving himself. He intended to go as quietly as he could so as not to disturb Sam in the bed next to him. He slid out from under the covers and made his way to the bathroom. He opened the door and closed it behind him before switching on the light. To his surprise, he came face to face with Sam. It was only then he realised that Sam wasn't in his bed. Sam was curled up on an armchair he had hauled into the bathroom. Wrapped in his duvet with toilet paper sticking out of his ears. Not the most comfortable of sleeping arrangements.

"Er sorry," said Gentleman George, "but can I get in for a pee?"

"Yes, no problem. I couldn't sleep for your snoring. That's why I came in here. I have heard nothing like it. I even stuffed toilet roll into my ears and I could still hear you from in here," Sam explained.

Gentleman George did the necessary and went back to bed. Sam went back into the toilet, stuffed even more toilet paper into his ears and tried to get some sleep. Not the easiest thing to do on an armchair crammed into the small toilet with the noise of a jumbo jet coming from the next room.

Gentleman George woke again at 6 a.m. He was bursting again (too many G&Ts). When he couldn't keep it in any longer, he chapped the door of the bathroom and asked to use the toilet. Sam stated he could not sleep anyway, what with the un-comfy armchair and the incredibly loud snoring coming from the bedroom.

George, being a gentleman, suggested Sam go back to his bed. He would get up and go downstairs and read the paper. He would then wake Sam before they stopped serving breakfast. That way Sam could get a sleep and not miss breakfast.

So it was again with a little surprise when Gentleman George saw Sam appear at breakfast less than an hour later. Sam yawned, rubbed his eyes and looked so tired he clearly had not slept.

"What are you doing up?" asked Gentleman George.

"My God," said Sam, "you were no sooner out the room when the phone rang, and someone said, 'George?' And I said, 'No' but before I could explain the caller hung up. He then called back every two minutes, and the same thing happened. Since I wasn't getting any sleep anyway, I just got up."

Shortly afterwards Sam and Gentleman George were joined by PC Penfold

"Where have you been George?" Asked PC Penfold.

"What do you mean?"

"I've been phoning you!"

"What were you phoning me for?"

"I wanted to know what room you were in."

"What for?"

"So I could chap your door to see if you wanted to come down for breakfast."

"I was in the room right next door to you. You saw me go in last night when we went up."

"Oh… I wondered what the noise was."

My misspent youth stood me in good stead when I joined the police. That I could swing a nine iron and point a cue using the correct end allowed me to compete in events on the green grass and the green baize. I had many trips away to play in Scottish and British events. Although, I studiously avoided sharing a room with Gentleman George.

I wasn't all that successful until I learned the secret of winning. A simple secret. While everyone else was practising day and night, I got there on pure natural ability. I had the ability to choose the best snooker player as my doubles partner. Jock, my snooker doubles partner, is a great snooker player, good enough to overcome my shortcomings and still win us matches. We had a formula for winning, Jock would pot the balls, and I would try not to do anything stupid. As a result, we regularly qualified for the Scottish Indoor Sports and subsequently the British Championships, representing Scotland.

These events are well organised and well attended. The standard of play is often incredible, and many of the players took their sport extremely seriously indeed. Jock and I didn't play to lose, but we didn't quite take it seriously enough to bother about things like a good night's sleep. Others were a little more professional and tucked themselves up in bed nice and early so they'd be rested and ready to play at their best the next day.

On our first trip to the British Police Championships, we gave it our best shot. We vowed to take it try hard to give ourselves the best chance of doing well in the competition. We arrived the day before the competition was due to kick off, and we had a plan. Our plan was to practice all afternoon, have our dinner, wash it down with a couple of beers and have an early night. It all went to plan - until we had a couple of beers. Greedy for more we ripped up the plan and flushed it down the loo.

About 1 a.m. I poured myself into bed. I'd last seen Jock about midnight hustling some Yorkshire cops on the pool table. It was a surprise that he could hustle anyone considering his couple of beers had multiplied into double figures.

Just as soon as I had entered a deep sleep, my prodigal partner returned. His key wouldn't work in the door. It wasn't the wrong key. His efforts to insert his key into the lock upside down had drawn me out of my deep sleep. Not fully awake, I lay there trying to comprehend what the noise was. The subsequent banging on the door and screams of, 'LET ME IN,' did the job.

I climbed out of bed, shook myself off and opened the door.

"AYE, WHAT'S HAPPENING?" he shouted, with a big drunken grin on his face.

"The same as always 'Jock,' I was sleeping, and now I am not."

Shortly after I had my own Darth Vader to contend with. Jock had stripped to his pants crawled on top of his bed and imitated the sound of a pneumatic drill.

I was awake now. Unable to nod off again. Insomnia brought on by the grunting and snorting from the next bed. Jock's snoring on this occasion was bad. I did what any other reasonable human being would do. I launched my shoe at him, but it bounced off his butt without so much as a grunt. I had a paperback beside my bed, and this too I tossed at him, it scudded off the back of his head, this time he grunted and rolled over. The pneumatic drill continued unabated. Nothing else for it, I extricated myself from my bed and held his nose. Jock ceased breathing altogether, struggled for air then gasped in air through his mouth. Fantastic - no more snoring. I returned to my bed and let the silence engulf me; sweet sleep would soon be mine.

One second after climbing back into my bed it started again. Jock reverted to his default position of snorting his way through a drunken slumber; he sounded like a hippo in heat.

Then I had an idea.

Our room had full-length patio windows and a small balcony with a plastic table and chairs. I opened the patio doors as wide as they would go and removed the plastic table and chairs. I then grabbed the end of Jock's bed and wrestled with it until I could manoeuvre it out onto the balcony. It was a bit of a squeeze, but I made it. Jock lay there in his bed, oblivious, in his lager induced stupor, to the fact he was now outside on the balcony. I closed the window, shut the curtains and climbed back into my bed with a contented smile on my face.

I woke in the morning and Jock was still there on the balcony. Snoring soundly and at the mercy of the elements. Other hotel guests passed by, confused at first then continued walking with a smile on their face. I quietly headed off to breakfast.

Jock eventually appeared at the breakfast table and called me for everything. He didn't seem to realise that he was lucky the bed didn't fit out the bedroom door. Otherwise, he would have woken up in a corridor in some distant part of the hotel.

An hour later, bleary-eyed, tired, suffering from shaky hands and a pounding headache we tossed a coin, and I broke off in the first game of the day in our doubles competition. The white ball spun off the reds and shot straight into the bottom pocket. Four points away and an easy red over the pocket for our opponents to take advantage. It didn't bode well. We lost the first game but Jock ground away and amazingly, we scraped a win in the next two games to win our first match.

It was time to take things seriously. We ordered a bottle of Budweiser each and kicked off our second match. Jock, hands now steady, focused and drifted into that deep state of concentration he called 'the zone'. The scores rattled up only to rattle down again once I messed up my shot. It was touch and go all the way - even on the snooker table. Steadily we progressed through each match until we got to the semi-final. I hadn't potted a ball.

The beers seemed to be working so my job was to keep Jock going with a fresh bottle every game. It worked, despite being the underdogs, Jock pulled off a fantastic forty-two break clearance to send us into the final. At the very least we were going to come runners-up in our first ever British snooker doubles competition.

"We can win this," said Jock.

I furrowed my brow. "How?" I said, "Are you going to take my shots for me?"

I wasn't playing well. I still hadn't potted a ball all day - at least I hadn't potted any other colour than the white. The guys we were up against were previous British Champions. Two good club players from North Wales. On a good day if I played my best I would have been lucky to score double figures against either of them. I'd be happy with the runners-up medal. Jock, however, had other ideas.

They went ahead. Jock closed the gap. They went ahead again. I increased their lead by fouling the black. They won the first game. They went ahead in the second game. I ballsed-up my safety shot and left the table open. They went further ahead. Jock stepped up to the table; I could see the determination in his eyes. He went back into the zone. One cracking shot after another. His break continued, and the points notched up. Our scores narrowed and then a bit of luck, Jock missed a difficult blue but went safe with the white. A full ball snooker. Our opponent missed and left me an easy red and all I had to do was roll it in, and I was in on the black. If I could score a few points, the game would be ours. Normally I could pot that red with my eyes closed. As it turned out, it would probably have been better if I had closed my eyes. The red was straight and easy, but I missed it by a comfortable distance. It was like driving past your exit on the motorway knowing that there wasn't another turn off for twenty miles.

Fortunately for me, I had Jock on my side. He returned to the table stayed in the zone and scraped a win. It was one game each. Now we had one more game. The winners would be crowned British Snooker Doubles Champions.

It was a blur. I don't know how it happened. Every ball on the table had been potted and there was only the black to go. The deciding black. Whoever potted that black would win. Jock had a go and left a difficult double up and down the table. Each of our opponents had a go and missed. The white was on left tight against the bottom cushion, and the black was diagonally opposite nestled against the side cushion. It was my turn. I hadn't sunk a single ball the whole match. Not one. My safety play had been dire, yet here I was left with an exceptionally long and difficult black across the nap of the table to win the game and the match and the trophy. I lined up my shot, somebody in the crowd shouted, "C'mon Malky," I was distracted. I stood up and carefully lined up my shot again. Bending down I lined up my cue to the white, my eyes flicked between it, the black and the distant pocket that I was going to knock the black towards. My right arm began a gentle sawing motion, and my cue slid silently back and forth across the V between my thumb and forefinger. I knew in my head that I had no chance of potting this. No chance at all. I couldn't pot an easy ball, far less this extremely difficult one. I could feel our opponents joy. They were happy that it was me taking this shot, grinning away in the full knowledge that I would miss it and hopefully leave them with an easy shot to finish us off.

I struck the white ball. It shot off towards the black, crossing the full length of the table from one diagonal to the next. It was to my great surprise that it even hit the black ball, but it did. It connected with the black ball with some force. The black blasted off from the white, overcoming its inertia and taking all the kinetic energy from the white. To the delight of the multitude of spectators, it shot straight into the corner pocket without touching the sides. The cleanest strike of the day. I turned to Jock with delight on my face, held my cue above my head in true *Dennis Taylor* fashion, and we looked at each other with disbelief. We had won.

Then I heard the crowd suck in their breath. A collective 'ooh' resonated around the room. I looked back at the table and time slowed. The white was still moving. It had struck the black and careened off it onto the side cushion. The rubber had bounced it back, and it was headed towards the opposite corner pocket from the black. Time almost stopped, I watched that white roll in slow motion as it took an undeviating path towards the pocket. *Go to the top pocket, go directly to the top pocket, do not pass go, do not collect the British Snooker Doubles trophy.*

Anyway, it stopped half a roll before it dropped into the pocket. Jock and I did win. I had potted the winning shot. Our claim to fame would be forever engraved on the silver cup for all to read and say, "Who were they?".

Later that summer, buoyed by my success on the green baize, I swapped my cue for a set of clubs and went on my second golf outing. I was one of about a dozen from my force who had qualified for the Scottish Championships, this time held in Dundee.

There are those that would argue that Police Golf Section was an excellent way for police officers to get together and socialise. The competitive setting of a golf tournament encourages sporting achievement, good etiquette and ultimately a feeling of accomplishment. The same people would argue that the friendly camaraderie and exchange of information was useful to take back to the work setting. The events were effectively team building exercises that benefited the officers, the players and the organisation as a whole.

Of course, there are some that would argue it was just an excuse for a piss up.

I enjoyed golf and, while I was never a great golfer, if I played in enough medal competitions throughout the year, I scraped enough points to qualify for attendance at the annual Scottish Police Championships (Scottish). PC Penfold was of a similar standard and also generally qualified for these events.

We made our way to Dundee. The accommodation on this occasion was student halls of residence, available as the student semester hadn't yet started. While the accommodation was somewhat Spartan; it did provide us with single rooms (usually we shared twin rooms to keep costs down).

On Monday we had a practice game. We played one of the courses we were due to play in the competition. The serious players took notes, worked out clubbing distances and practised every putting angle to get a feel for the greens. We tended to ignore all that palaver, make a few side bets and laugh derisively at every duffed shot and missed putt.

The evening after the practice was spent in witty banter at the bar. Our numbers dwindled as the night wore on. Those with a serious chance of doing well in the competition took themselves off to bed for a good night's sleep. The rest, including PC Penfold and myself, found our way to a kebab shop before returning to the halls of residence and kicking off a game of three card brag. The kebab being washed down with more beverages of an alcoholic nature.

By midnight, eight of us were crowded into one of the bedrooms as we sat in a circle around the single bed, which doubled as a card table. The drink continued to disappear with abandon, and no real thought was given to the state of our golf the next morning. It is an interesting thing that Police Officers, in general, are trustworthy souls. Your money, jewellery or any valuable prized possession would remain safe and untouched in any circumstance. The exception to that rule is biscuits and cakes. Don't leave those lying around the office - they will be hoovered into hungry mouths. There won't even be the slightest pretence of an effort to hide the evidence. The empty packet will lie on the table ripped apart and covered in crumbs. The other occasion where you have to watch your colleagues is when drink is consumed and a pack of cards produced. Otherwise reliably honest and upstanding boys in blue are transformed into veritable shysters. Not only do you have to contend with bad luck and bluffing but you also have to keep yours eyes open for the occasional card squirrelled away up a sleeve. One particular inspector had such a reputation that he was not allowed to deal the cards or remove his hands from sight, not even to scratch his bum. Inspector McThomson was unembarrassed by this restriction he just smiled and said, "Hah! I always win in the end."

Everyone watched Inspector McThomson like he had a soft steaming turd in his hand and was willing to throw it at the first person who looked away. History taught us that to take our eyes off him was to sanction his card sharp skills. Brief glances away signalled the moment for him to produce a prowl of threes from thin air. It was hard work trying to keep an eye on him all the time. It was to everyone's delight when Inspector McThomson eventually retired from the game; he'd lost a fiver. As he walked out of the door, he took a bit of ribbing for losing his money. There were grins present on every face that had benefited from his loss.

"Hah! I always win in the end," he told us as his face disappeared out the door.

About 2 a.m. PC Penfold, who was now about four hours past his normal bedtime, declared that he had played his last hand of brag and was going to bed. Unsteadily, he got to his feet and stumbled across the room, found the door and disappeared out into the corridor closing the door firmly behind him.

"That's strange," said Bert.

"What's that? PC Penfold leaving to go to bed?"

"No," he replied without looking up from the cards, "this is his room, and this is his bed!"

There was expectancy for PC Penfold to arrive back and reclaim his bed. However, he never re-appeared. We finished up an hour or so later. I don't recall there being any great concern for PC Penfold or his whereabouts. There was, however, some consternation from Bert.

"The bastard!" Bert shouted as he stood up and looked at the floor.

"What's the matter, Bert?"

"That bastard has done it again."

"Who? What?"

"That bastard McThomson, he's drunk all my bloody whisky."

A quick inventory was carried out. Before long we realised that while we had been keeping an eye on Inspector McThomson cheating with the cards, all the time he had been consuming as much of everyone else's drink as he could stomach. Aye, he always wins in the end.

At nine the next morning I was waiting to tee off at the first when PC Penfold came wandering across from the clubhouse. He wasn't due to play for another hour. I felt rough. I was tired, hung-over and during the night someone had replaced my tongue with the insert from a marathon runners training shoe. Despite that, I must have looked like an Adonis next to PC Penfold. He didn't look good. His normally rosy cheeks had taken on the pallor one shade whiter than I had seen on a corpse the week before. His eyes were squinting in the light, but I could still see the telltale bloodshot sclera. He was grappling with his shirt tail, which wasn't quite tucked in properly. All the way across to me, he was trying to force it back down his trousers. About five yards away the stench of his breath hit me. Mustard gas alert! You didn't need to be a bloodhound to know that last night he had consumed a dubious kebab and washed it down with a fourteen lagers and a bottle of whisky.

"You will never guess what happened to me this morning," he said desperately keen to relate his story.

"What happened?" I asked wondering what ills had befallen him.

"I was lying in my bed when this big guy came into my room and started raking through my wardrobe."

"What did you do?"

"I said to him - 'Hey! What are you doing in my wardrobe?'"

"What did he say?"

"He said, 'Son, this is my wardrobe, this is my room, and you are in my bed!'"

I couldn't help laugh, "Yup, we did all wonder where you had got to, it was your room we were playing cards in."

It turned out the guy had got up in the middle of the night to go to the toilet along the corridor. His trip to the toilet had coincided with PC Penfold leaving the card school, finding an open door and making himself comfortable. On returning to his room, the guy found the comatose PC Penfold lying naked, hairy bum in the air, atop his bed. His dogged efforts to rouse him without touching the drunk furry Neanderthal failed. He gave up. The poor guy spent the rest of the night in the dormitory kitchen huddled up on some chairs that he had pulled together into a makeshift bed.

"You are looking a bit rough," PC Penfold told me as he eyed me up and down.

He was right, I did feel rough, but I was a bit indignant that he was telling me I looked rough. Were there no mirrors in the halls of residence?

"You know what you need?" he asked me.

"What?"

"You need a wee drink of this," and he pulled out a hip flask from his back pocket, opened the lid and pushed it into my face.

The industrial strength aroma of brandy almost made me gag.

"Er, no thanks."

"Suit yourself," and he took a big slug from the hip flask, "I love golf outings, don't you?"

Chapter 11

WHAT'S YOUR AGENDA?

One of my jobs as a sergeant was to go to meetings.

There were regular daily meetings, weekly meetings, monthly meetings, yearly meetings and even biannual meetings. We had appraisal meetings, training meetings, performance meetings, emergency planning meetings, event planning meetings, even non-event planning meetings. I could go on.

Some meetings were worthwhile, the purpose was clear, everyone contributed and left focussed on the task in hand. Most meetings were akin to being dumped from a landing craft at Normandy where I had to fight my way across a barbed wire strewn beach while avoiding the bullets fired by the bosses from their fortified positions. I will go into those later.

Chief Inspector Able, however, ran few meetings but when he ran them, they were models of efficiency and good practice.

He only ever called a meeting if it was necessary. He only ever invited persons relevant to the meeting and could provide input. A week before his meeting everyone got a copy of the agenda and a brief note detailing what he expected them to research and contribute. People were in no doubt what he required of them and what they were there to do. After his introductions, he explained why the meeting was important. He made it clear he didn't care about what happened in other meetings or what had gone on in the past; he expected his meeting to be productive and for the result, whatever the topic, to have meaning or make a positive difference. It was motivational. He made us feel we were doing something worthwhile.

It was with some dismay then when Chief Inspector Able came to the end of his service and retired. Chief Inspector Bungle took his place. He was a nice enough fellow. He bustled around the office with sheaves of papers stuck under his arm looking busy, but never too busy to stop and chat to everyone. I would see him leaving his office to walk the twenty yards to the typists' room with folders in both hands and one under his chin. He wouldn't get past his office door without having to re-adjust the folder to talk to someone in the passing. An hour later I would walk back along his corridor and see him still struggling with the folders, five yards short of the typists' office, talking to someone else.

The time came for his first monthly meeting. There was no pre-notice agenda sent out. I entered the meeting room curious about what we would discuss, and just a little peeved that the meeting would delay me from getting on with running the shift.

Chief Inspector Bungle sat at the head of the table with sheaves of paper and folders in front of him. I sat down at one of the two remaining chairs in what was already the largest gathering for a meeting I had seen. A further half dozen attendees appeared before we could get started. The last five having to exit for a short time while they hunted down a spare chair from somewhere else in the station.

When Chief Inspector Bungle eventually got the meeting underway, some twenty-five minutes late, he passed round his agenda, and it was only then I learned that this was to be a new monthly 'Supervisors Meeting'. The agenda consisted of items he thought were pertinent to the running of the station.

The scheduled hour for the meeting overran somewhat. Three hours and twenty minutes to be exact. That wasn't entirely the fault of Chief Inspector

Bungle, not unless you blamed him for inviting three, 'I-like-the-sound-of-my-own-voice' inspectors and two, 'bollock-speak' community sergeants - both of whom had mastered the art of talking endlessly in management jargon without actually saying anything whatsoever.

"What are we prioritising in the community team this week?" Chief Inspector Bungle addressed one of the bollock-speak community sergeants.

"Sir, yes, we are adjusting the frame this afternoon. It is a matter of routinising ingenuity within the team. I think you will agree that we need to ensure our community officers are cut from a different cloth. We don't generate good ideas without firing the synapses, and we can't get them firing on all cylinders without sparking the imagination. We are at the concept stage at the moment, but there will be a piece of work going on to widen the net and catch the big fish. It is all about internalising the external effects of the inspiration process. So we are seeking to identify what solutions are out there because it is easier to find a solution to a problem if we know that there is already an answer in the ether." … blah blah blah.

When bollock-speak community sergeant No. 1 finished he there was a chorus of approval from the three 'I-like-the-sound-of-my-own-voice' inspectors.

"It's new waters we will be exploring, indeed."

"Spot on, couldn't agree more."

"Yes, work in progress, getting there, well done."

Seriously!

What the feck did he just say?

Whatever it was it was a mystery to me. I happened to call into the community team office later that afternoon and gathered that *'Routinising ingenuity,'* must have meant sitting about on their arses drinking tea and 'firing the synapses' required copious amounts of biscuits and a wee blether.

My only contribution to this trail-blazingly unproductive meeting was at the end when Chief Inspector Bungle politely asked me to pick up and dispose of the used agendas that littered the table. I gathered up the copies but spotted one that had been scrawled upon by an attendee. The author in question had been as engaged in the meeting as I had or, at least, thinking about things a little too literally. This was the agenda and the comments he had written:-

SUPERVISOR'S MEETING
6th JANUARY

AGENDA

1. Vehicles – *There are 12 of them, some have blue lights, one or two dinnae.*

2. Courts – *Pain in the butt, just send them straight to jail and save the hassle.*

3. Monthly return – *Aye, I come back monthly for the pay.*

4. CS* Management – *I think we manage the Chief Super quite well.*

5. Special Constables – *I have a few officers who are special.*

6. Sergeant support – *C'mon the Sergeants!!!*

7. SPR** – *Is it not the SPL***?*

8. Crimefile – *I try not to use it, takes up too much time.*

9. Community Team – *That would be a great idea, when are we playing?*

10. CID – *Suits-R-Us!*

11. Event planning – *Think that's a bit radical, why start now?*

12. Transfers – *I hear Caldwell, McMitch and Robson are going to Middlesborough, Boyd to Birmingham.*

*CS is that spray stuff that makes your eyes water.
**SPR is a Standard Police Report.
***SPL is the Scottish Premier League

Chapter 12

IN LOO OF NOTHING TO DO

For years I was a member of the Police Support Unit (PSU). (The guys with the shields and helmets). With all the specialist training we underwent, we were a well-honed public order policing machine. Ready for any eventuality. We trained twice a year. Two weeks of constant drill, developing our skills until we were a co-ordinated unit capable of dispersing any mass disorder in an efficient and professional manner.

The only thing was, in Scotland, we did not get a lot of major disorder. It was rare for the Police Support Unit to get a call out. When it happened, it was most often to extricate a violent prisoner from a cell or assist the drug squad to gain entry to a house. (We had a big key).

PSU training involved donning our protective gear and shuffling about behind shields while the instructors lobbed wooden bricks at us and set off petrol bombs at our feet. Exciting and fun, for the young ones. For the old hands, it was just an arduous experience we tried to get through the day without breaking a finger or straining an ankle. Overzealous instructors made sure we always hobbled out of our PSU training with a patchwork quilt of bruises.

When called out on a job, it was often as a 'just in case' for a major event. It meant sitting about in a van hidden away from those attending the event, so as not to intimidate anyone. Just waiting for something to happen. Invariably nothing happened. We were always on hand in the marching season - 'Orange Parades' always attracted the worst of both sides of the divides. One year they even called us out to be on hand for the New Year firework display - Sitting in a van, helmet at

215

the ready watching the sky light up a mile away - just in case.

On one occasion our force was host to an event which had the potential to attract hate-mongers. If enough of them turned up, it would be a problem, so they asked the PSU to be on standby. The event was to last a whole week. The full PSU drafted into headquarters where we remained on standby in the gym. We were to be there for twelve hours a day for the full seven days.

In the first hour of the first day, bosses briefed us in the potential problems that might arise. New members of the team were eager to get involved, keen to see action. The rest of us had a much more pragmatic approach. We checked our kit to ensure everything was there and functional. Kept ourselves up to speed with intelligence reports, but all the time we knew there would be little reason to use us. The PSU is the last resort. If we did get called into action, it would be the final desperate acknowledgement that something had gone wrong - badly wrong.

By the second hour, boredom crept across the gym and the unit became restless. Some wandered off to the canteen and lounged there, drinking coffee and chatting. The lack of activity from us did not go unnoticed by our senior officers. Miffed that they had to stand in a queue behind several PSU officers in boiler suits before they could order their usual morning coffee and scone. By the end of the first day, the order came, from high up, that we should be gainfully employed. As a result, the next day they us assembled in the rear car park at headquarters and marched us out to practice our drills and cordons.

The noise from all the barked orders and marching up and down soon became a bigger inconvenience to the senior officers. Within half an hour the order came back down for us to shut up and get back into the gym. We remained there for the rest of the week.

A resourceful young officer acquired a TV and PlayStation and those inclined spent the twelve hour days racing cars with their thumbs and playing shoot-'em-up games. Others brought in newspapers found a comfortable mat and spent the time reading their paper from cover to cover. I sat whiling the hours away chatting with a group of friends, including PC Molly.

PC Molly made me laugh, the way he chuckled at his own stories and his boyish outlook on life. He also had a natural bent towards having nonsense. He was forever winding me up. I had been the target of many a prank of his over the years.

On our second day PC Molly headed off to the toilet, and I decided I could also do with a pee. I got up and followed PC Molly to the loo, but he didn't notice me behind him. As I entered the loo, PC Molly locked himself in a cubicle. He was clearly oblivious to the fact I had followed him in. I carried on with the job in hand, in silence. I then washed up at the sink. At the last moment, I cupped some water in my hands and threw it over the top of Molly's cubicle. He didn't make a sound. No protest whatsoever. I too remained silent. I sneaked out without saying anything and headed back to the group I was sitting with in the gym.

When Molly returned, he sat down beside us and omitted telling us of his soaking. Then another member of our small group asked, "How come your shirts all wet Molly?" at which point I burst out laughing and Molly pointed an accusatory finger at me.

"I knew it was you, McEwan."

"Why didn't you say anything then?"

"I wanted you to think it might have been someone else in there."

The next morning we were mulling around the gym doing the daily crossword and chatting when the urge took me. I made my way to the gents and chose a suitable cubicle. Dropped my trousers and contemplated the meaning of life. I heard the toilet door open. There was a bit if shuffling about; a tap spurted out water. Then a hand appeared over the top of the cubicle. In that hand was a plastic cup, the hand twisted and a full cup of water was dumped on my head. I couldn't go anywhere and couldn't help but burst out laughing as did PC Molly from the other side of the door.

The next morning, Molly I saw, was contemplating his next movement but eyed me suspiciously. So he sneaked out and wandered headquarters to find a safe haven away from the gym. I missed the opportunity for the next two days and pretended indifference. However, on the fifth day, I spotted Molly making his way into the same gents toilet as he did the first day. I nipped into the cleaners cupboard and found a bucket. I filled the bucket full of tepid water. I then sneaked into the gents. There was only one cubicle in use. PC Molly was interrupted in the middle of his ablutions by four gallons of water being poured over the top of the cubicle door and onto his head.

I spent the next ten minutes guffawing and the following twenty minutes with a bucket and mop getting rid of the evidence. I might have swabbed the floor dry, but I couldn't wipe the big cheesy grin off my face.

Every night we bagged up our gear in our big black holdalls and took them home just in case a call out came during the night. Our kit bags were a pain in the backside to lug around as they were so heavy. I took every opportunity to moan about it. On the last day, the bosses stood us down an hour early. There had been no trouble, and we had sat in the gym twelve hours a day for seven days on the trot without so much as a whiff of action. I lugged my kit bag to my car and headed off home. All that sitting around for a week had taken its toll, my kit bag felt heavier than ever. Despite the occasional bit of nonsense, it had been a tedious week, and I felt exhausted.

When I got home, I emptied my kit bag to ensure my overalls were cleaned and aired before their next outing. It was only then I found the four bricks that PC Molly had deposited there – no wonder the damn thing was so heavy. Yes, he liked his nonsense too.

A couple of weeks later I took one brick, wrapped it up in brown paper and sent it to PC Molly through the internal mail. I didn't include a message as I presumed he would realise it was from me. I deposited the brick parcel in the internal delivery tray. The driver/cleaner must have wondered what the heavy parcel was, but he transported the parcel from my station through to headquarters and deposited in the office mail boxes. In due course, the duty sergeant picked it up, scratched his head wondering what it was then delivered it to the custody suite. A curious custody suite sergeant took the heavy parcel and dutifully placed it on top of Molly's in-tray.

About two weeks after that I called at the custody suite with a prisoner. PC Molly was at his computer processing a line of prisoners. I noticed the brick I had sent him sitting on the windowsill behind him.

"What are you doing with a brick on your windowsill?" I asked him with a mischievous smile.

PC Molly looked at the brick and then looked at me. A sudden realisation crossed his face, and we both burst out laughing again. He told me that, until that moment, he didn't know who it was from and had decided he better keep it in case it was a production.

Chapter 13

HE'S THE BACK END OF A SEWAGE OUTLET!

It is not all fun and games in the police.

One weekday night shift I was in the office early preparing the briefing for the troops when a call came in. The control room took the details and passed it as a petrol theft. They told me a male had walked into a petrol station, on the far side of town, and filled up a plastic petrol canister before walking off into the adjacent housing scheme. He made no attempt to pay for the petrol, so the control room passed it as a minor theft.

A canister of petrol valued about £5 - not the crime of the century. The suggestion from the control room was that as we, the night shift officers, were about to start we could attend the call after I had completed the briefing. I had an odd feeling that something wasn't quite right about this one.

We call petrol thefts 'drive-offs'. Committed by people who fill up their car or motorbike then speed off without paying. I hadn't heard of anyone walking into a petrol station, filling up a petrol canister and walking off. Why didn't he run off?

I didn't like the idea of someone wandering about a housing scheme with a canister full of petrol. I didn't wait until I had completed the briefing. I sent two officers to the call right away. I thought we had a better chance of catching the guy if we got there sooner rather than later.

While the two officers were on route to the petrol station a further call came in. A woman who lived two streets away from the petrol station had seen a male carrying a petrol canister. Something about concerned her. She watched him stop outside her house, undo the cap on the canister and then pour some contents over his head.

I had just started the briefing when this second call came in. Seconds later I had my jacket on and issued instructions for all the crews to head down to the housing scheme. I also called on the radio for the back shift officers to stay on and head down too. As I made my way to the locus, I instructed the officers to plot up at various points so that if the male headed into town away from the petrol station, there would be a crew at every corner to intercept him.

Within ten minutes the strategy had worked. Two young cops, who had parked their car down by the river, near the old folks' home, spotted our thief coming towards them. He was walking across an expanse of waste ground. He still had the petrol canister in his hands, and as soon as he saw the officers, he poured more petrol over his head, pulled out a lighter from his pocket and threatened to set himself on fire. The two cops relayed all this via radio.

I made my way there, tyres squealing.

Several other crews arrived with me, and I instructed each to bring their fire extinguishers from their cars. While we surrounded the male, I expressed my desire for them to keep a safe distance.

The male had moved, so he was just a few yards away from the edge of the river. We spread out on our approach, and I instructed my officers, again, to keep a safe distance from him. They formed a semi-circle with the male at the centre, keeping about thirty yards away. I moved in a little closer towards him.

The male was about twenty, had a shaven head and was wearing a woollen jumper and jeans. He still had the petrol canister in his hands and wasn't talking much sense. He seemed angry and was directing this anger towards the police. Experience told me to engage with him in a non-threatening manner. I told him my name and asked him his. He told me his name was John Magno. I listened to what he was saying and tried to empathise with him and keep him talking. Then he went off on a rant, "I'm not guilty, I've been charged, I'm not guilty, I'll set myself on fire, I didn't do it, I'll set myself on fire."

As if to prove a point he poured more petrol from the canister, over his head and then held his lighter out in front of himself. It was a little white plastic disposable lighter, the ones that are hard to stay lit outside in even a light breeze. Unfortunately, there wasn't a breath of wind. He pulled his thumb down on the lighter and the rotation of the striker caused a spark, which lit the gas. A flame appeared, and he held the lighter at arm's length until the metal striker became hot, and he had to let it go before he burnt his thumb. I knew I'd better do something quick.

Malky, why would anyone want to set fire to themselves?
I don't know.
Why don't you know?
I'm not a bloody mind reader, am I?
You're the sergeant you're supposed to know things like that, aren't you?
Why am I supposed to know that?
Didn't they teach you that at the Scottish Police College?
On my sergeant's course?
Yes.
No, they didn't, you should know, you were there!
Just do something okay!
Okay, I'll talk to him.

"Come on John," I coaxed him, "put the lighter down. Don't do anything stupid."

John Magno ranted again, "I'm not guilty, I've been charged, I'm not guilty, I'll set myself on fire, I didn't do it, I'll set myself on fire."

I had radioed in a request for a trained negotiator to attend but I knew they would be at least a couple of hours to get out to us (I think that is their first tactic - wait long enough before attending, and the situation resolves itself before they get there). I had been in enough stand-off situations with negotiators to have picked up a few of their tactics. Get them talking, get to the heart of the problem and gain their trust.

"How is it that we had ended up here?" I asked him.

He ignored me.

"I'm not guilty, I've been charged, I'm not guilty, I'll set myself on fire, I didn't do it, I'll set myself on fire."

"What didn't you do? What started this all off in the first place?"

He ignored me again; he mumbled under his breath, I couldn't make out what he was saying.

I tried a different tack.

"How can we resolve this situation?"

None of those questions seemed to work. John Magno wasn't listening; maybe he was psychotic or high on drugs. I wasn't sure. He continued to mumble and rant, not making any sense. I gathered from his outbursts he had been charged with a fraud. He protested his innocence, but the details of it were not clear as he kept going off on tangents. Agitated and angry.

I continued to talk with him. In response, he poured more petrol over his head. This time he grabbed his jumper with his left hand and pulled it away from his body. He lit the lighter again and put it nearer to his petrol-soaked jumper, far enough away so as not to set himself on fire, but close enough that any slight movement could ignite it.

A lot of things went through my head; I thought furiously, all the time trying to appear calm and persuade him not to do anything stupid.

Malky, maybe you could rush him. If you wait until the lighter burns his finger and if he switches it off, you might have a chance. Just rugby tackle him, the river is just behind him. If soaked he wouldn't be able to set himself on fire, would he? Even if he set himself on fire before you got him into the river, the water would put the flames out wouldn't it? That river is deep, and it is flowing fast, what if you got stuck in the mud? What if he drowned? You might end up on trial for murder. Okay, okay. I'm confident I can talk him out of it.

I had loads of experience dealing with suicidal people. I had always talked them round. I adopted my softly-softly approach. I am a likeable guy; I knew my charms would eventually work on him. If I showed genuine concern for his welfare, sympathy for his predicament and compassion for what he was going through, he would come round and see sense. It required me to remain calm and use all my experience. Let's face it nobody really wants to set themselves on fire. That would be just stupid.

I coaxed him into giving me his name, sweet-talked him into providing his address and used as much charm as I could muster to persuade him to put the lighter and petrol canister down. I was making progress. My softly-softly approach was working. I had skills. Maybe I should have been a salesman. I can talk anybody out of anything. My natural ability to win over people came to the fore, and I was getting through to

John Magno. He recognised my empathy and appreciated my concern for his well-being. This would be my greatest triumph, my magnum opus. Here I was talking a man out of setting himself on fire, surrounded by my shift all eyes on me. They were standing watching in quiet admiration. Proud to have such a capable leader as their sergeant.

At which point John Magno set himself on fire.

He pulled out his jumper put the lighter to it and whoosh, up in flames he went. John Magno stood before me engulfed in flames from his petrol-soaked jumper. The flames grew startlingly quick and reached high above his head; his face obscured by the red and yellow glow.

John ran around like a headless chicken, screaming in agony. I don't think anyone who pours petrol over themselves and sets themselves alight truly appreciates just how excruciating a thing like that is until they do it. If they did - they wouldn't do it. He ran around for what seemed like ages but could only have been about ten or twelve seconds. Training took over, I shouting at him to get on the ground and this time my negotiating skills worked. He collapsed and lay on the ground. I bellowed at him to roll on the grass and at the same time motioned to the two cops holding fire extinguishers to move in. They were on him as quick as they could, spraying him with foam. It put the fire out and probably saved his life.

My failed negotiating skills had resulted in John Magno getting badly burned around his torso and neck. We had already summoned an ambulance and got their help to get him to the hospital for treatment. I followed in my car and sat in the waiting room while the Accident and Emergency staff tended to him.

After a few hours John, sedated and bandaged, could see me. The look he gave was full of pain.

"How are you, John?"

"Ooh ya bugger!" He said. "That was sore. I'll no be doing that again."

To my knowledge, John Magno never set himself on fire again. I suppose it is not the kind of thing you do twice. I made the occasional enquiry as to how he was doing. I knew that he pleaded guilty to his fraud and received a fine of £100.

I also attended a case conference. There were social workers, psychiatrists and health professionals present. The purpose was to assess whether or not John Magno was sane enough to remain in the community. He was married and was the father of two young boys. Their safety was a big consideration. There were a lot of discussions. John Magno had been the subject of a lengthy psychiatric assessment, and the psychiatrist concluded he was sane. Social workers had visited him at home three times a week since the incident and had concluded he didn't present a danger to himself anymore and, more importantly, to anyone else. His wounds had left him with much of his neck and torso scarred - a gruesome reminder of his utter stupidity.

After much debate, the chair realised that I hadn't spoken. He sought my opinion.

"Sergeant McEwan, why do you think he did it?"

John Magno may have been mad (or at least had a temporary psychosis), but I don't think he was a bad person. He committed a fraud, and he self-harmed, that was all. Everyone had downplayed the fact that he had self-harmed in a spectacularly frightening fashion. People get inured to the craziness that is around them sometimes.

I tried to remain serious when I replied, "I think it was just a smokescreen to get off with his fraud."

Increasingly the police seem to deal with the mad and sad rather than the bad. We are a civilised society, and that demands we take care of each other. The police are often the first to come into contact with those that are sad or a bit mad and not just when they are bad. We can all be a bit sad, a little mad or even a tad bad at various times in our lives. So maybe we should have more compassion. Sometimes it is just our circumstances that send us off in that direction. Those that get dealt a bad hand in life can find themselves at the bottom of a hole and find it hard to climb out. That was certainly the case with Morag McMaddie.

Morag McMaddie was a troubled young girl. Brought up in foster care, having been abandoned by her mother at the age of seven. Those important formative years, for her, were bereft of the care and true love a normal parent would extend to her child.

More spitting snake than cuddly toy, Morag's foster carers couldn't give her the love she needed to feel wanted. So Morag ended up in trouble from an early age. The lack of love in her formative years skewed Morag's view of humanity. She got into fights, vandalised the town and scorned anyone and everyone who crossed her path. It was hard for teachers, social workers or the police to feel any sympathy for her. Her response to anyone's attempt at being nice to her was undisguised venom. She was one bad-tempered bloody nuisance of a young lady.

Despite early intervention and direct Social Work involvement, there were too many issues to resolve. It became an almost daily occurrence that Morag came to our attention. If she took a dislike to someone, she would spend her every waking minute making their life a misery. She could be truly awful to other people. A glance in her direction could be misinterpreted by her and offence taken. The perceived slight, no matter how minor, would make Morag swear vengeance. Day and night she would go out of her way to turn up at that person's house to hurl abuse, or stones, destroying the peace and damaging windows. There wasn't a day went by she didn't end up being complained about, investigated and invariably arrested.

Because she was a juvenile when Morag got herself arrested her foster parents had to attend the police station on every occasion. In Scot's law, an adult has to be present when a child charged. A time-consuming paperwork nightmare for the police. It became a major inconvenience for her foster parents. We asked them to come in, but the more Morag got herself into trouble, the more her foster parents dragged their heels. Initially, it took half an hour for them to get themselves extricated from the comforts of their home make their way to the police office, then it was an hour and then two hours. We ended up sending a crew straight to their house to hurry them along. The crew would wait, arms folded tapping their feet, while they put on a pair of shoes and a coat. Morag would go out the next day and cause further mayhem for those that had complained about her, the cycle repeating itself. No wonder they got fed up with her.

No surprise then that the day Morag McMaddie turned sixteen her foster parents took her to the council housing offices and presented her as homeless. They had had enough. Just as her mother had abandoned her, Morag McMaddie got dumped by her foster parents as soon as they could.

The state now had to take care of Morag McMaddie. That very same day the council housed her in a flat of her own and gave her an emergency loan until they could sort out her proper benefits.

Those benefits amounted to more money than she had ever seen before but instead of financing her heating, food, and clothing, all it did was finance her growing drinking problem. The more she drank, the more she got into trouble.

An angry young lady. She spent her days drinking and then singling out someone for a supposed wrong they had done to her, and she would focus all her attention on making their life miserable. One fast food takeaway owner ended up having to get a court order to prevent her from coming anywhere within one hundred yards of his premises. She ignored this, smashed his windows, scratched his car, abused his customers and wrote racist graffiti about him all over the town.

"Why did you do it Morag?"

"Because he didnae gie me enough chips wi ma haggis supper!"

A young single mother received similar attention. Morag McMaddie called at her house and banged on her door at all hours of the day and night. Mostly drunk, sometimes sober but always looking for the poor woman to come out and fight. She stalked her to the local nursery picked a fight with her. But she came off the worse, so Morag phoned us to complain about the young mother!

The police received thousands of calls about Morag McMaddie over the years. Where there was evidence, she was charged and ended up in court. The courts, however, rarely dealt with her firmly. The next day she would cause mayhem again and make someone else's life a misery. Morag McMaddie was a perpetual frustration and, understandably, we had little sympathy for her.

By the time she was twenty-five, Morag McMaddie had been the suspect or accused person in over two hundred different complaints. Many of these had multiple charges; mostly for vandalism or breach of the peace. Short spells in prison reduced her offending, but she became an even bigger nuisance by calling in to report feeling suicidal at least once a week.

The first job of a police officer is to protect life. The legislators have listed this way down at part 20(1)(c) of the relevant legislation, but any good police officer worth his salt knows that protecting life is their primary purpose. Chief Constables have spun this principle and turned it into the catchy slogan 'keeping people safe'. It serves as a reminder to everyone within the service that no matter how many times Morag McMaddie phones to report, 'I'm going to kill myself', we have to devote many officers' time and efforts to trace her. We had to make sure she wasn't in a life-threatening situation. She demanded a lot of time and effort. Despite her cry for help, she seemed just to bugger off and make it difficult for us. A day or two later she'd be traced at some other reprobate's house, where she would be drunk and deny making any such call.

Yes, Morag McMaddie was a pain in the neck, but one incident left me with feeling a slight chink of sympathy for her.

Winter was drawing in; the clocks had just turned back the requisite hour signalling the full onset of winter. The average person felt a little down. Lack of sunshine darkened the thoughts of the Seasonal Affective Disorder (SAD) brigade. A time to turn to friends and family for support.

Morag McMaddie didn't have friends or family. When she got depressed, she called the police, "I'm going to kill myself," she'd say through her tears.

Despite the attention seeking nature of the appeal, she refused to say where she was or how she would kill herself. The call taker persisted in trying to get more information, but Morag hung up. Once again we tasked cops to make enquiries to find her.

First port of call was her flat and, for a change, the crew in attendance could confirm that she was there. Despite knocking repeatedly, Morag refused to open her door to them. The two young cops spent some time talking to Morag through her letter-box trying to get her to open her door, but no amount of coaxing worked. That's when they called me up on the radio seeking authority to force open the door. They wanted to make sure she was safe.

I clarified the situation with them. The crew had not seen Morag with any weapons or means of causing herself harm. I also established that Morag had not stated how where or why she would commit suicide. Without there being any evidence of an immediate threat to her wellbeing, I asked them to wait until I got there. I wanted to talk to her myself.

On my arrival, the cops still conversed with Morag through the letter-box. She sounded a little drunk, and she was undoubtedly feeling sorry for herself. I took over at the letter-box and told her who I was. I explained that if she didn't open the door, we would have to force entry.

She shouted, "I don't want you to see me like this."

A strange thing to say.

I have a useful little trick for these situations. I shouted to Morag I'd give her ten seconds to open the door or I would force it open. I told her she would be liable for the cost of damage and the council would take it out of her benefits. Less money for her to spend on drink.

I counted to ten, but the door remained firmly locked and closed. So I turned my back to the door and slapped the door with the sole of my shoe. The noise this makes is deafening. It echoes through the block of flats and sounds as if you are actually forcing the door open but because it is just a slap of the whole sole, it does no damage. Morag fell for it and in a flash she opened the door.

Morag McMaddie stood facing me on her threshold, I couldn't help myself, I burst out laughing. I know it wasn't professional. The two cops couldn't help themselves either, they followed my lead and let go with some hearty guffaws. Well, you couldn't blame us because what we saw was hilarious.

Earlier that day Morag McMaddie had purchased a self-tanning lotion. It was of the cheaper variety. After returning to her flat and consuming large quantities of strong cider Morag applied the tanning lotion. This she did with her bare hands. As a result, her face was a bright orange, but she had left big white panda eyes and a big white clown mouth. Her hands were completely black, giving her a look was not dissimilar to the kind of thing you might have seen on a light entertainment singing show in the 70s (for those of you who remember *The Black and White Minstrel Show*). The result of her effort to give herself a tan had caused Morag to contemplate suicide.

Morag McMaddie looked up at me laughing at her. I couldn't help myself; it was such an unexpected sight to behold. I guffawed as hard as I had ever done in my life. Morag's sad face changed ever so slightly; her lips curled up at the sides, she couldn't help herself either. My guffaws and the hearty laughing from the two cops with me was infectious. She could not keep from laughing along with us. Once she laughed we guffawed all the more, tears rolling down our faces and sides sore. It was ten minutes before we composed ourselves enough to sit down and have a chat.

Morag McMaddie and I came to an agreement. She promised not to kill herself if we didn't tell anyone about her fake tan escapade.

I mentioned that one of the first tactics of a Police Negotiator is to stall for time. To a negotiator that is an outrageous accusation. If you are a negotiator, please don't take offence; it was just my experience.

I'd called out Police Negotiators on many occasions. Twice for hostage situations but mostly for those threatening suicide. Whether it was night or day, the negotiator seemed to take hours to get there. I used to think it was part of their training to roll over and go back to sleep, finish their book or continue their marathon session of watching the *Game of Thrones* box set before they made a move. I lost count how many times we had the situation resolved before the actual Police Negotiator turned up at the scene. However, in their defence, any situation that required us to call out a Police Negotiator is a stressful time. Five minutes can seem like hours. There weren't any occasions I wasn't pleased to see a Police Negotiator (when they eventually appeared). Like a puppy, you could lock me away in the boot of a car for two hours - I'd be wagging my tail when the Police Negotiator let me out.

Being a negotiator is not an easy number. It is a tough post and takes a certain type of person to do it well. You need patience, determination, and tenacity. A little humour doesn't go amiss either. The selection process for a prospective Police Negotiator is difficult. Those applying for the position must first have the support of their line managers. That filters out a lot of officers deemed unsuitable; they don't even get the opportunity to go on the course.

The Police Negotiator's Course is one of the most intensive training an officer can undertake. Mock scenarios can sometimes extend into days to reflect real life situations. Imagine a hostage situation where the police negotiator knocks off at 5pm. That can't happen in real life.

The failure rates are high. The instructors don't care if no-one passes. They are brutal in weeding out unsuitable candidates. They have to: lives could depend on it.

Those who make it through possess incredible amounts of stamina, patience, determination, and emotional intelligence.

Johnny passed.

No ordinary pass mind you. Johnny walked out with the highest score ever recorded.

The live scenario they put him through exhausted even the instructors. It lasted 52 hours. At the end, they were all spent forces. Johnny stood up to everything they threw at him, and more. When it finished, Johnny suggested they give the instructors a debrief, and physiological assessment. He saw drained faces, burnt out souls, he worried for their mental well-being. His empathy for the people who had put him through the ordeal was outstanding.

Johnny went back to his job as a detective sergeant with deep respect from all involved.

It isn't until there is a real life situation it becomes clear why they get such intensive training.

One balmy summer evening a call came in stating that Frankie Foster had a knife and was threatening to kill his girlfriend. I made my way to the scene.

Frankie was standing at the top of a flight of stairs, the only access to the two uppper flats in the building. The stairs, at the rear of the block, split the building in the middle. There was a metal handrail on either side and a landing area at the top leading to two flats. Frankie was pacing back and forth on the landing. The door to his flat on the left was open. A heavy solid wood door.

Frankie had a large kitchen knife in his right hand and a litre bottle of cheap vodka in his left. He'd ripped off his shirt and was standing on the landing topless, swigging from the vodka bottle and threatening to stab any cop who came within arm's length.

I established that his girlfriend had made the call; she stated she was inside the flat in a back bedroom. My first concern was for her.

Had he stabbed her? Was she injured, or dying? Did we need to force our way up the stairs past Frankie to save her?

I asked for a Public Order team to attend (the guys with helmets and shields).
If we needed to get in, we needed to get in quick. It was part of their training to enter a building and deal with those carrying offensive weapons. You might have the biggest, baddest knife in the world but it won't do you any good against a rushing wall of shields with six burly cops behind them.

The control room confirmed they had been in contact with the girlfriend via her mobile phone and that she was uninjured. She could not escape from any window, her only exit was past Frankie, so they had asked her to barricade herself in her bedroom.

The first cop to arrive stood at the bottom of the stairs and engaged Frankie in conversation.

It wasn't going well.

Everything he said seemed to rile Frankie. Frankie swigged his vodka and threatened serious injury to anyone who tried to come up the stairs towards him. I radioed in and asked for a Police Negotiator to attend.

I knew that the best way to keep everyone safe was for us to keep our distance from Frankie but it was also important to keep him talking at the top of the stairs to prevent him from going back inside the flat where he might be a danger to his girlfriend.

Frankie, volatile and angry, was getting drunker by the minute. He slugged the 40% proof vodka and the fire in his belly gave him enough bravado to make him believe he was invincible.

It was a tricky situation.

These are resolved only when something gives; when the protagonist realises the futility of his situation and gives up or, more often than not, does something that requires our immediate intervention. We react, and he gets tackled to the ground.

Frankie, however, stayed at the top of the stairs. Pacing on the landing, knife in hand and hurling abuse at us.

The public order team arrived suited up, helmets on and shields at the ready.

I positioned them out of sight at the side of the building. If Frankie came down the stairs, they would be on him quicker than a defensive line-up from an American Football team.

Intense situations slow time.

It seemed ages before the Police Negotiator arrived, but I smiled when Detective Sergeant Johnny Connelly arrived. His reputation preceded him.

Johnny was born to be a negotiator. Patient, determined and full of wit.

It was always a pleasure to have him join my company in any situation. I briefed Johnny with all the information we had. The cop talking to Frankie was getting frustrated, and Frankie was reacting by firing more threats at him.

Johnny took in the situation, happy that we had the backup of the public order team should things go askew. We agreed that it might be best for Frankie to stay out of the flat by keeping him engaged in conversation.

Sergeant Johnny Connelly strolled out from the side of the building into Frankie's view. Johnny didn't look up at our knife wielding thug; he dismissed the cop at the bottom of the stairs, who breathed a sigh of relief, happy to surrendered his position.

Frankie went quiet, watching us from high. A sharp clawed common buzzard ready to pounce.

Johnny sidled up to the banister at the bottom of the stairs and leaned against it. Getting into a comfortable position as he could, knowing he might be there for some time.

Still ignoring Frankie, he took out a packet of cigarettes. He extricated a single smoke from the packet, tapped the end on the box before inserting it in his mouth. He then laid the packet down on the bottom step, in full view of Frankie. I watched from the side as Johnny exaggerated the search of every pocket on his person, looking for a match. The whole time the cigarette dangled from his mouth.

After his second pat down he looked up at Frankie for the first time, "Got a light?"

Frankie switched from loud and abusive to quiet and curious. He laid down his half-finished litre bottle of vodka on the landing, reached into the pocket of his jeans and produced a disposable lighter, which he held up in proof he had such a thing.

"Em, can I get one of those, please?" he asked Johnny.

"Sure," Johnny responded.

They traded by throwing the packet of cigarettes and the lighter between them.

Johnny went back to leaning on the banister and blowing the occasional smoke ring before engaging Frankie once more, "So, what's this all about Frankie?"

And for the next two hours, they chatted to each other.

Frankie drank his vodka and smoked Johnny's cigarettes until the packet was empty.

Johnny listened and responded. Always appropriate, building rapport. He extracted information from Frankie like a skilled surgeon removing a gallstone. It is all about engagement and empathy. It is how a negotiator gains trust. Only when there is trust can he look to use persuasion and suggestion. The only break in the conversation between the two was when Johnny turned and asked me if he could get another packet of cigarettes.

The police car took me to the nearest shop. I purchased a packet of twenty *No.6* and headed back, pondering what an order of twenty *No. 6* would get me in a Chinese takeaway, hunger gnawing at my stomach.

I arrived back at the block of flats with the cigarettes. Johnny, leaning against the banister chatting to Frankie, looked up and nodded to me, calm as you like. I walked out into sight to hand Johnny the cigarettes. Frankie sat on the top step of the staircase. Three-quarters of a litre bottle of vodka taking its toll. He saw me and stood up.

Volatile all over again.

"WHO THE FUCK IS THAT?" he shouted to Johnny.

"This is Sergeant McEwan," Johnny replied, nonplussed.

"WELL, HE'S A FUCKING ARSEHOLE!" Frankie shouted at the top of his voice straining every sinew in his neck in the process and putting as much effort into the emphasis of the word 'arsehole' as he could.

Johnny remained expressionless. He turned looked me up and down, before turning back to the enraged Frankie and replying,

"So you've met him then!"

I raised an eyebrow, but kept quiet, turned around and walked back out of sight.

I had seen enough.

Frankie's bottle was almost finished, and I knew that a litre of that stuff in such a short space of time would finish Frankie off. I predicted that he would collapse in an alcoholic stupor within half an hour and said as much to the public order team.

It wasn't as long as that.

Ten minutes later Frankie finished his vodka. Struggling to stay awake he stood up to shake himself off. He staggered, put his hand out to stop himself from falling, forgetting he still held a large kitchen knife. The knife struck the banister and caused him to lose his grip on it. As the knife tumbled from his hand, Frankie made to grab it and missed. In doing so, he spun around losing his balance. He teetered over the top step before slumping backwards and falling head over heels all the way down where he crash landed at the feet of Sergeant Johnny Connelly.

The public order team had Frankie surrounded in a blur, but there was no need. Frankie was out for the count and didn't come round again until he woke up in his cell a full thirty-six hours later.

The demon drink had relaxed his body so much that he hadn't felt a thing. Unscathed from his fall other than a scrape to his face and a sore rib.

Although, he did have the Granddaddy of all hangovers.

Chapter 14

NOT AS DAFT AS HE LOOKS

PC Gary Gorman was a man whose standing within the police was as short and stocky as his physique. A legend in his own lunchtime. Long before I ever met Gary Gorman I had heard stories about him. Stories that had made me smile but also made me shake my head.

A member of the public handed in a football. PC Gary Gorman filled out a Found Property Report. He entered the name of the finder, taking care to spell his name correctly and write it as neatly as he could. He completed the address of the finder in a similar fashion; Gary asked where he found it and entered the time, date and location. Once he had noted all these details, he copied the reference number onto the property tag, and the finder watched in astonishment as PC Gorman completed the lodging process by stapling the tag to the ball.

Well, I suppose it was easier to store flat.

On another occasion, an office clerk attended to the counter one evening to a man carrying four planks of wood in one hand and four planks of wood in the other. The man dropped them in the reception then disappeared out to his van; he brought in a further eight similar loads. The last load was felt roofing. Only then did he approach the counter.

"What's this?" the office clerk asked.

"Well, my next door neighbour had this shed in his garden and wasn't using it. I spoke to an officer, and he advised me that if I brought it to the office as found property and nobody claimed it in six months, I would get it back to keep. I would like it for my garden – so here it is.

"Which officer told you that?" the office clerk asked, disbelievingly.

"I can't remember his name, but he is short and stocky, looks like a gorilla."

"Gary Gorman!"

I used the same tone as the office clerk when my boss told me that PC Gary Gorman had got into a little bother and they were going to transfer him to my shift. I hadn't met Gary before, I like to take people as I find them, but from the stories I had heard, I had a little groan to myself.

"What has he done now?" I asked.

"Oh. It was just a little misunderstanding."

PC Gary Gorman's escapades with found property paled into insignificance when I heard why he was getting moved onto my shift:

Gary came from a big family. He was the youngest of eight children, and his family had a poor upbringing. His dad was a council gravedigger and his mother a housewife. It is hard to bring up children on such a low wage and with so many mouths to feed, but they did their best. There were no thoughts of university or college for any of the kids; there was no money or inclination for such lofty goals. As soon as they reached school leaving age, they went to work.

Gary had three older brothers, all of whom had followed their father into the council grave digging squad. It was accepted that Gary would end up working there alongside them when he too left school. Every weekend his father and brothers worked overtime, Gary would go along with them and dig in, literally. Gary's squat frame ideally suited to digging. The hard slog of digging holes in the ground helped build a stubby frame of hardened muscle. By the time Gary left school, he had the build of a small Russian shot putter and no qualifications other than he could dig a hole faster and deeper than anyone alive.

It was a surprise then when instead of following the footsteps of his father and brothers he walked into his local police station and filled out an application form. It was a bigger surprise to his folks that he was accepted into the police family.

Plain old civilian Gary Gorman became Constable Gary Gorman. He worked for a few years, met a nice girl, got married and had four lovely children. Gary decided enough was enough. He didn't want his children to be as poor as he and his siblings had been, his wages wouldn't extend to coping with any more children on the payroll - so he had a vasectomy.

These days a vasectomy is a fairly minor procedure. In and out in a day. A couple of days to recover and 'how's your father,' you are back to work.

Gary's operation was a snip - that's true. He was in and out in a clip. Unfortunately for Gary things didn't quite go as smooth after that. On returning home he felt a little discomfort, he presumed that such twinges were normal. The next day, however, that little discomfort had increased to the extent that he was getting a regular shooting pain. There was an even bigger problem. His right testicle had swollen up. It was not dissimilar to the size of a pear. Gary tried to ignore it, took painkillers and went off to bed.

He woke the next day and found his pear sized testicle had grown further. It was now the size of a 'Galia' melon. Gary realised that he needed to do something about it. He put on his dressing gown and went to see Shirley, his next door neighbour.

Shirley opened her door to see Gary standing there in his blue towelling gown. His anguished expression concerned her.

"What's the matter Gary?"

"It's this!" said Gary, and he opened his dressing gown, dropped his pyjama bottoms and out plopped the 'Galia' melon. A great big hairy sac of throbbing pain confronted Shirley. She recoiled in disgust. Aghast and appalled by the swollen scrotum.

"What do you think?" Gary asked.

"It's awful!" was all Shirley could muster. She pulled her eyes away from this horrible mammoth testicle and looked Gary in the eye.

"But why on earth are you showing it to me?" she asked, concerned that he had lost his mind.

"Because you are a nurse," said Gary.

"I'm a dental nurse," Shirley informed him, "I hand tools to a dentist so he can look after your teeth."

Shirley phoned the police and asked to speak to a supervisor. She related the incident and demanded that PC Gary Gorman be warned never to darken her door again, with or without his gargantuan gonad. There were a flurry of phone calls, and the powers that be decided that Gary would be transferred to as far away a station as possible and thus force him to move home, away from his traumatised neighbour.

So that was how PC Gary Gorman ended up attached to my shift. His reputation preceded him and I, as his supervisor, was naturally wary of there being any further embarrassing incidents. He was now my responsibility, and I had to check everything he did. On Gary's first day I called him into my office for a chat. Gary entered, shut the door on my instruction, and sat down. He looked like the stub end of a cigar. Short and wide. His hair grew only from a small mound on top of his head and struck out at all angles. Despite swearing he shaved every morning, a rough growth of stubble adorned his face at all times. His legs were short and squat like tree stumps. His body was as wide as it was long, his early years spent digging holes had given him his broad muscular physique. He would not have looked out of place on the slopes of Kilimanjaro.

We had a welcome chat, and I found him to be forthright and honest with me. PC Gary Gorman had no ambitions to be anything other than a cop. He would never sit his promotion exams and never admit to having any inkling for advancing his career. All he ever wished for was to be a cop. That kind of thinking is quite liberating for a person. You simply get on with the job. No need for political point scoring. No need for back stabbing. Gary had no pretence about him, no airs and graces. Gary was just proud to be a serving officer earning a decent wage. He did what he was told to do, got on with the job and didn't care what others did or didn't do. Only concerned with himself and what he had to do. I was careful never to give him anything too complicated, and he was always happy to get on with it.

It was his eating habits that drew the most attention and not his work. PC Gary Gorman was the hungriest man I have ever known. During briefings, he would produce an apple from his pocket and eat it in four or five hearty crunches, devouring the core, seeds and all. It was mesmerising to watch. The whole shift turned and stared at him as he devoured it. Ten seconds and the apple was gone. Often a second apple would appear from his pocket, and this too would be devoured like a kid eating a marshmallow.

At break times Gary would arrive in the canteen with two items from the chip shop. A sausage supper as his starter, followed by a fish supper as his main course. He would then dip into his bag and produce a plated meal (mince and tatties) that his wife had made him. The mince and tatties would receive a cursory warming in the microwave before also being demolished. Then he'd crunch through a never ending supply of apples, eaten whole. Then it would be back to work, and I would be on tenterhooks waiting to see what his next predicament would bring.

The first problem I had with Gary was when he went missing. We were working the night shift, and after his break, I had asked Gary to patrol the town centre. It is generally quiet in those early hours so I didn't expect the task to be too much of a hardship and I certainly didn't expect any dilemmas.

On a night shift, it was normal for officers to filter back into the station about six in the morning, they would complete their necessary paperwork and get ready to make a sharp exit when the early shift came in at seven. Gary wasn't the best timekeeper when starting his work, but he was punctual at finishing. So when it came to 6.30 a.m., and he hadn't arrived back in, I gave him a call on the radio. There was no answer. I kept trying. The clock ticked on to a quarter to seven. Gary still didn't answer his radio. I instructed my shift to get back out in their cars and find him. One I sent to tour the periphery of the town centre; one I sent to scour the far outreaches of the town. I grabbed my jacket and went out on foot straight to the High Street.

While the cars were searching the main streets, I searched the back alleys, and entrance closes. I suspected that Gary had found somewhere comfortable to curl up and pass the night away. I hoped it was just that and not something more sinister.

The office clerk continued to call PC Gorman on his radio every two or three minutes, but there was just silence.

I checked an alley just off the High Street, and when I came back out, a bakery van drove past me. My eyes did a double take. I wasn't sure at first, but it looked like PC Gary Gorman was driving it. The van carried on to the bakery at the top of the street, about fifty yards away from me. It stopped, and sure enough, Gary jumped out the of driving seat, went round to the back and opened the van doors, before lugging two large trays onto his shoulders and heading into the bakery. I radioed to control that I had found our missing officer and walked towards the bakery. Just as I reached it, PC Gary Gorman walked back out and saw me. With no embarrassment he smiled at me and said, "Hi Sarge."

"I'll 'Hi Sarge' you," I said to him angrily, "what do you think you are playing at?" Although in truth I was relieved to see him alive and well.

"Oh. I just did a wee favour for the bakers here. Their driver phoned in sick, and I offered to do the run for them."

"Why didn't you answer your radio?"

A quick check revealed his battery was flat.

"You and I are going to have some serious words when we get back to the office PC Gorman," I informed him, still trying to convey a message he had caused concern.

"Ok Sarge," he said. Still none too concerned, "but look what I got for the shift."

Gary produced two paper bags one laden with about a dozen pies and the other stuffed with an assortment of cakes. He had a great big delighted smile on his face and no threat of 'having serious words' was going to spoil his good mood. He seemed consumed by the fact that he knew he could munch his way through most what the bags contained. Honestly, he was like a kid looking at all his wrapped presents at 4 a.m. on a

Christmas morning. I felt like that tired dad who had to tell him to go back to bed.

There was a nervous tension that came with having to supervise PC Gary Gorman. It was always with some relief when we made it to the end of the shift, and no disaster had befallen him. There were always minor incidents that kept me on my toes.

We had a cold spell one winter and, for this purpose, we kept sacks of road salt inside the garage. Great big five kilogramme bags of the stuff. I asked PC Gorman to salt the rear yard to ensure we could get our cars in and out. Gary returned about ten minutes later to tell me he had finished. In his right hand, he held a small, empty salt cellar he had taken from the canteen.

He stopped a motorcycle for having a noisy exhaust, he charged the driver under the Construction and Use Regulations but also brought the exhaust back to the office as a production. I resolved it by getting an ex-mechanic to go back and put it back on.

He got banned from the police rugby team because he had a tendency just to stop and take a pee on the pitch whenever the urge took him.

He went out on the night shift, cut down a fir tree and used the police van to transport it home. The garage complained when the pine needles left in the van caused their vacuum cleaner to pack in. All minor stuff but all warranting a shake of my head and a wag of my finger.

One day PC Gary Gorman and I had to attend court as witnesses: A necessary part of the job of a police officer. We interview people, gather evidence and present that evidence in a report to the Procurator Fiscal. The Procurator Fiscal decides which cases have merit. Where there is merit, the accused receives a 'copy complaint' or 'indictment'. These detail the charges and affords the accused the opportunity of pleading guilty or not guilty. When a 'not guilty' plea is submitted, the case goes to the court where it is the job of the Procurator Fiscal to present the evidence to a judge (or in serious cases, a jury).

The Procurator Fiscal presents the evidence by producing witnesses who tell the court what they saw and did. He cannot enter a piece of evidence without someone (a witness) speaking to it. A fingerprint, for example, is just a pattern of greasy marks left on a surface by someone's digit. To present it as evidence the victim of a housebreaking will first detail how his house was broken into. A Scene of Crime Officer will then detail how he found a fingerprint at the point of entry. A forensic scientist will show how that fingerprint was compared to those on the Police National Database and found to belong to the accused. A police officer will spell out the action he then took in arresting the accused and what he replied when he charged him with the housebreaking. It can be a long drawn out process.

The housebreaking won't be the only case in court on any given day. There will be dozens of other court business to get through. Police officers are routinely cited for court and have to sit around waiting for that nerve-jangling call to the witness box. The police officer is the last in the process too. So even if the case gets started he will have to sit in a witness room all day and sometimes into the next.

It is a frustrating experience. We have to be in attendance at the court because without our evidence the case could not go ahead. It is dead time. We cannot do any other work. We sit on uncomfortable plastic chairs waiting.

Gary and I were listed as witnesses No. 62 and 63 respectively. It looked like it would be a two or three-day trial. Two or three days of sitting around just waiting. If you are going to become a police officer, you better get used to waiting.

By mid-morning I'd read my newspaper cover to cover. Completed the easy crossword and guessed several answers in the hard crossword before giving up. The court officer popped in and informed us the trial was adjourned for lunch.

I made my way to the canteen and bought myself a coffee and a sandwich. PC Gorman took the decision to keep me company and joined me at my table with his vast spread of mince and tatties, half a loaf of buttered bread and his obligatory apple. We were just killing time until we had to go back to the witness room and kill more time.

It was a pleasant surprise then when Gary entertained me with a story about his dad. It was a riveting story about how good a footballer his dad was. A footballer turned gravedigger; this is what Gary told me:-

'When my Dad was young, he played for his local team, 'Thistle United' and was a highly rated and respected striker. They were halfway through the season and had been winning everything because my Dad had scored in every game. He had in fact scored more goals than the rest of the team put together. They were having a nice run in the cup and got to the final. The final was a home match, which they drew. The replay was re-scheduled for mid-week in Ayr.

They made arrangements for the team to hire a bus to pick them up at 4 p.m. on Tuesday and travel to Ayr together all in plenty time for the 7 p.m. kick-off.

My Dad worked as a gravedigger with the local council at the time. So to get the time off to play in the replay he went to this boss on Monday morning and explained his predicament. He requested that he be allowed away early from work the next day to meet the team bus. Now whether his boss didn't like him, or didn't like football or needed him, we were not quite sure, but his boss categorically refused to give him the time off.

My Dad went to his football coach that night and explained that he wouldn't be able to play in the replay. The coach thought otherwise and devised a plan.

The plan was that on Tuesday at 5 p.m. my Dad was to leave work jump on his bike and cycle like fury to the train station where he would meet a friend. His friend would hand him his football kit and take his bike off him. My Dad would then board the train to Glasgow. At Glasgow Queen Street Station he should get off and run as fast as he could to Glasgow Central Station. If he were fast enough, he would make the train to Ayr. He was to get changed into his football kit on that train and on arrival at Ayr a taxi would wait for him to take him to the ground. That meant he would arrive at the ground at 7.15 p.m. The plan was to start the game with only ten men and play the first fifteen minutes without him. That way when he arrived at the ground, they could bring him straight on and not have to carry out any substitutions. It might save time and wouldn't impact on them if they needed substitutes later.

The plan went well initially. My Dad left work at five, cycled to the station handing his bike to his friend and took his football kit from him in good time. Then, on route to Queen Street Station, the train got delayed a few minutes. When he got off, he ran as fast as he could to Glasgow Central Station but was seconds too late. As he ran into the station, he was just in time to see the Ayr train setting off. He checked the timings and realised that there wouldn't be another train for forty-five minutes. If he waited on that, he would not be able to get to the ground in time for the second half. So he jumped into a taxi and, despite the cost, asked to be taken to the football ground in Ayr.

The taxi set off and weaved its way slowly through the busy Glasgow traffic until it found the A77 to Ayr. Time was ticking away, but my Dad was confident he would make it by 7.30 p.m. and at least get some of the first half to make an impact. Then, disaster, the taxi had a puncture. By the time they changed the wheel, and they were on their way again my Dad wondered if he was going to make it at all. The taxi driver sensed his urgency and put his foot down to accommodate him.

They arrived at the ground at 8.15 p.m.; there were less than twenty-five minutes to play in the game. The coach had played with only ten men up until then, and they were losing 2 - 0. My Dad was brought straight on and put right up front as a centre forward.

He only got to play the last twenty minutes.

PC Gary Gorman seemed to think that was his story finished. He pulled out an apple and distractedly munched his way through it. I waited on him telling me more, but he seemed to have finished at that. I was eager to know.

"What was the final score?" I asked him impatiently.

"Oh, they lost 6 - 0," he told me as he devoured the last of his apple pips and core and all.

Aye, no as daft as he looks. He caught me hook, line, and sinker.

Chapter 15

A SIGN THAT YOU ARE GETTING A WEE BIT TETCHY

There was the occasional frustration with PC Gorman, but on the whole, I liked him fine. He wasn't the worst. There are some people I came across that just made me mad. I would like to think I am a pretty level-headed person and not one to lose my temper. There are occasions, however, when I can't help it. There is always one person in life who can rub you up the wrong way, get under your skin and make you fly off the handle. And that person, for me, was Sidney Bain.

Sidney Bain was the irritant who caused me to lose my cool. Sidney had the job title of driver/cleaner. It was simple really, his job was to drive and clean. His job description clearly stated he had to do two things:-

1. Drive the cars.
2. Clean the cars.

We asked nothing more of him. We didn't ask him to do odd jobs or the like. His only responsibility was to deliver mail, drive from point A to point B and return. Then he could choose any police car and clean it.

I suppose I'd been spoiled by the willingness and versatility of previous incumbents of the post. Good guys who, of their own volition, started work at 5 a.m. because that was when the cars were in the yard and available for cleaning. They not only cleaned them but maintained their tyre pressures, windscreen wash, oil, etc. They delivered the mail and came back. Prompt and willing. Always on the lookout for other ways to help out they would fix things around the office, clean paths of dirt or snow, tidy garages - anything to help.

Sidney Bain wasn't like that. No sooner was he appointed to the role of 'driver/cleaner', the cars slid into dirty disrepair. Rarely did he wash a car, he always had an excuse.

"I'm too busy driving and dropping things off here and there," he would say if asked to wash a car.

"I'm too busy washing cars," he would say if asked to deliver something somewhere.

Unfortunately, whenever we radioed him to ask him to do these jobs, he never answered the call. Either he didn't have his radio with him or, if he had it with him, it was switched off. When we needed him, we had to go searching for him and sometimes it was quicker making the delivery ourselves.

It became my mission to get him working. I sat him down in front of me and told him, in as clear terms as possible, when on duty he must carry his radio with him and have it switched on. His tendency towards buggerliness (a contemptible person's tendency towards the annoying) meant that he ignored this instruction and Sidney Bain continued to wander around the office without his radio.

I referred the matter to Inspector McTaggart who also called him into his office. Inspector McTaggart sat him down and told him this was no longer a joke he must carry his radio and keep it switched on. There would be no excuses. That very afternoon I radioed Sidney to ask him to do a job for me. Lo-and-behold there was no reply. I searched the office for Sidney, but couldn't find him anywhere. I called into the inspector's office to make him aware. There on the chair, where Sidney Bain had sat to get a telling off for not being available, was his radio.

I submitted a memo detailing the circumstances, Inspector McTaggart added his scathing comments and handed it to Chief Inspector Euphemia Miller.

Chief Inspector Miller took action. She called Sidney Bain into her office, sat him down and checked that he understood how to use his radio. She made him show her that he could operate it. Chief Inspector Miller then handed him a belt clip that acted as a radio dock. She watched him attach it to his belt. Now he had no excuses. He could attach the radio to his belt, and it would always be with him. She then made it clear to him that this was his last chance. Either he carried the radio with him and kept it switched on, or the matter would be taken further. It was his formal warning.

The next day I heard Inspector McTaggart radio for the driver/cleaner. "Inspector to driver/cleaner Bain, Inspector to driver/cleaner Bain."

There was no reply.

Inspector McTaggart tried a few more times, but on each occasion, there was silence. At that precise moment, I saw Sidney wander past my window in the back yard. I knocked on the window to grab his attention and shouted to him that Inspector McTaggart was calling him on his radio. I could see that Sidney wasn't carrying his radio. Sidney marched off. I shook my head and sat down at my desk. A few seconds later Sidney blustered into my office.

"What do you mean the inspector has been calling me on the radio? He has not been calling me," he was most indignant about it.

I turned in my chair to face him. Calmly I told him, "Look, you have been told a hundred times to carry your radio and keep it switched on. I told you two weeks ago. Inspector McTaggart told you a week ago. The Chief Inspector told you yesterday and made it clear that was your last warning. When on duty you carry your radio with you at all times and keep it switched on. You do not have your radio with you now, so how on earth would you know if the inspector had been calling you on the radio or not?"

He looked at me searching his mind for an excuse.

"You don't expect me to carry it to the toilet do you?" he asked.

"Yes I do. I carry my radio to the toilet. I expect you to carry your radio to the toilet with you. You don't have to answer it right there and then in mid flow, but you could listen to it, and as soon as you have finished, you could call anyone back that has been calling you." I let that sink in before continuing.

"In any case when Inspector McTaggart called you just now, you were wandering aimlessly out the back yard without your radio and nowhere near the toilet."

"Look, son," he said, "I'm just trying to help you."

"Well, you are not helping. Now get your radio and then go see what Inspector McTaggart wants you for." My voice soft like a Dad speaking to an errant toddler.

"Look, son," he said again, "I'm just trying to help you."

"Well, you are not helping. Now go and get your radio and then go see the inspector and see what he wants," I told him again.

"Look, son," he said for a third time, "I'm just trying to help you," he stood there looking at me as if I had a massive plook growing from my forehead.

This wasn't getting my work done.

"Well, you are not helping. Now get your radio and then see what the inspector wants," this time a little louder and a little more firmly.

"Look, son," he said, "I'm just trying to help you."

"Get out of my office."

"Look, son," he said, "I'm just trying to help you."

"Get out of my office. I have work to do," I told Sidney again raising my voice so he would be in no doubt that he was now beginning to rile me.

"Look, son," he said, "I'm just trying to help you."

Sidney Bain stood there in my office looking at me like a demented frog. His job description was to drive and clean, he rarely did the former and never did the latter. We could never get a hold of him when we needed him because he wouldn't carry his radio with him. I had spoken to him, and it made no difference, and the inspector had spoken to him about it, and it made no difference. The chief inspector had given him a formal warning; this had gone in one ear and out his backside. Now I was having this surreal conversation with him, stuck in a loop. I had told him to get out of my office six times, and each time he had inexplicably ignored this instruction and told me he was 'just trying to help me'. It wasn't helping it was making me mad.

I couldn't quite put my finger on it, but there was something about him that rubbed me up the wrong way.

"FECK OFF OUT MY OFFICE!"

"Look, son," he said, "I'm just trying to help you."

I then told him to "FECK OFF OUT MY OFFICE!" ten times in a row. Each time I raised my voice louder and louder and each time he replied, "Look, son, I'm just trying to help you."

On my last "FECK OFF OUT OF MY OFFICE!" I realised I could be heard all throughout the entire police station and that this wasn't a good situation. I got up and leave before I ended up losing it completely. Murder carries stiff penalties, what went through my mind could put me in jail for thirty years - and that might not have been a deal-breaker.

As I left my office to escape the irritating imbecile, I slammed my door shut so hard that the

'Sergeant' sign on the outside came flying off and bounced down the corridor.

Now that is a sign you are getting just a wee bit tetchy.

As soon as I stepped out of the office, I saw every eye on me. John, the custody sergeant, had stepped out of the cells to see what I was shouting at and looked at me as if I had gone mad, several cops had poked their heads out of the report room and were eyeing me warily. I calmed down, forced a smile onto my face and ushered them back to their offices. John approached me, "What's going on?" he asked.

"Feckin Sidney Bain is what is going on," I explained, "I pulled him up for wandering outside without his radio, and he marched into my office as if I was telling him to piss on his mother's grave. So I asked him to leave about a million times, but he just stood there saying 'I'm just trying to help you'. That is what is going on. He is still in there. I had to get out before I hit him."

John nodded, opened the door to my office and saw Sidney standing there in his dishevelled clothes, rough growth, and glaikit expression.

"Why didn't you leave the office when Sergeant McEwan asked you?" John asked him.

"I was just trying to help him."

"What exactly were you trying to help him with?" John asked.

Sidney Bain stood, and his eyes rolled upwards, searching his brain for a reason. Only now did he seem even to understand what he had been saying. A full twenty seconds passed as John and I watched Sidney try to come up with a reason for his disconcerting presence in my office. Sidney frantically darted his eyes around, looking for inspiration. His eyes settled on the 'Sergeant' sign lying on the floor.

"I could help him put that sign back up on the door," he said, as if it explained everything.

Despite Sidney Bain making me a little irritable, I was never as bad as Ian Angry. Ian Angry was a sergeant famous across our area for having a rather volatile temperament. He seemed to get less and less tolerant as the years went by. He was a good thief catcher in his early days, and his efforts were rewarded by a position in the CID, where he stayed for many years. Once promoted to sergeant, he went back to uniform and took charge of a shift.

Once back in uniform every little thing irritated him. The least little inconvenience got under his skin. Bosses ignored complaints from the public regarding his behaviour as best they could. They ignored his occasional rants when he attended meetings. They ignored him when he vented his feelings about something or other as he passed in the corridor.

They stopped ignoring him when he turned up in their offices and ranted about this that and the next thing. Their patience with him dried up. Sergeant Ian Angry found himself transferred to the furthest station away from headquarters they could. His new station was a small outpost in the middle of nowhere. Out of sight and out of mind.

Sergeant Ian Angry's new station became a place to avoid. Cops who worked there spent most of their shift out on patrol, returning only at his beckoning. Often just to deal with someone who had dared to call at his office with their 'trivia'.

Nobody from headquarters phoned Sergeant Ian Angry, and nobody was available to speak to him when he phoned in. He sat in his chair within his office in his little outpost seething away waiting for the day, which couldn't come soon enough, when he could retire.

One day an unfortunate cop was sitting in the office with Sergeant Ian Angry when the phone rang. The cop had only ventured back to the office because he had a report to write. The phone ringing was an unusual event. It resulted in both Sergeant Ian Angry and the cop staring at the phone for several rings before Sergeant Ian Angry moved into action. He picked up the receiver and put it to his ear, "Hello, police, Sergeant Ian Angry speaking."

The cop later described the next few moments as being surreal. Sergeant Ian Angry had a short conversation with the caller on the other end then screamed, "FUCKING WHAT!"

He slammed the receiver down on the phone, so hard that the Bakelite simply shattered. He then grabbed the phone cord and pulled it with all his might causing the wall socket to dislodge itself. Sergeant Ian Angry picked up what remained of the phone and threw it as hard as he could muster against the back wall of the office. The phone smashed against the wall leaving a clear indentation where it had struck. The vibrations of the impact caused a picture (Sergeant Ian Angry in full regalia) to fall to the ground and crack.

"THE BASTARDS!"

The cop sat in dread of what might happen to himself but curiosity eventually overcame his fear, and he plucked up the courage to ask.

"What's the matter, Sarge?"

"THEY'VE ONLY FUCKING GONE AND CANCELLED MY ANGER MANAGEMENT COURSE AGAIN!"

Sergeant Angry may well have benefited from knowing Big Bob's anger management technique. Big Bob had an anger management technique that worked like a Swiss watch. When he had a bad day, he didn't take it out on those he loved. He didn't take it out on his friends or colleagues. Big Bob was always mellow and cheery. I never found Big Bob in a bad mood, irritated, or annoyed.

"How come you are always in a good mood," I asked Big Bob one day.

"I've got an anger management technique."

"Tell me more."

"I discovered this technique by accident. One day I was sitting at my desk making a phone call. A man answered, and I asked to speak to the person I was phoning. The reply I got was shocking. The man screamed down the phone:-

"'GET THE RIGHT FUCKING NUMBER!' and he verbally abused me, my mother, my father and even questioned my gender orientation. At the end of his tirade of abuse, he hung up. I stared at the phone in disbelief, astonished at his outburst, indignant at his unwarranted outburst. I couldn't believe anyone could use such language with a complete stranger. I checked the number and realised I had accidentally transposed the last two digits. Yes, it was my fault I had called the wrong number. However, he didn't need to speak like that. The manner of his abuse was outrageous. That is when I came up with my 'anger management technique'. I called the same wrong number again. When the same guy answered I told him, 'You're a plook* on the face of humanity,' and hung up."

A plook is a Scottish word for a large nauseating facial pimple.

This amused me no end and nodded in encouragement, and there was more. Big Bob continued.

"I then wrote his number down and kept it in a drawer by my desk. Two weeks later I was having a bad day. The sergeant had lumped more work on me, and I was under pressure. I went to my drawer to get a pen and noticed the number I had written. So I picked up the phone dialled the number, and when he answered I said, 'Is this the householder?' He said, 'Yes, what do you want?' I asked if I could speak to his wife."

I was almost laughing already. I could just picture Big Bob with the phone to his ear and a mischievous grin on his face.

"What did he say?"

"He told me he wasn't married. So I replied, 'That's because you are a big plook!' And hung up. It made me feel a little better. I had a smile to myself and got on with my work."

That was funny; I laughed as Bob continued.

"It became a lovely little support mechanism after that. Whenever a big credit card bill came in, or came up against life's other frustrations I called his number. I would do it even just to cheer myself up. I did it at random, and so quickly he never had the chance to say anything back as I would immediately hang up. Occasionally I varied the message, 'Hi, this is John Smith from BT, I am calling to see if you are familiar with our friends and family system?' 'NO. I AM FUCKING NOT. SO PISS OFF!' he said and slammed down the phone. He was still as big an arsehole as he had always been. With my conviction re-invigorated I called him back moments later, 'That's because you are a big, yellow headed plook!' That cheered me up no end."

I was holding my sides with glee.

"Then one day I was at the supermarket waiting for a car to reverse out of its parking spot. A black

BMW drove in, cut me off and pulled into the spot I had been waiting for. I stuck my head out the window as the driver got out and told him I had been waiting for that spot. The driver turned told me to 'fuck off' and walked away. 'How rude' I thought."

"What did you do to him?"

"I noticed he had a for sale sign in the back window of the BMW so after I found another parking spot I went back and noted the number. Now I had two therapeutic numbers to call. Their attitude warranted me reminding them that they were the acne on the face of humankind. So that night I called the owner of the BMW. This is how the conversation went.

'Is this the man with the BMW for sale?'

'Yes, it is', he replied.

'Can you tell me where I can see it?'

'Yes. I live at 5 Greenbank Crescent. It's a bungalow, and the car's out front?'

'What's your name?'

'John Carmichael.'

'When is a good time to catch you, John?'

'I am home every evening after six, and I am home right now.'

'Listen, John, can I tell you something?'

'Yes.'

'John, you are a bit of a plook!' and I hung up.

'I then phoned my first therapeutic number, 'Hello,' he answered.'

'You are a plook!" I told him for the umpteenth time, but on this occasion, I didn't hang up.'

'Are you still there?' He asked.

'Yes.'

"STOP FUCKING CALLING ME!' he shouted.

'Make me!'

"IF I EVER FIND OUT WHO YOU ARE, I WILL FUCKING MAKE YOU!"

'My name is John Carmichael,' I replied
'YEAH! WHERE DO YOU LIVE?'
'I live at 5 Greenbank Crescent. It's a bungalow, and my black BMW is sitting right outside. Not that a big plook like you could do anything about it?'
'I AM COMING OVER RIGHT NOW, JOHN. YOU HAD BETTER START SAYING YOUR PRAYERS!' he roared down the phone.'
'I will recognise your big yellow head then!' I said to wind him up a little more.
I then called back John Carmichael.
'Hello.' he answered.
'Hello plook!'
'If I ever find out who you are...'
'You'll what?'
'I'll kick your backside!' and he directed a tirade of verbal abuse at me.
'Well here is your chance because I am coming over right now!' I then hung up."

Big Bob's anger management technique worked. I had never seen him get even the slightest bit tetchy.

If such an anger management technique isn't quite to your taste, or you worry about 'caller ID' then there is a much more composed method you can use. If, like me, you are prone to getting two or three items of junk mail in your post: fret at the waste of another tree here is what you can do. Use the pre-paid reply envelope to send other company's junk mail to them. It never fails to put a smile on my face. I think of it as a service to the sender. I'm not interested in learning how to make an extra £500 per week on the 'forex', but you never know the person who opens the letters at the forex company might just need a loan. After all, he or she should have easy access to their investment opportunity.

Tearing up and binning all that sales material seems to be a dreadful waste of good trees. Posting unwanted mail back to those companies is much more therapeutic. One looks forward to the next pre-paid envelope to drop through the letter-box, especially when you get a nice *'free pen just for getting a quote on your insurance'* letter waiting to pop it in.

Hell, even if it is not a pre-paid envelope, make sure your name and address isn't on it and just send it back anyway. It might make the sender think twice if he has to pay the postage twice - and still get no sale. I suspect that if more people did this as a courteous service, there'd be more trees for us to hug.

Chapter 16

CIVILISED SOCIETY HUH!

As a constable the sergeant often sent me out to patrol the streets on foot - Groan. I always felt I had more important things to do, places to go and people to charge. Why should I wander aimlessly around the town centre when I had investigations to follow up and enquiries to do? Walking the beat was boring. It was often cold or wet or both.

Why did I always get this crap job?

Over the years, my opinion changed. Plod the beat? Sure. I realised that it was my chance to slow the pace. When I went out walking in uniform people stop and talk, and they seemed pleased to see an officer on the beat. Reassured by my presence. Well, that was what the law-abiding members of the public felt.

I learned things too. It is surprising what people would tell me simply because I was there. Little nuggets of information that could help put the bad guys away. Most people are lazy in telling the police stuff that matters. We had to seek the information we required - unless walking the beat. Then they couldn't wait to let you in on the fact that Johnny tried to sell them a stolen lawn-mower or their neighbour always drove home from the pub at 11.05pm on the dot and staggered into their house as drunk as a lord. There was never any thought of phoning the police at the time that was too much like hard work. But bump into a uniform three weeks later, and they would open up like an overripe avocado.

So it was relaxing and fun to walk the streets during the day. Not so much when there was nobody around. When it was quiet walking the streets and checking property was boring. It helped when a colleague accompanied me. I liked a bit of banter.

One quiet Sunday afternoon I was sitting at my desk catching up on my paperwork when the duty inspector called into my office. Inspector Susan (Sue) Rennie was a prim and proper person and not one for nonsense or spontaneous humour. Respected for her professionalism but regarded as somewhat standoffish and unapproachable (not least because she always smelled of garlic). It was a surprise then when she asked me to go on foot patrol with her for an hour. I willingly abandoned my paperwork, and we headed out to walk the town. I wondered if she had an ulterior motive so remained on my guard.

Despite my initial suspicions, Inspector Rennie was laid-back and seemed to have no secret agenda. She wanted to enjoy a pleasant walk and have a chat. I learned that she was due to retire in less than a year and that she had no plans to do anything else. Perhaps she was already on the wind-down. The nearer you get to retirement the more you long for it and the less hassle you seem to want. And the less hassle you want to dish out. Inspector Rennie and I chatted about all sorts. There was no mention of work, no gossiping about colleagues and no moaning about bosses. The three topics all police tend to veer their conversations towards. Instead, we covered a gamut of subjects. I learned that we shared a love of reading. However, our literary tastes were somewhat out of sync. She loved gardening; I didn't - so we moved on from that. Her favourite TV programme was Coronation Street or was it Eastenders? Anyway, it was some inane soap she liked to switch her brain off to watch. Not my cup of tea. Then we found a topic we both liked - dogs. Sue had been looking for a dog for some time. She told me she was keen to get a dog when she retired. Pictured an idyllic life for herself walking the dog twice a day, catching up on her reading and pottering about in her garden.

"What breed of a dog would you like?"

"I'm not sure," she replied, "I don't want a big dog, although I think those Labradoodles are just gorgeous. I don't want anything too boisterous either. I don't want to be walking for miles every day. Maybe just a little lap dog that will keep me company."

There were lots of people out walking their dogs, and as we carried on with our leisurely patrol, I saw two pug-like dogs coming towards us. I turned to Inspector Rennie and asked, "What about a Shih Tzu?" correctly identifying the breed of the two dogs headed towards us.

Inspector Sue Rennie turned towards me with a puzzled look on her face and in all seriousness responded, "No... I'm fine thanks."

I nearly peed myself. It was, in fact, some minutes before I could stop laughing and even longer before Inspector 'Tzu' Rennie realised what she had said.

A few years later I was driving through; the now retired, Inspector Rennie's hometown and saw her walking into the local park with a little fluffy, grey and white Shih Tzu on a lead. It seems that Sue wanted a Shitz after all.

As a sergeant, I didn't get much time to walk the streets. Every time I extricated myself from the office someone would need me for something. It happened again. A quiet Tuesday evening and I had just managed five steps out the door when my radio interrupted what would have been a pleasant summer evening stroll.

"PC McTear to Sarge, come in over,"

"Go ahead, Tommy."

"Sarge, that's us arrived at the mortuary with our sudden death, would you like to join us to examine the body?"

"I'll head back to the office and get a car, be with you shortly," I informed him.

If you can't be bothered with frauds,
Thefts, assaults and all that palaver -
Go and examine a cadaver.

In every death where a doctor is not prepared to certify the cause - for whatever reason - the police take possession of the body and investigate. Unless there is something obvious that would suggest a wrongful death the investigation is limited to getting details of medical history, finding out the deceased's last movements and examination of the body for any signs of violence. Sergeants are supposed to be experienced in these matters, so we get the job of double checking.

I was now heading to the mortuary to view PC Tommy McTear's cadaver. A sixty-five-year-old ex-miner who had smoked since he was twelve. He had been suffering from various bronchial complaints, but the doctor who had came out was not his usual doctor and had no knowledge of his previous medical history. Thus he was not prepared to certify the cause of death. It all sounded routine. I was going to examine the body with my usual solemn deference then get back to my paperwork.

It is a basic principle of civilised society that we treat the dead with respect. The measure of how far we have come along the path of evolutionary progress is surely best measured on this principle. The ancient Greek philosopher Diogenes professed that he didn't want buried when he died. He asked that his body be

270

thrown over the city wall so wild animals could devour it.

"What harm can the mangling of wild beasts do to me if I am without consciousness?" he asked.

What does it matter to him when he is dead? He's asking. His body is but an empty shell. His remains will feel no pain. Why not discard it so other animals can use it for sustenance? It will make no difference to him whether his remains are buried or not, for he will not know the difference. Diogenes thought it stupid and wasteful to spend time and money in the ritual burial of the dead. No need to fuss. Diogenes's life, therefore, was one of extreme simplicity, inured to want and without shame.

Diogenes's way of thinking perhaps has some merit. Maybe he got it right. Why should any of us care what happens to us when we die? We will be dead, and there will be no more conscious thought. Our bodies will reduced to dust and returned to the earth.

Diogenes was a real grumpy bastard when it came to his beliefs.

Unfortunately for those around him, Diogenes was also a man who also professed that people should not be embarrassed to do private things in public, it is recorded that he masturbated and defecated openly in front of others.

"Meeting one's natural needs cannot be shameful or indecent," he espoused.

Tell that to the judge!

Despite the logic behind Diogenes's thinking, it is unimaginable to us that we would leave our dead to the animals. We have come far from our hunter/gatherer history and our basic survival needs. The dead matter to us for we have lived with them loved them and wish to remember them.

We can measure our development against where we were in the past. Our ancestors became more educated and recognised our obligation to treat our dead with deference. Further along our civilised route we not only treated our dead with reverence but erected monuments to mark their final resting place on earth. These final resting places we adorn with words of veneration and refresh with flowers in commemoration. Thus we live in a civilised society watched over by police officers who have high moral standing. They are the respected members of our civilisation. We look up to them and their humanitarian stance.

Sometimes, however, humans can revert to their roots. In times of war, in times of drought, when there is severe poverty or disease, the remains of our fellow man are occasionally discarded without pomp or ceremony. Our respect for the dead simply abandoned. A time when all decency and regard is momentarily put to the side.

There are other times when people show no reverence. Sometimes this is out of an innate evilness in the person, a psychopath, for example, has no feelings for a person alive, far less dead. A corpse is just a lifeless lump to them. It may be due to nurture - disrespect for the dead, born from being dragged up by parents who know no better.

Then again sometimes, in the case of the police, it can be a coping strategy to make light of what will happen to us all. The police can become inured to dealing with death. Out of a need to go home and exist without bad thoughts in our heads. We have to make light of death. It is a survival trick that ensures good mental health. Thus cops, on the odd occasion, are not so respectful of the deceased.

I called into the mortuary and met PC Tommy McTear. He and his probationer had taken the initial call. They had obtained all the necessary details at the deceased's home, contacted the undertaker and had the body removed to the mortuary. My expectation was that they would have stripped the body, tagged the toe, completed the details in the big black book and would be ready to slide the man into the large mortuary fridge once I had a cursory look. I entered through the rear roller doors, which allowed the undertakers to drive right in and remove the body from their hearse without being seen by any passersby.

The rear of the mortuary, as you would expect, is a clinical area. Tiled floors allow for easy cleaning. The mortuary refrigerator extends down one wall offering three levels of compartments where the corpses are stored. A trolley sat in the middle of the floor, at one end of the trolley a handle extended upwards. The handle pumps the hydraulics and sets the tray to the correct height for sliding into position in the appropriate compartment of the refrigerator. At the far end of the mortuary is a small desk and chair where they keep the black book. Details of all bodies, coming or going, are recorded.

My initial confusion started with the trolley. It was empty.

Surely they hadn't put the body into the refrigerator already? Tommy Toolbag should know better than that. If they had, I would have to ask them to get the deceased out again, that would be a bit embarrassing for Tommy, showing him up in front of his probationer because he didn't know the procedure.

Then my confusion changed. Who was the man sitting on the chair by the desk? Why was he wearing sunglasses? Why was he smoking a cigarette in here? Why did he look so pale?

Then it dawned on me. As my facial expression changed from bewilderment to astonishment, Tommy Toolbag and his probationer burst out laughing. Big hearty guffaws at my bewilderment. I couldn't help it. Fortunately for them, I'm not without a sense of humour. I couldn't help myself either, my face cracked into a smile, then I too burst into laughter. Guilty laughter. Almost as quickly I straightened my face.

"Get that cigarette out of that bloody corpse's mouth and get him on this trolley before someone comes in and catches you."

On the drive back to the office I couldn't help but shake my head at the thought. I mean, who else but Tommy Toolbag would think of propping up a dead man on a chair, putting a pair of sunglasses on him and sticking a lit a cigarette in his mouth.

Chapter 17

HOW TO DEAL WITH DRUNKS

The busiest pubs and clubs hire bouncers or 'door stewards', to give them their preferred title. Their job is not to stop people from getting in. Getting in is not a problem. The job of the bouncer is to kick them out once they have become drunk and argumentative. The pubs and clubs serve them with copious amounts of alcohol, and some punters become a problem. So the bouncer ejects them from the premises. That drunk and argumentative person is no longer their problem, he (or she) become a problem for the police.

Beer battered drunks are a cop's bread and butter. Most incidents the police deal with during the night will result from over-indulgence in alcohol. Dealing with drunks is notoriously difficult. You can't reason with them, they can be belligerent, they make no sense, they argue, they think they are invincible, and you still have to make sure they do not come to any harm.

It is against the law to be in a public place if you are drunk and incapable of taking care of yourself. (We used the abbreviation 'D&I'). In days gone by police would scoop up drunks from the streets and pour them into a cell for the night. There they would remain there until they dried out and were fit to go back into the community. They left the Police Office with nothing to look forward to but a court appearance and fine. It made for an expensive night out for them. If it didn't deter them from doing it again, it would ensure they were less likely to afford it.

Then things changed. Procurator Fiscals concluded that dealing with D&I offences were wasting their time. Thus they decreed that unless it was a third offence, committed within a calendar year, they were not interested. There would be no prosecution unless they met that criteria. It didn't matter that this wasted more police time, we still had to deal with them and record the offences. We had to ensure their wellbeing, provide a safe cell for them to sleep it off and process them as we would a normal prisoner. Then, once they had sobered up, we issued them a warning letter.

Dear Mr Drunk,

On this occasion, we will not be taking any further action. Don't do it again otherwise; you may receive a fine.

Signed

The Chief Constable

No need to bother the Procurator Fiscal with a report. With no monetary punishment, they would still have money to spend on more booze. The only thing they had learned was that if they got into the same state again, we would take care of them. They'd get a bed for the night and a cup of tea in the morning.

With the lack of deterrent, drunkards continued to get drunk. Their offences totted up until they triggered the three times in one year rule. Then we had to report them to the Procurator Fiscal. The Procurators Fiscals found even this too onerous a task for them. It was such a waste of their time. So they changed the system again.

We were issued with a fixed penalty book to avoid any Procurator Fiscal involvement. Drunks ended up with a £40 fine. Drunks would rather spend their money on drink than pay fines. So in due course, the Procurator Fiscals had to get involved again and issue warrants for non-payment of the fines. It didn't matter that this tied up many police officers executing these warrants, but it was sufficiently irksome for the Procurator Fiscals to change the system once more.

So the system nowadays, instead of being reported to the procurator fiscal, or totting up offences until they trigger the criteria for reporting or issuing of fixed penalty fines, the police were simply instructed to go back to giving drunks a warning letter. The police still have to go through the process of arresting them, making sure they receive medical attention and check on them every fifteen minutes as they sleep it off in the cells. When they waken they get a shower and some breakfast and we'd hand them the new standard pro forma letter on their way out.

Dear Mr Drunk,

Gonnae no dae that!

Signed

The Chief Constable

I was always more concerned with the wellbeing of a drunk. It wasn't about notching up another charge. It was all about making sure we left no-one in harm's way. We don't want people freezing to death on the streets or choking on their vomit. My concern reflected in the 'keeping people safe' police philosophy. What if the person is ill and not drunk? Some people who have diabetes can appear drunk when suffering a diabetic complication that can cause unconsciousness. How can we tell for sure? The simple answer to that, 'we can't'.

So these days cops have to take all drunks straight to the hospital. Custody Sergeants don't want to the responsibility for someone who might be ill. They want every drunk seen by a medical practitioner to confirm they are fit to be detained.

At the hospital, cops have to wait in the Accident and Emergency Department (A&E), often for several hours, until a doctor becomes available to examine their charge. The doctor will invariably take one look at the drunk and declare him 'fit to be detained'. The cops, armed with medical confirmation, can then return to the drunk to the custody suite.

Cops can spend more than half a shift dealing with one such person, and it can take years to learn the secrets of dealing with them without tearing your hair out. Drunk people can be arrogant, indignant, argumentative and infuriatingly thickheaded. It is often an effort to get them into a van, either because they don't want to go or physically have to be poured in.

In time, I developed a foolproof method for dealing with drunks.

The drunk was lying with his feet stretched out on the pavement and the rest of his body supported by the pillar box. It was a tricky balancing act for him as the cylindrical pillar box meant any slight movement left, or right sent his head careering towards the hard stone pavement. With no little perseverance, the drunk hauled himself back up only to remain balanced for a few seconds and fall in the opposite direction.

The object of the exercise, for me, was to get this drunk into the car, take him home and deposit him in the care of a more sober family member. I didn't want to arrest him. The offence of being drunk and incapable is only complete if there is no suitable person to look after them. Find a suitable person, and it can save a lot of time and hassle.

I tried a liberal dose of gentle persuasion to get the drunk up and into the car. I failed. Trying to be his best friend resulted in him telling me he loved me but didn't get him off the ground.

I then gave him a right good rollicking. I failed again. He considered a rollicking to be an invitation to fight and while this got him to his feet his attempt to punch me only unbalanced him and sent him clattering back down to the ground.

I tried to lift him into the car; this resulted in him being entered head first onto the backseat but with his legs still dangling outside. I failed again. He now thought he was being arrested for nothing and became argumentative and obstructive. He wouldn't put his feet into the car and repeatedly asked why he was being arrested.

I tried patience, explained that he wasn't being arrested and that I would take him home. I failed again.

"For the 16th time YOU ARE NOT BEING ARRESTED, get in the car tell me your address, and we will take you home."

"SSHWHY ARSH YOU FUGGING ARRESTING ME?" He replied.

I considered brute force - a tactical option. With much effort, I lifted his feet and pushed them in the rear door before slamming it shut, a millisecond before he could stick them out again. I failed spectacularly. He caught his little finger in the door, and he spent the next fifteen minutes abusing me and threatening to sue, rather than telling me his address.

Eventually, I extricated his wallet from his trouser pocket and found a driving licence with his address on it. I conveyed him home and deposited in the care of his 'loving' wife. She left him on the hallway floor and went back to bed.

The secret to dealing with drunks is, therefore, this:-
The next time you see the Detective Inspector lying drunk on the pavement - call an ambulance and let them deal with it. (Nothing worse than a D&I DI).
No wonder I needed a break.

Chapter 18

HOW TO GET PROMOTED

In 1829 the Home Secretary, Sir Robert Peel, introduced the first London policemen. They became known as 'Peelers' or 'Bobbies'. We don't use 'Peelers' anymore but we still occasionally refer to the police as 'Bobbies'. More frequently used nicknames make no reference to Sir Robert Peel but infer that police officers are parentless lotharios.

Scotland was thirty years ahead of Sir Robert Peel with the City of Glasgow Police being introduced in 1800 along with six other forces across Scotland shortly after. All those years of extra experience have stood us in good stead. In modern times English detection rates hover between 20% - 25%. In Scotland, they are double that. With that in mind, I was surprised to hear two of our senior detectives were heading off down south to attend a conference at the top English force, held in high esteem for a detection rate of 27%. They were so proud of their record they were keen to pass on their working practices and knowledge to others. Considering that our force held a detection rate of 52% I presumed that our senior detectives headed down for a jolly good gloat - the emphasis being on the word 'jolly'.

So in 1800, the first Chief of Police was Mr John Stenhouse, appointed on a salary of £200 per annum; also appointed were two sergeants and six officers. I am not sure why they appointed Mr John Stenhouse to the role as his background was as a City Merchant. His salary of £200 per annum is equivalent to less than £12,000 today, so it would appear that he didn't do it for the money. His small force was a great success. Many of the city's criminal inhabitants had to up and leave. It promoted demands for similar forces across other areas on the outskirts of Glasgow - where the ousted criminals turned up.

It would suggest that Mr John Stenhouse was a motivated, honest, and hardworking man and that these qualities had been instrumental in his appointment as Chief of Glasgow City Police. Good qualities such as those should be a prerequisite for promotion.

It is not until circa 1840 that we get an idea of what our police officers looked like. The arrival of the daguerreotype camera giving us yellowed photographs of our early police officers. There are limited images available, but there are still sufficient in existence to make an educated guess on the criteria used for promotion.

This is my theory:-

From the 1840s to the 1870s you had to be male (there are no female police officers on the scene until the 20th century). From the pictures available, the one and only criteria used after that was the size of your pipe. (Not a euphemism). The larger the pipe you smoked, the more likely you were to be sitting in the middle of a group of police with rank insignia on your arm and hat. Pipe-smokers rejoice.

The twentieth century saw a change. An era that provided much more evidence from old photographs and written accounts for getting that extra rank. Out went the pipe smoking prerequisite for promotion and in came the facial hair formula.

The facial hair formula is the best way to work out the rank of a police officer from the 1900's to the 1930's. A small wispy moustache, nothing more than bum fluff on an upper lip, would indicate a low ranked young lad. A fuller moustache, like a caterpillar glued beneath the nose, would be a sign of a more experienced constable. A full blown 'Magnum PI' chevron moustache would coincide with a chevron on the epaulette and shoulder. A painter's brush, capable of whitewashing an average sized room in a couple of hours, would confirm the rank of inspector. Finally, the man in charge, the Chief of Police, would sit in the middle of the photograph, walrus moustache pride of place covering his entire upper lip and Garibaldi beard covering his lower lip. If there was any doubt about who had the most hirsute face, then you could be sure that the deciding factor for promotion would come down to the severity of expression. The less happy you were about life, the further up the ranks you go.

The war years saw an increase in the age and flat-footedness of the average police officer. The war required young men to fight it. A lot of police officers were ex-forces, men who had been soldiers. Trained men were essential to the war effort and returned to old units. The police had to make do with the leftovers, those that managed to dodge the draft. They still made promotions during the war, so for a long time after if you see a picture of a group of police, in amongst the newly sworn-in strapping men would be a weedy old fellow looking decidedly uncomfortable in his senior rank.

The tide turned.

In due course, through the 70s and 80s, the promotion criteria changed. Height became the benchmark to which to aspire. The taller you were, the more likely you would end up in a higher rank. It is a well-known phenomenon in just about every occupation (jockeys excluded) that, on average, taller men earn more and achieve a higher position in every organisation. The police were no different. It was a prejudiced perception that perpetuated. Who wants bossed by Hitler or Napoleon? They even have a syndrome named after those short-arses.

283

When I joined the police in the early eighties, I didn't pay that much attention to the promotion process. When I think back, I recall that my sergeant was quite tall and my inspector even taller. I wasn't all that conscious at the time; When I think back, I am sure that there was a link between height and rank.

In the nineties, there was a general move away from the correlation between height and rank. A new trend was emerging. There was a definite suspicion mooted amongst the ordinary polis that you had to have a connection with the police football team. It was no coincidence that the recruiting sergeant, at the time, was in charge of the police football section. Anyone with any professional experience in the football arena could swap their football kit for a uniform. Days off to play in the Force Football Team granted from day one.

Such was the success of our soccer boys that our good chief constable showed his appreciation in the form of awarding stripes, pips, and scrambled egg. In turn, nepotism dragged other teammates into positions of higher rank. Senior officer meetings often took place in a four-four-two formation. Their meetings ran smoothly only if there were a referee and a whistle present. I paid no heed. I was getting on with learning the job. I never rolled my eyes when I heard a twat got promoted, how did I know if they deserved it or not? It was the people who commented negatively about others being promoted that I used to think were the ones I wouldn't put in charge of a toilet brush.

The dawn of the 21st century would signal yet another new era. It was the start of the equal opportunity movement. Education can only do so much - once a racist, homophobic, misogynist always a racist, homophobic, misogynist.

Left to their own devices kids include anyone in their circle of friends, no matter their colour, background, sex, or sexual orientation. To end up a racist, homophobic, misogynist back end of a sewage outlet, they have to learn that behaviour from another racist, homophobic, misogynist rear end. So it perpetuates.

Police forces came in for some scathing criticism for their lack of diversity. Something needed done. The police were under-represented in all ethnic minority groups. The police did not mirror the communities they served, did not promote enough females to balance the demographics, had a culture that bordered on the homophobic. Police forces showed institutional racism. In a time when women were reaching the south pole, they were being discriminated against in all walks of life. Despite all their achievements, women couldn't get paid the same as men for doing the same job. The Prime Minister at the time,Tony Blair, was on the receiving end of their wrath and received a hostile reception during a speech at the Women's Institute - heckled and slow hand-clapped by the members. No change there then, Tony.

It was time to do something about it. It required positive action. Positive action differs from positive discrimination. Discrimination is, in fact, illegal. What positive action did was level the playing field - or at least try to. Ethnic minorities, disadvantaged by years of negative discrimination, got a leg up to the starting post. Education, tools for learning and other resources provided to those who didn't have access to those things before. Then, and only then, were they thrown in with everyone else to go through the recruitment procedures or the promotion processes.

It worked, more women got promoted, and once again facial hair became an indicator of rank (just joking). It worked to a certain extent.

So how did I end up getting another promotion in this climate?

Well, it was easy. I hedged my bets, bought a large pipe, grew an extra four inches, a handlebar moustache and goatee beard. I had a sex change, scored a goal in a five-a-side game, got diagnosed with flat feet, and et voila - Inspector here I come.

In truth - I had an idea. I put that idea into practice, and I received my promotion. I'll tell you all about my idea in my next book, so keep your eyes open for:

'How to be the most OUTSTANDING COP in the world - in a silly way'.

It has even more tales of Derring-Do, dopey goings on and hilarity.

ADDENDUM

In the interests of plausible deniability, one of these stories is totally untrue. If you have any issues with any particular story - that was the one I fabricated.

A wee note from Malky.

Oh good, you made it to the end. I hope you enjoyed it. Would you be so kind as to give it a rating on Amazon, please? One way to help establish this book's status as an entertaining source for others is to read your esteemed opinion and review of the book.

Many thanks.

Malky

Malky McEwan writes to tickle, inspire, and make you think.

For police humour to tickle and delight:

'The *really* FUNNY thing about being a COP'

The exciting things, the funny incidents, the strange goings on, and the comic situations are what remains of a thirty year and two-month career in the police. So here they are, guaranteed to make you laugh out loud.

How to be the most OUTSTANDING COP in the world
(In a silly way)

The hilarious conclusion to a thirty-year and two-month career in the police. Meet Constable WTF Jones, the legendary Tony Maloney and PC Wally Walker. Learn about the sweetie jar principle and even why you should never keep a kiwi under your bed.

Keep your colleagues amused and never be bored at work again with the *Lateral Thinking Puzzle* books:

'Outstanding' Fiendish & Fun Lateral Thinking Puzzles

My favourite puzzle here is 'The milk container' which always gets the biggest 'AHA' moment.

'Even Better' Fiendish & Fun Lateral Thinking Puzzles

'My favourite puzzle here is 'Skiving' which was an absolutely, fit to burst, hilarious scenario that really did happen. It still makes me smile to this day.'

'The Ultimate' Fiendish & Fun Lateral Thinking Puzzles

My favourite puzzle here is 'How to deal with time wasters' which has such an elegant solution. I genuinely used at work to stop time wasters in their tracks. It never offended anyone and worked every time. There is a slight twist if you want to get to the right answer.

Now, he's turned his attention to Scotland.

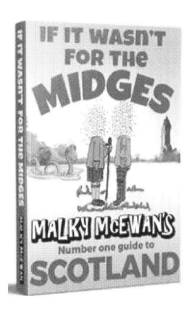

'If it Wasn't for the Midges' will keep you entertained from the first page. The fascinating history is mixed with dollops of information and twists of humour. It includes:

- Why visitors to Callander never smile.
- How a serial killer convention thwarted his quest for scallops.
- What B&B will give you puppy hugs.
- Which whisky is the same as a 15 year old malt at half the price.
- Where the views are so good they take your breath away.
- How his poor French got him in a spot of bother.

- Where you would die happy if there was an apocalypse.

Be warned: you will laugh out loud and surely smile. You'll learn a little about Scotland and it might just tempt you to visit - just to taste the water.

Here is a review:-

Kaleidoscope Down Under
(A blog about life in Australia viewed through the somewhat crazed eyes of an ancient Quoran).

Book Review:
'If it Wasn't for the Midges'

If it Wasn't for the Midges is the latest book by our very own Scottish policeman, Malky McEwan. I had the opportunity to read it this week and found it to be every bit as entertaining as his Quora posts.

Although my heritage is Welsh, it is Scotland that lives in my imagination. Now I'm looking at Scotland through another set of eyes—those of Malky McEwan, a retired policeman—and Malky's eyes sparkle with humour as well as with a love for his country.

*I had expected **If it Wasn't for the Midges** to be a straight travelogue. Boy, was I ever wrong. The book is alive with personal anecdotes that give it a unique fascination.*

This book is not a dry tramp through Scotland, but a tour

in which the reader has time to meet the people as well as to see the sights. Written by a man who has spent a lifetime in the country he obviously loves, it will delight you: it is a book sprinkled with fairy dust.

As I discovered, Scotland is a place where history and the modern world co-exist. The side trips into the past and its characters, are as interesting as the interaction with the locals Malky met during his journeys.

The humour is infectious and the writing style intimate. It's a good read.

David Evans

Printed in Great Britain
by Amazon